Existential and Ontological Dimensions of Time In Heidegger and Dōgen

SUNY Series in Buddhist Studies
Kenneth Inada, Editor

Existential and Ontological Dimensions of Time In Heidegger and Dōgen

Steven Heine

State University of New York Press

Published by
State University of New York Press, Albany

© 1985 State University of New York

For information, address State University of New York Press,
State University Plaza, Albany, NY 12246

Library of Congress Cataloging in Publication Data

Heine, Steven, 1950–
    Existential and ontological dimensions of time in
Heidegger and Dōgen.

    (SUNY series in Buddhist studies)
    Includes bibliographical references.
    1. Heidegger, Martin, 1889–1976.   2. Dōgen, 1200–1253.
3. Time—History.   I. Title.   II. Series.
B3279.H49H36 1985   115'.092'2   84–16433
ISBN 0–88706–000–5
ISBN 0–88706–001–3 (pbk.)

10 9 8 7 6 5 4 3 2 1

Contents

Page

Abbreviations   vii

Preface   ix

Chapter 1. The Question of Time   1

   The Significance of the Question   1
   Formative Elements in Heidegger's Philosophy of Time 13
   Formative Elements in Dōgen's Philosophy of Time   22
   Issues in Methodology   29

Chapter 2. The Origin of Derivative Time   35

   Problematics of Derivative Time   35
   Heidegger's Analysis of Derivative Time   40
   Dōgen's Analysis of Derivative Time   49
   Comparative Examination   60

Chapter 3. Finitude and Impermanence   71

   Problematics of Finitude and Impermanence   71
   Heidegger's Disclosure of Finitude   77
   Dōgen's Disclosure of Impermanence   86
   Comparative Examination   96

Chapter 4. Primordial Time   105

   Problematics of Primordial Time   105
   Heidegger's Understanding of Primordial Time   111
   Dōgen's Understanding of Primordial Time   125
   Comparative Examination   137
   Conclusions   144

Appendix   A Translation of Dōgen's "Uji" (Being Time)   153

Notes   163

Glossary of Japanese Terms   187

Index   197

Abbreviations

SZ (BT)   Martin Heidegger, *Sein und Zeit*, Tübingen, Niemeyer, 1953. Trans. *Being and Time* by John Macquarrie and Edward Robinson, New York, Harper and Row, 1972. (Page numbers are cited from both German and English editions).

SBGZ   Dōgen, *Shōbōgenzō*, 2 volumes, edited by Terada Tōru and Mizuno Yaoko, Tokyo, Iwanami shoten, 1970 and 1972. (Translation is my own).

Preface

My aim in this work is to establish a basis and framework for philosophical dialogue between Heidegger and Dōgen through an examination of their analyses of the true nature, structure and meaning of time in terms of a convergence of existential and ontological dimensions. Heidegger and Dōgen each seem uniquely suited for critical comparative and cross-cultural study for two interrelated reasons: they both attempt to overcome their respective philosophical traditions which, they feel, express unacknowledged and deficient presuppositions concerning time; and they reorient our understanding of all phases of existence and experience in terms of time and temporality, death and dying, finitude and impermanence, issues of universal meaning which influence and determine but are not necessarily restricted by any particular historical or cultural context.

The present study has a threefold significance. First, it seeks to advance Western scholarship, still in its formative stage, of Dōgen's philosophy of Zen, which clearly has a monumental importance in the history of Japanese thought and Buddhist thought as a whole, and remains singularly contemporary in its exploration of the dynamic nature of temporal reality. Second, it focuses attention on the matter of time as the central clue to the question of Being in Heidegger's *Sein und Zeit* and throughout the various phases of his philosophical enterprise that is frequently overlooked or relegated to secondary status. Finally, the work attempts to ground comparative philosophy and religion in a specific yet universal issue, underscoring the differences between Heidegger's theoretical approach to ontological disclosure and Dōgen's insistence that philosophy can and must spring from direct religious experience.

I express my deepest and heartfelt gratitude to my mentors, Charles Wei-hsun Fu and Kenneth Inada, for their invaluable and ever-challenging guidance and support.

Chapter 1

The Question of Time

The Significance of the Question

Both Heidegger in *Sein und Zeit* and Dōgen in the *Shōbōgenzō* (particularly "Uji," "Busshō" and related faciscles) maintain that the problematics of existence and the limitations of metaphysics are fundamentally and directly related to basic misconceptions concerning time. Human understanding and activity tend to be fixated with the apparent stability and constancy of phenomena which are conceived in terms of serially-connected instantaneous time-units forever and irreversibly "passing us by," as if independent of existence. Time is viewed as a static substratum "in which" events transpire from the standpoint of a substantive and actual, yet fleeting, current moment linked in an endless series to past moments which have gone away and future moments which are yet to come. This static, linear conception of time, so deeply ingrained as to be considered self-evident and beyond question or doubt, is manifested in man's preoccupation with the chronology and calculation of time in terms of hourly and seasonal sequences. It also haunts supposedly more sophisticated philosophical claims of permanence or an eternal time conceived of as an abstract, changeless realm outside of the limitations of contingent time.

In the seemingly innocuous phrase rife with misconceptions that "time flies"[1] or "time keeps passing on," for example, which both thinkers cite as illustrative of the conventional view of time, there is expressed a particular ontology derived from the entanglements of existence which, in turn, further debilitates that

1

existence, impeding genuine self-realization and self-understanding. It reveals man attached to a supposedly actual "now," fragmenting time into three isolated and independent tenses. The past and future, in contrast to a particular time-point in the present and revolving around it, are not actual and therefore are not considered real. The past comes before the present and has been fully exhausted when the present takes place; and the future which has not yet arrived is equally empty of actuality. Man constantly refers back to the past and ahead to the future in the expressions "old and new," "beginning and end," "before and after," but only relative to the supposed stability of the present. In divorcing himself from time, man thereby disperses time into separate slots or entities which are mutually exclusive: one point (t2) cannot begin until the first (t1) is finished; once completed, (t2) has no bearing on the next point (t3).

Dōgen illustrates the conventional view of time by citing the example of someone who lives in a valley, crosses a river and climbs a mountainside to reach a palace at the summit. When the goal is sought and attained, the tendency is to relegate the mountain and river to things of the past which have no relation to living in the present. "Although the mountain and river are indeed here right now, I [from the standpoint of the average person] seem to think that I have left them far behind and I act as if I occupy a palace made of rubies, thereby believing that there is a separation between myself and the mountain and river [as great] as that between heaven and earth."[2] Where is time to be found in the movement from the valley (t1) to the river (t2) to the mountain (t3) and finally to the summit (t4)? Although man is fixated on the present at any particular time, he feels that all the while now-points proceed incessantly and in rapid succession; the nows are connected in a linear series which moves on its own like a conveyor belt, sweeping man away as it rushes by him. Human events occur in time and are controlled by it. Time cannot be stopped, although it can be calculated with increasing accuracy.

"Time flies" just barely expresses, but cannot fully articulate the sense of subjugation and conflict which man experiences with regard to time. Time appears to have an inevitability and unstoppable movement which is free from man and yet which continuously victimizes him. It is as if time were in pursuit of man and capable of overtaking him should he relinquish his hold on the present — so he attempts to seize it all the more firmly without realizing its fabricated nature. Despite man's fixations, he always seems to be losing time or he can never get enough of time as he watches it speed by him. The movement of time seems to be remote and unreachable; no matter how diligently he chases after it or how accurately he measures it, man cannot prevent or dissuade, subdue or forestall the irreversible sequential tide. In fact, it is just these attempts which further remove man from a genuine experience of what Heidegger calls "primordial time" (*ursprüngliche Zeit*) or what Dōgen calls the "truth of [being-] time" (*uji no dōri*).[3]

The ordinary view is self-limiting or lacking of a primordial basis, according to Heidegger and Dōgen, because although it holds that at any given time-point the present is unrelated to past and future, the present instants themselves are seen as connected in a linear series of coming along and going away, arising and desisting. The present is vainly grasped as something stable, but the continuity of time is conceived of as a ceaseless and relentless marching forward on its own. The fact that man is constantly measuring time and trying to refine his sense of calculation, and then lets himself be controlled by this reckoning, as if it were absolutely real, indicates how he feels victimized by time, taking it for granted as something given and not subject to inquiry without ever really understanding it or trying to become aware of the source of his bondage to it. Caught in an entanglement of seeking more time while losing his grasp on what he has, and of taking one particular moment to be appropriate or not for reasons dictated by external circumstances, man conceals from himself primordial time in insidious yet all-pervasive ways.

Both thinkers agree that the conventional view of time is not to be considered "false" in that it does have a certain justification and can even be useful in an everyday context. But, they argue that calculative time is derivative of primordial time, springing from and yet concealing it. They insist that we constantly reexamine, reevaluate and revise our viewpoints concerning time in accord with its truly dynamic and unified existential and ontological nature. They consider unnecessary any recourse to Augustine's famous dictum that while everything seems to be known about time, once one is questioned, nothing is really known.[4] The matter of time is too basic and essential to be lightly dismissed, and its true nature can be penetrated and appropriated through proper analysis and understanding.

Although critical of misconceptions about time, Heidegger and Dōgen certainly do not negate time itself, but investigate the meaning and structure of contingent lived-time. They do not deny the reality of the present now, of the three tenses, of change and movement, or of continuity and duration, but reorient our understanding of these dimensions of experience by pointing to the basic, pervasive and inviolable relation between time and the existence of self and world. Heidegger and Dōgen differ significantly in their respective views of the nature and constitution of primordial time, yet they do concur that it must be conceived of as a fluid, flexible and integrated process inseparable from human activity. Primordial time does not mean that there are fixed things in an ever-changing realm called time; nor that time is merely the various transformations of an essentially constant entity. It is not the meeting of one changeless substance with something changing so that the first is thereby altered. An understanding of the primordiality of temporal existence demands the overcoming of any notion — whether explicitly or unwittingly expressed — of actuality or constancy in traditional Western metaphysical conceptions of Being, and of substantiality or permanence in Mahāyāna Buddhist approaches to Buddha-nature.

The conventional view of time is problematic precisely because it is so familiar and taken for granted as self-evident. Not only are the predicaments of existence inherently connected with time, but they are intensified because they are generally analyzed either without regard for the issue of time or in terms of the conveniently accepted sequential view. Human activity is misdirected so long as the question of time remains unexplored, and fundamental presuppositions are continually overlooked and not overcome.

Heidegger and Dōgen challenge and attempt to expose the

limitations of the conventional conception in two interrelated ways: ontologically, by surpassing deficient or misleading doctrines in their respective philosophical traditions which are based on sequential time; and existentially,[5] by analyzing the possibilities of human freedom in terms of a genuine encounter with time in existence. First, in *Sein und Zeit* Heidegger charges that the Western metaphysical tradition has been forgetful of the meaning of Being because it has always accepted and built itself upon the most naive and opaque definition of "now-time" (*Jetzt-zeit*). Being is represented as a present-at-hand (*vorhanden*) being and conceptualized as the highest and/or first entity. That is, the disclosive presence of Being (*Anwesenheit*) is mistaken for one aspect of time — the most obvious one, the present (*Gegenwart*). Being, the primordial ground and structure of existence, is thus rendered indistinguishable from a substantive being which Dasein manipulates that is present-at-hand or that bears a "constancy of presence" (*ousia*), because entities are grasped in their Being exclusively with regard to the present tense. This everyday, derivative view is systematized and rigidified in Aristotle's definition of time as the substantive duration of the now in relation to the receding no-longer-now and the approaching not-yet-now ("For this is time: that which is counted in the movement which we encounter within the horizon of the earlier and later").[6] Aristotle's definition can never fully disguise its derivative basis, but it has tragically been taken over unchallenged by subsequent thinkers, including the great modern philosophers.[7] It is not sufficient, however, for a thinker to merely emphasize the significance of time in order to escape the stranglehold of the conventional view. Even Kant, who alone analyzes the transcendentally idealistic origin of time in terms of its synthesizing and creative epistemological function, accepts the traditional conception and leaves veiled the decisive connection between the Cartesian *cogito* and time.

Heidegger asserts that Being always has a "temporal determinateness" (*temporale Bestimmtheit*). Being is not an abstract, independent realm in contrast to or transcendent of time, but is dynamically and illuminatively revealed by the horizon of time in the most profound, basic and pervasive respects. The temporal nature of Being is continually ignored in metaphysics because Being is conceived of either in terms of sequential time, or as outside of time, or as some entangled combination of these views. Three categories are presupposed which use time to naively discriminate various realms of entities: the temporal (natural processes and historical events), frequently contrasted with Being; the non-temporal (spatial and numerical relationships), which supposedly has little to do with Being; and the supra-temporal (that which has no bridge to the temporal), which is generally identified with Being. Heidegger maintains that the latter two categories are misleading and that the temporal category has been poorly conceived largely because it has been separated from the others. He insists that claims of eternity made from Plato to Hegel and Nietzsche are based on the untenable notion of an "endless" series of now-points without beginning or end, and thus do not go beyond the conventional understanding. Nietzsche's doctrine of "eternal recurrence of the same," for example, represents the will to power's futile attempt to perpetuate the now forever. By reducing eternity to the world of becoming, Nietzsche presupposes the fundamental bifurcation of Being and now-time and thereby reverses — without overcoming — traditional metaphysics.

Dōgen is critical of particular ways time has been ontologically portrayed in the history of Buddhist philosophy. Time is a fundamental issue in Buddhist thinking because the Buddha's analysis of existence, which Dōgen feels is frequently overlooked or misinterpreted, states that all factors of experience (Skt. *dharmas*; J. *hō*) are non-substantive (*anātman*; *muga*) and non-permanent (*anitya*; *mujō*) events which do not move in time, but are thoroughly temporal in nature. The elements of experience comprise a perpetual, mutually conditioning flux of arising/desistence, appearance/disappearance, life/death (*pratītya-samutpāda*; *engi*) each and every moment of which, if staticized by desire and ignorance, generates suffering (*dukkha*; *ku*) resulting in *karmic* bondage to cyclic death and rebirth. Despite the merits of the basic Buddhist view, the genuine significance of impermanence is somewhat neglected in subsequent historical developments of philosophy. The Abhidharma scholastic controversy concerning the essence and duration of the momentariness of *dharmas*, for example, seems to reduce impermanence to a speculative issue. The Mādhyamika refutation of time as a conceptual fabrication (*prapañca*), an important corrective to the Abhidharma view, does not account for the deeply existential nature of impermanence. Even the Hua-yen (J Kegon) notion of the simultaneous interpenetration of ten phases of time, a doctrine which Dōgen largely incorporates into his thinking, is overly speculative and somewhat removed from existential considerations. It is idle to discuss time, Dōgen strongly feels, as a philosophic topic divorced from one's own immediate and continuing temporal activity and response to impermanence. Dōgen seeks to explain the truth (*dōri*) of time only on the basis of the utmost exertion of the "skin, flesh, bones and marrow"[8] of the True Man (*shinjin*) who has fully penetrated and realized the meaning of impermanence.

Dōgen most vigorously protests the betrayal of the meaning of impermanence in the tendency to seek awakening in a non-temporal or supra-temporal realm. In the Abhidharma categorization, time is considered problematic and associated with the conditioned (*saṃskṛta*) realm, whereas *nirvāṇa* is non-temporal and associated and with pure space (*ākāśa*) as the unconditioned (*asaṃskṛta*). The Mahāyāna refutation of conceptual polarities and identification of conditioned and unconditioned, *nirvāṇa* and *saṃsāra*, however, does not fully overcome this tendency because the sequential view of time is frequently unchallenged. The central Mahāyāna ontological doctrine of Buddha-nature (*busshō*) is represented in much of the sūtra and śāstra literature and accepted by the orthodox Japanese Tendai teachings of Dōgen's age as a permanent absolute, undefiled by change and conditions, which paradoxically manifests itself in-and-through the relative world at the point of complete enlightenment.[9] While Buddha-nature is considered to be originally *beyond* time, the process of actualizing enlightenment is depicted in terms of the linear sequential development of now-points leading to a future goal *in* time, compared to the seeds of plants which when nourished by rain issue forth branches, leaves, flowers and fruits with new seeds. Dōgen attempts to overcome this sort of static eternalism which he terms the "Senika heresy" (sennigedō), the view that busshō is untouched by time in that the "house is changing but the masters are still the same."[10] Senika refers specifically to the Ātman doctrine of the Upanishads of an eternal Self which sits like a passive and impartial witness in the chariot comprised of mind, body and senses. It also designates the tendency toward a subtle, often disguised staticization of Buddha-nature which haunts Mahāyāna thought, including Zen. For example, Dōgen applauds the dictum attributed to Hui-neng that "impermanence is the Buddha-nature," but also criticizes the sixth patriarch's doctrine of "seeing into [one's own-]nature" (kenshō) which may be interpreted as an eternal substance or substratum.[11] Dōgen also refutes the "naturalistic heresy" (jinen-gedō) which presumes that Buddha-nature will arrive on its own independent of the sustained effort of dedicated discipline.

Heidegger and Dōgen also show that ontology based on calculative time derives from existentially deficient encounters with time in one's own life. Man is so intimately related to and determined by time in terms of death, contingency and vicissitude that he tends to deny or fearfully flee from his awareness of temporal limitations, which only heightens his bondage to them. In a sense, the expression "time flies" is justified; it is actually closer to the truth than the one who utters it realizes in that the certainty of death does suggest the irreversibility of and man's dependence upon time. In Heidegger's notion of finitude (Endlichkeit) and Dōgen's interpretation of impermanence (mujō), however, contingency is stressed more deeply and radically than in the conventional view, and from a willingness to accept, confront and find freedom in terms of it rather than by fleeing it. Without such existential resolve, ontology remains misguided. So long as death is seen as an actual end to life that will arrive in the not-yet-now of endless time, primordial time is concealed. A profound awareness of and perpetual confrontation with death within existence as the extreme possibility of one's impossibility is the most convincing and significant evidence of the interconnectedness of man and time. Although seemingly nowhere to be found and the least tangible of elements, time is the most

basic and undeniable aspect of experience; whether acknowledged and genuinely realized or not, it can never be avoided.
Death is disclosed by Heidegger and Dōgen as the urgent, immediate and inescapable signpost of time which disavows any
attempt to divorce time from existence, and betrays claims of permanence which bypass this relation.

In highlighting the existential significance of death in terms
of disclosing the ontological meaning of finitude and impermanence, Heidegger and Dōgen do not propose that man submit to fate or be overwhelmed by the flow of time, which is
precisely the attitude expressed by the conventional view that
"time flies." Nor do they attempt to stop time, but to uncover
and analyze — and thereby resolve — the source of conflict between man and time which generally causes him to fear or to
wish to escape time. Awareness of death is not a cause for nihilism
or dismay, but a unique affirmation. The human predicament
is not generated by death, but by an unwillingness to authentically accept and confront it. By calling for a continual encounter
with death within one's existence, Heidegger and Dōgen insist
that time can neither be denied, the conventional attitude, nor
transcended, the more philosophical yet equally misguided view.
Rather, they accentuate and illuminate the singular significance
of time in its inseparability with human existence as the basis
of freedom.

Thus, an understanding of the nature and structure of primordial time is the aim of ontological disclosure, which liberates
any fixation with the substantive and actual now-points by revealing the elements of existence to be dynamically interrelated
through the temporal process. Concrete, active realization of primordial time rather than the attainment of a goal either "in"
or "out" of time is the basis of Heidegger's view of authentic
existence and of Dōgen's approach to Zen enlightenment.
Although Heidegger and Dōgen agree that primordial time is
the starting point of philosophical reflection, the ground of existential freedom, and the basis for the convergence between these
dimensions, they reach this conclusion on the basis of different
conceptual aims, methods and perspectives. The reasons which
lead to their strikingly similar philosophies of time have quite

distinct historical and theoretical foundations, and it is necessary to clarify the divergent approaches and central goals before critically comparing their doctrines.

Heidegger's ultimate concern is ontological as he attempts to solve the ever-puzzling Western metaphysical question of Being (*Seinsfrage*) which he maintains is "the *question* of all authentic questions, i.e. of all self-questioning questions, and whether consciously or not it is necessarily implicit in every question."[12] He turns to an analysis of Dasein's finitude and the possibilities of its temporal existence in order to prepare a fundamental ontology and not, he maintains, to offer an existential imperative or moral pronouncement. It is essential for his task to undertake an investigation of the finite transcendence of Dasein's way-to-be as the best access to the meaning of Being, but not to propose definite ontical modes of behavior. Heidegger asserts that while an *existenzial* analysis is not possible without *existenziell* decision, fundamental ontology cannot in turn provide guidelines for action. "*Existenzial* Interpretation will never seek to take over any authoritarian pronouncement as to those things which, from an *existenziell* point of view, are possible or binding."[13] Although in his later works Heidegger does speak of "saving"[14] the modern post-metaphysical epoch from the apparent global dominance of technology, which is a consequence of the withdrawal of Being, he generally shies away from discussing any soteriological import in his thinking, and he maintains that the existential question is subsidiary to the *Seinsfrage*. Nevertheless, it seems that in *Sein und Zeit* especially, there is an existential emphasis on Dasein as thrown-projection and a soteriological implication in the notion of anticipatory resoluteness that are beyond Heidegger's stated or explicit intentions. This tension in the structure and execution of *Sein und Zeit* raises the question of whether there is a deep-rooted and problematic ambivalence in Heidegger's thinking.[15]

Dōgen's concern is primarily soteriological. He seeks personal emancipation from the existential anguish of suffering through insight into the truth of impermanence. The ontological question about the true nature of time is raised by Dōgen only in light of his religious quest, which motivates him to comprehend real-

ity from the ever-flexible middle way perspective without presupposition or one-sidedness. In turn, the question of time is fully
resolved only on the basis of complete existential fulfillment
through sustained practice of his soteriological aims. To understand and express the inexhaustible meanings of the Way is
necessarily to live and to continually renew and enhance one's
authentic experience of time through the concrete here-and-now
activities of True Manhood. Therefore, the three dimensions —
soteriological (the quest for enlightenment), existential (dedicated
exertion in pursuit of the Way), and ontological (clarification of
the truth of being-time) — are inseparably and simultaneously
attained by Dōgen as ultimately one and the same reflection of
"the immediate and complete manifestation of Zen realization"
(*genjōkōan*): "For whoever expresses the Way, Buddha-nature
must be nothing other than the attainment of Buddhahood
(*jōbutsu*). Buddha-nature is the majesty of attaining Buddhahood.
Furthermore, the attainment of Buddhahood and Buddha-nature
must be simultaneously realized as the same life and the same
practice."[16]

Dōgen insists on bringing Buddhist philosophy in accord with
his intensely and dramatically personal experiences of all-
pervasive impermanence, and he is dissatisfied with those views
which overlook or discount the full significance of existentially
realized transiency. In the opening paragraph of "Genjōkōan"
(which is in most editions the introductory chapter of *Shōbōgenzō*), Dōgen notes that although the Buddhist Way is originally
beyond the bifurcations of life/death, delusion/enlightenment,
sentient beings/Buddha, fullness/lack, still there is the continual
unfolding of generation and extinction, arising and desistence
and consequent sense of sorrow and suffering. "And yet, even
though this [ultimate non-differentiation] has been said," he
writes, "blossoms scatter in sadness and weeds spring up in
dismay."[17]

The existentially experienced and pervasive ontological reality of impermanence generates the twofold sense of dejection and
despair or of longing and aspiration in the pursuit of soteriological
deliverance, attitudes which themselves must be either uprooted
or cultivated even while they cannot alter the course or resist
the incessancy of change. Any attempt to negate or transcend

impermanence is ontologically untenable, existentially misleading and soteriologically unsatisfactory. Dōgen does not propose a termination of impermanence, but demands genuine realization which penetrates to the true existential and ontological meanings of transiency and change prior to man's obsession with "time flies." It is the tendency to deny impermanence in the thought that there are no blooming flowers or falling leaves in the world of "the true nature of *dharmas*" (*hōsshō*) that must be abated, and not the temporal vicissitudes themselves.

Thus, Dōgen philosophizes on the basis of his liberation experience. He writes in "Uji" that without clearly perceiving and expressing the truth of time, it is impossible to "reach the moment of breaking through the barrier [to realization],"[18] for *bodhi* and *nirvāṇa* would be seen as the mere coming and going of sequential time and nothing else. Understanding true time is not only a matter of clarifying metaphysics, but of personal awakening, transformation and deliverance. To misconceive time is to be unenlightened and to mistake oneself and/or phenomena for constant substantiality, as one who rides in a boat either thinks that he is still and that the riverbank is moving or vice-versa, but fails to experience the continuing dynamic and harmonious interplay of boat, water and bank.[19] Although Heidegger discloses the unified ground of care (*Sorge*) as prior to bifurcations of *theoria* and *praxis*, his "thinking" (*Denken*) is by his own claim primarily "theoretical" (in the sense of emphasizing *existenzial* disclosure) and not "practical" (by not advocating any specific *existenziell* mode of behavior). Heidegger philosophizes, according to the method of fundamental ontology, to the exclusion of his or any particular person's experiences. The *existenzial* structures of Dasein are not necessarily derived from or applicable to anyone's practical life, and yet are meant to constitute a theory which is universally significant for the very basis and meaning of existence itself. Heidegger asserts that "time must be brought to light — and genuinely conceived — as the horizon for an understanding of Being and for any way of interpreting it . . . in terms of the temporality of the being of Dasein which understands Being."[20] Yet, his aim is the liberation of Being from its objectified status, and not of himself or even of the universally conceived Dasein.

Formative Elements in Heidegger's Philosophy of Time

Like Dōgen, Heidegger's thinking is propelled by one fundamental question concerning the existential and ontological meanings of time. The question of the primordial meaning of time been long neglected by his philosophical tradition; its very asking generates the overcoming or destruction of previous statically-oriented ontologies. But in contrast to Dōgen, who stresses the existential and soteriological basis of his philosophy of impermanence and being-time, Heidegger downplays any personal involvement in or significance for his "fundamental ontology." Although existential and soteriological implications can be drawn from his discussion of authentic Dasein, he believes that these are restricted to the ontic level of inquiry and do not pertain to the essential nature of his thought. Heidegger expresses disinterest in or a neutral attitude towards the question of personal involvement, emphasizing *theoria* in uncovering the foundations of *logos*. He insists that his thinking responds not to an existential quest, but to the question of Being which has been forgotten by the Western metaphysical tradition. Dōgen's philosophical career began with his intensely personal realization of impermanence and culminated in his universalization of the meaning of time based on this experience. Heidegger's central concern is not personal reflection or emancipation in a soteriological pursuit in the experiential sense, but the disclosure of Being. As opposed to Husserl, however, who sought to establish phenomenology as an objective scientific discipline, Heidegger argues that phenomenologico-ontology can never be a rigorous mathematical procedure, nor should it seek to be one, because it presupposes the hermeneutic circularity of Dasein's *existenzial* comprehension of Being and *existenziell* potential for authenticity as essential to the philosophical endeavor.[21] Thus, Heidegger's "hermeneutics of facticity," to a limited degree, does stress the existential (in the sense of *existenziell* decisions which are explored for *existenzial* disclosure) foundations of ontological understanding.

Heidegger attempts to lay the foundation for metaphysics and scientific investigation by rendering the *Seinsfrage* problematic and worthy of the asking, and he comes upon the issues of time and human finitude as the best and necessary ways to accomplish this task. "In contrast to [the ways time has been ordinarily understood]," he asserts, "our treatment of the meaning of Being must enable us to show that *the central problematic of all ontology is rooted in the phenomenon of time, if rightly seen and rightly explained,* and we must show how this is the case."[22] This involves demonstrating, first of all, that "temporal" can no longer mean simply "being in time." Indeed, Being and its modes and characteristics have their meaning determined primordially in terms of time, and the conventional view of linear sequential time reveals this even as it conceals it.

Heidegger considers afresh the meaning of Being because, he maintains, it has been trivialized by the Western metaphysical tradition's dogma that Being is the most universal, indefinable yet self-evident concept. Being is said to no longer require an investigation of its meaning since it is always "used" whenever one cognizes or asserts anything either about entities or about oneself, as in the expressions, "The sky *is* blue," and "I *am* merry." Heidegger finds this dogma self-contradictory and problematic because it takes Being for granted as the most readily apparent concept and yet resists any attempt to define Being. The traditional view conceals the fact that Being has been veiled in darkness and never explicitly disclosed. This has resulted from a tranquilization of understanding, a self-alienating flight from the disturbing, thought-provoking and enigmatic nature of Being. Anxiety is subdued, though not authentically resolved, by concern with the seemingly obvious and actual, rather than being troubled by the remote and the possible. The inflexibility and false sense of clarity of this dogma demands that the question of Being, the most concrete and significant of questions, be directly confronted. "The very fact that we already live in an understanding of Being and that the meaning of Being is still veiled in darkness proves that it is necessary in principle to raise this question again."[23]

Heidegger was initially stimulated in his thinking when, as a young theology student, he read Brentano's work *On the Manifold Sense of Being in Aristotle*, which explores the Greek philosopher's phrase, "A being becomes manifest (sc. with regard to its Being) in many ways."[24] Why, Heidegger wondered, had Being come to have a multiplicity of seemingly irreconcilable meanings for Aristotle, the founder of ontology proper, such as, Being as property, as possibility and actuality, as truth, and as schema of the categories. And, Heidegger also asks in this context, "What is the pervasive, simple, unified determination of Being that permeates all of its multiple meanings?" What is the relationship between the primary and derivative senses of Being? Why also, he asked, has Being generally been conceived in contrast to time? Heidegger soon abandoned his theological studies because he felt that the development of theology as an ontical science of faith is derivatively made possible by and must therefore be primordially grounded in genuinely conceived ontology: *"Philosophy is the possible ontological corrective which can formally point out the ontic and, in particular, the pre-Christian content of basic theological concepts. But philsophy can be what it is without functioning factually as this corrective."*[25] It is thus imperative to uncover the meaning of Being as *logos*, from which theology as well as traditional ontology and logic have sprung.

In *Einführung in die Metaphysik*, Heidegger notes that Western metaphysics since Aristotle has been haunted by bifurcations between Being and becoming, Being and appearance, Being and thinking, by which Being is objectified through human representation as an abstract, independent realm which stands over and against human and temporal existence. Heidegger concurs with Nietzsche that the traditional conception of Being has become in modern times an "evaporating mist" or an "empty fiction," but he rejects Nietzsche's attempt to reduce Being to the "innocence of becoming" through the doctrine of eternal recurrence. Rather, he is compelled to clarify the heretofore obscure relationship between Being and time, indirectly revealed in that: (1) time appears in a fundamental yet unclarified way in all metaphysical doctrines from Anaximander to Nietzsche; and (2) philosophers for the most part have unquestioningly and unreflectively accepted Aristotle's definition of now-time so that they are never free from it without even being aware that they are bound to it. In "Der Rückgang in den Grund der Metaphysik," Heidegger writes, "Thus Time becomes the first name, which is yet to be heeded, of the truth of Being, which is yet to be experienced. A concealed hint of Time speaks not only out of the earliest metaphysical names of Being, but also of its last name, which is "the eternal recurrence of the same events." Through the entire epoch of metaphysics, Time is decisively present in the history of Being, without being recognized or thought about."[26]

Thus, for Heidegger to speak of "Being and time" is not to propagate one more limited dichotomization; for example, to substitute time for becoming or thinking in the traditional bifurcations. Instead, "it points in an entirely different direction of inquiry,"[27] one which is more basic and fruitful "because in the beginning of Western philosophy the *perspective governing the disclosure of Being* was time, though this perspective *as such* remained hidden — and inevitably so."[28] The importance of time is established in *Sein und Zeit* because the sanctioned neglect and presumed self-evidence of Being is directly related to fundamental misconceptions about time; that is, to the everyday sense of "derivative" time carried over into metaphysics in the thought of Being as eternity and independence from the apparent passing away of time. The derivative view, given justification by Aristotle, though not false, conceals primordial temporality (*Zeitlichkeit*). "Must not one as much as the other, Being as much as time —," Heidegger challenges metaphysics, "must not both become questionable in their relatedness, first questionable and finally doubtful? . . . The question of Being and Time points to what is unthought in all metaphysics. Metaphysics consists of this unthought matter . . ."[29]

Although Heidegger's basic ontological question is the Aristotelean one — *ti to on*, what is a being in its Being, or the twofold of Being's presencing through beings-present — his approach is greatly influenced by modern philosophical perspectives, which in itself suggests to him that the *Seinsfrage* is historically determined and can never be abstracted from its temporal-historical context. The central clue for Heidegger's inquiry is that the question of the meaning of Being is to be worked out "concretely," that is, in terms of the structural unity of Dasein, that being which is factical yet projective in its understanding of Being and whose constituents of selfhood, including care, death, guilt, conscience and they-self are in no way present-at-hand (*vorhanden*). Being is eminently temporal though not as "beings in time," but because Dasein, although generally preoccupied with now-time, is a dynamic temporal totality, a futural or transcendent potentiality permeated by its finitude or factical nothingness.

Dasein is the being for whom Being is an issue which is in each case "mine" (*je meines*) and which can be authentic (*eigentlich*, something of its own) by choosing and winning itself from out of the ensnarement of misconceptions of the anonymous they (*das Man*).[30] Although "proximally and for the most part" Dasein is not itself, its Being is never fully lost. Dasein's Being emerges, for example, in the mood of anxiety toward one's death and as the call of conscience which strip Dasein of its disguises and reliance on the they, impelling it toward self-confrontation and self-discovery. The question of Being as the ownmost matter for Dasein is neither an arbitrary objective revelation nor a subjective or solipsistic projection, but "the radicalization of an essential tendency-of-Being which belongs to Dasein itself — the pre-ontological understanding of Being."[31] Dasein is its own disclosedness, its own illumination, the basis for the determination of its authenticity or inauthenticity. Being is not a superior power, but symbolic of the self-attunement by which Dasein discloses to itself its possibilities.[32]

In his analysis of Dasein's temporality as the best access to the meaning of Being, Heidegger incorporates influences from other philosophical approaches to the nature of human existence, including those of Kant (epistemology), Dilthey (history and hermeneutics), Scheler (philosophical anthropology), Husserl (phenomenology), and Nietzsche (existentialist-oriented metaphysics) in addition to Plato and Aristotle. He is also greatly influenced by the religious reflections on man's ultimate choices of Augustine and Kierkegaard. As Otto Pöggeler notes, "Heidegger forces into harmony here the metaphysical tradition, which thinks Being in a hidden manner in the light of time, and a nonmetaphysical and anti-metaphysical tradition, which brings the temporality and historicity of man's factical ek-sistence into view."[33] Yet Heidegger does not merely abstractly or artificially synthesize two disparate traditions so as to present a static ontology modified by historicism. Rather, he absorbs, enhances and supercedes his influences in a unique way in that he does not subscribe to any particular standpoint, but fashions from the various ones the creative discipline of fundamental ontology. Heidegger's inquiry is relentlessly concerned with the essential ontological issue prior to the ontic dimensions of human experience which alone, he maintains, guide the above thinkers. Still, fundamental ontology must be and is grounded in the concrete elements of existence in the world of beings.

Heidegger is perhaps most significantly influenced by Kant's investigation of the transcendental structure of *a priori* conditions for the possibility of rational and scientific knowledge in terms of the finite human subject. Kant, he says, is the "first and only person who has gone any stretch of the way towards investigating the dimensions of Temporality or has even let himself be drawn hither by the coercion of the phenomena themselves. . . ."[34] Kant, however, never questions the traditional understanding of now-time or its relation to the subjectivity of the subject, which he depicts in Cartesian fashion as isolated and detached from the world of everyday concern. Offsetting Kant's strickly epistemological analysis of finite knowledge, Heidegger recognizes the significance of Dilthey's "critique of historical reason" which emphasizes that human existence must be hermeneutically grasped in terms of the *Erlebnis* (lived-experience) of its entire historical reality in all its manifestations and complexities. From Scheler, Heidegger draws upon the notion that the person is "not a Thing, not a substance, not an object . . ."[35] merely thought of behind and outside what it immediately experiences; nor is it a subject of rational acts which follow certain laws. Hosserl's investigations, from the standpoint of Heidegger's fundamental ontology, overcome the psychologism of Dilthey and the axiological thrust of Scheler. Phenomenology is a nonevaluative discipline which illuminates the multi-dimensionality of intentional consciousness, attempting to thereby bypass the traditional dichotomies of subject/object, realism/idealism. Husserl's quasi-scientific outlook, however, is offset in Heidegger's thought by Dilthey's interpretative stance, which calls into question the possibility of a purely "objective" description of transcendental states of consciousness.

Heidegger believes that traditional metaphysics is unable to free itself from its preoccupation with constantly abiding presence, by which it reduces man and Being to the status of something *vorhanden*. He is thus profoundly drawn to the evocative portrayals made by Kierkegaard and Nietzsche of guilt, dread, despair, loneliness — the imminent and pervasive though generally concealed abyss of everyday existence — as formative experiences in the development or achievement of selfhood. He maintains that Kierkegaard alone has articulated the notion of a dynamic present moment-of-vision (*Augen-blick*) experienced in man's encounter with dread, in contrast to the conventional static now-point. Yet the sense of urgency and immediacy in the existential imperatives which Kierkegaard and Nietzsche propose (and which presuppose an "ideal" human subject) remains secondary in Heidegger's ontology.

Heidegger is also moved by Augustine's thinking which functions on the basis of factually realized life-experience. Augustine is not interested in the measuring of "within-time-ness," by which man orders the objects of ordinary external perception. Rather, his concern is the time that is constituted by concrete decision-making human experiences, from which he reflects on the complex interrelatedness of the three tenses: "And thus passeth [time] on," Augustine writes, "until the present intent conveys over the future into the past; the past increasing by the dimunition of the future, until by the consumption of the future, all is past."[36] Heidegger is critical of Nietzsche for his attachment to the metaphysics of eternity, and of Kierkegaard for not conducting a meaningful ontological investigation of time. Whereas Kierkegaard unreflectively opposes ontology, however, Heidegger contends that Augustine uncritically allows an overlay of Neo-Platonism in his thinking to distort and falsify basic life-experience.

None of the previous philosophers or thinkers, Heidegger

feels, were aware of or reflective about the traditional and misconceived ontological framework of their thinking. They were
unable to liberate themselves from bondage to Aristotelean
substance ontology based on the supposed endurance of *ousia*.
The focus of modern thinkers on the human subject conceived
of as a static substratum only disguises, but does not overthrow
reliance on *ousiology* (substance ontology). Heidegger's fundamental ontology is not a synthesis of their still misguided positions,
but it represents a radical breakthrough from its influences
through digesting and transcending them. Heidegger stresses
that human existence is the unitary phenomenon of care as
"Being-in-the-world thrown-projection." Dasein's understanding
of Being is always accompanied by its mood, its selfhood is
grounded in the world of everyday concern, and its *logos* is
historically and hermeneutically determined. In contrast to the
metaphysical tradition's anthropological and/or theological definition of man as the rational animal who by the gift of *logos* reaches
beyond himself to "eternal truth," Heidegger maintains that
understanding is not a purely abstract capacity of reason or facil-
ity for discourse, but a power of Being (*Seinkönnen*) which must,
in turn, be conceived of and rooted in the concrete factical *existenzial* structure of finite Dasein's temporal and historical environment. Dasein is essentially finite, not as an accumulation of
imperfections or as opposed to the Infinite, but in its very nature
and basis as Being-thrown-unto-death and permeated by the
nothingness of anxiety and guilt. Yet Dasein is also futural and
transcendent or ahead-of-itself in that its understanding consists
of a fore-structure which is already involved in the area of its
concern and inquiry.

Thus, the *Seinsfrage* is a "matter of thinking" (*Gedankesache*)
deeply involving a hermeneutic circularity. The hermeneutic
circle which Heidegger acknowledges is not a problematic ontical vicious cycle created either by an impossible goal or self-
contradictory thinking, but "is the expression of the *existenzial
fore-structure* of Dasein itself . . . [in which] is hidden a positive
possibility of the most primordial kind of knowledge."[37] Dasein,
always already ahead-of-itself as its own possibility, constantly
"more" than it factually is, has a view and grasp of Being as well

as of the world and itself in advance of the meanings it projects. The circle represents a "productive logic" (which lays the foundation for traditional logic that "limps along after it") that leaps ahead into the midst of Being. Dasein has an ontical priority amongst beings in that its Being is determinative for its existence by virtue of its ontological priority — that it is always already familiar with its Being. Because of its ontico-ontological priority as the basis for any and all ontologies, however, Dasein is thrown and for the most part lost or fallen in the world which is then "reflected back upon the way in which Dasein itself gets interpreted."[38]

Fundamental to the hermeneutic circle is the profound interrelation between the *existenzial*-ontological and ontic-*existenziell* dimensions of the inquiry. Ontological disclosure of Dasein's *existenzial* structure prior to particular attitudes and decisions is intimately connected with its choice to either be or not be its authentic self. Heidegger asserts, "Not only, however, does an understanding of Being belong to Dasein, but this understanding develops or decays along with whatever kind of Being Dasein may possess at the time."[39] Also, "The question of existence never gets straightened out except through existing itself. . . "[40] One implication which may be drawn from this is that successful phenomenological ontology requires the authenticity of Dasein and vice-versa, a view which would approach Dōgen's insistence upon the simultaneity of the understanding of Buddha-nature and the attainment of Buddhahood. Yet, it is clear that Heidegger does not wish to be drawn into such a conclusion. He denies that ontology is wholly dependent upon Dasein's *existenziell* decisions, and claims that he is interested only in the matter of Being and not in any doctrine concerning or imperative for man. James Demske has suggested in *Being, Man, and Death* that there are two "sides" or two possible ways of reading *Sein und Zeit*: the "appropriate" reading according to the demands of the text itself focuses on "what the book really intends and accomplishes at its most profound level, even though this may not adequately come to light," which is the philosophy of Being; the "inappropriate" reading, however, "gives rise to the dark and forbidding picture of a being who achieves his true greatness by the joyfully stubborn affirmation of his own nothingness."[41]

While Demske helpfully cautions against losing sight of the all-important *Seinsfrage* in *Sein und Zeit*, it would be unfortunate and misleading to overlook the existential import of the book and thus accentuate the separation of theory and practice, ontology and existence suggested therein, *despite* the fact that Heidegger of course does encourage Demske's position. In his later works such as *Humanismusbrief* and *Gelassenheit*, he adamantly denies that he is to be associated with "existentialism," which he views as a consequence of the metaphysics of *subiectität*. There, he maintains that thinking is dependent upon and will come to pass through man's poetic homecoming to the unveiling of a remote and withdrawn Being whose self-revelation can only be "awaited," and he reinterprets key passages from *Sein und Zeit* to reflect his new stance.

Formative Elements in Dōgen's Understanding of Time

Dōgen's understanding of time is shaped by several important personal realizations of the permeation and meaning of impermanence which he later interprets as unique existential "occasions" (*jisetsu*) for the spontaneous manifestation (*genjō*) of the *Dharma* in lived-time. Dōgen is deeply aware of impermanence not only because of the basic Buddhist doctrine of the three signs of existence (*ku*, suffering; *muga*, non-self; *mujō*, impermanence), but also because of the Japanese cultural context as well as dramatic experiences in his own life. Medieval Japan was keenly attuned to the sadness and poignancy of fleeting existence. There also developed a widely held belief which considered Japan inextricably bound by the Age of Degenerate Law (*mappō*) that arose due to the corruption and hypocrisy of the rapidly changing and troubled world and man's apparent failure to elevate himself above the sense of decay, hopelessness and dismay. Although greatly influenced by the Japanese ethos, Dōgen understands *mujō* even more fundamentally and radically than as an unfortunate historical epoch, due in large part to the early death of his parents. It is recorded in the traditional biography of Dōgen, *Kenzeiki*, that as Dōgen at age seven observed the smoke ascending from the incense at his dear mother's funeral,[42] he was profoundly stirred by the incessant mutability of the life-death process which consumes all phenomena, the conditioned nature of existence underlying any particular experience of sorrow, loss or lamentation. "When I was quite young," Dōgen says in reference to this incident, "the realization of the transiency of this world stirred my mind toward seeking the way."[43] He was both grieved and inspired by impermanence as Śākyamuni was once moved by the sight of old age, illness and death to renounce the idle luxury of the palace and seek refuge from *dukkha* through the cultivation of insight and meditation.

The suddenness and tragedy of death created a sense of urgency about the need to seek the Way which continued to motivate Dōgen throughout his life. In his exhortative/autobiographical works such as *Zuimonki* and "Gakudō-yōjinshū," he constantly reiterates the themes that life is as ephemeral as a dewdrop, that death claims the king and pauper alike, and that there is no time to waste on superfluous matters which obstruct realization. "The thorough clarification of the meaning of birth and death → this is the most important problem of all for Buddhists."[44] Dōgen does not see impermanence as a cause for fatalism or as a reason to seek enlightenment outside of the life-and-death process. In fact, he strongly rejected such efforts to deny the flux both as un-Buddhistic and, more basically, not true to the nature of his own quest and longing to find release from suffering within — rather than in contrast to — the unstoppable transiency of lived-time. Rather, impermanence impelled Dōgen to become an avid, persistent seeker who refused to let anything interfere with his resolve to penetrate to the true nature of time. He used the ever-changing flux to enhance enlightenment by transmuting his raw sense of *mujō* into lucid insight into primordial time — being-time (*uji*) or impermanence-as-impermanence — which led him to revise or overcome many commonly accepted Buddhist doctrines. "Our body already does not seem to be our own," he later writes in the *Shōbōgenzō*. "The moment-to-moment passing away of transiency never ceases."[45] Observing the fact that life is invariably altered by changing circumstances and that the mind itself is continually affected, the average person feels that there is nothing on which to rely. But those who resolve to seek enlightenment use this constant flux to deepen the meaning of their realization.

Haunted by the tragic death of his mother, Dōgen rejected his family's refined, aristocratic life-style to enter the monkhood at age twelve, and eventually he went to the Tendai monastery at Mt. Hiei. His path to awakening was impeded there, however, largely because the orthodox monastic teaching of the doctrine of Buddha-nature was problematic with regard to time. As a diligent and studious young monk, Dōgen's experiential understanding of impermanence immediately came in conflict with the Tendai interpretation of Buddha-nature as everywhere present though generally yet-to-be-realized. Awakening depicted as a metaphysical process of the self-realization of an unchanging absolute Buddha-nature, distinguished in terms of its innate and acquired, complete and partial dimensions, seemed to Dōgen to negate the importance of practice and of his own existential appropriation of the Way. Dōgen was also disturbed by sectarian controversies at Mt. Hiei and other Buddhist centers over the preeminence of *kōan* or *zazen* practice, self- or other-completed enlightenment, and mind- or body-actualized enlightenment.

The problem was that enlightenment was said to be unitary and all-pervasive, and yet was continually divided and subdivided into its various aspects. Sorrowful about the transiency of the world and seeking release though disdainful of the romanticized fatalism of the aristocracy, Dōgen found the doctrine of Buddha-nature contradictory and self-defeating, reduced to facile solutions or pat formulas that left untouched his profound personal longing. He was told that the Way is, was and always will be right here, a view which can lead to a naive affirmation of the phenomenal world before it is authenticated by sustained practice. Why then, he asked, have all Buddhas been committed to spiritual exercise and physical discipline? On what basis was he — Dōgen — compelled to cultivate a meditative discipline? Buddha-nature was also said to be originally beyond time, and yet it could be approached as a goal to be attained in time. Neither of these points successfully accounted for the significance of impermanence. Was there a barrier between an eternal Buddhanature and the world of transiency and sentience? Dōgen suspected not, but he was as yet unable to surmount this impasse. He did not recognize that his heightened sense of urgency in the quest for enlightenment due to the swift passing of time was itself a partial barrier to the realization of primordial time. The orthodox doctrines did not help him fully uproot his misconceptions; rather, they tended to reinforce them and obstruct awakening.

"Originally, the Way is complete and all-pervasive. How does it depend on practice and realization?"[46] This was the fundamental question plaguing Dōgen, what has been termed his "great doubt"[47] which he forced himself and all Buddhists he met to ask in their study and training, but he did not find it answered on Mt. Hiei. Dōgen challenged the conception of Buddha-nature as a potentiality possessed by all beings somehow separable from the everyday self, or as an unactualized possibility awaiting the appropriate time for fulfillment. He was wary of any misleading objectification of Buddha-nature either as something static and eternal that did not require self-effort or as an attainable goal fulfilled only at the completion of practice. The profound and troubling soteriological dilemma which Dōgen faced, aggravated by the apparent gap between his existential experience of impermanence and the Tendai ontology of an eternal Buddha-nature, is succinctly illustrated in the following *mondō* (Zen dialogue) related in "Genjōkōan": A monk approaches Zen master Hōtetsu, who is fanning himself, and asks, "The wind-nature is constant. There is no place it does not circulate. Why do you still use a fan?" The master replies, "You only know that the wind-nature is constant. You do not know yet the meaning of it circulating everywhere";[48] and he continues fanning himself. That is, the permeation of wind, symbolic of Buddha-nature, seems to render superfluous any human action, such as waving a fan. But if the fan, symbolic of sustained practice, is not used, the coolness and freshness of the wind will never be felt.

Dōgen journeyed to China with a sense of shame and disillusionment about the weakness and inadequacy of the Buddhist

Dharma as taught in Japan.[49] He soon found himself on the receiving end of such a conversation as cited in the *mondō* above. While living on board a docked ship, he was visited by an old monk who quickly terminated his visit despite Dōgen's insistent request that he stay the night. The monk retorted that he must return to his job of cook at the monastery, but Dōgen protested that someone of his position could easily escape this obligation. The cook made the point, however, that his monastic duty was indeed the "practice of the Way" (*bendō*), something to be eagerly pursued and by no means to be avoided.[50] This encounter shocked Dōgen into a new perspective of time and its relationship to Buddha-nature. He realized that enlightenment is not a matter of waiting, anticipation or expectation, but is to be actualized right here-and-now through continuing practice. The Way is everywhere, but it must be affirmed and renewed through the cultivation of sustained exertion (*gyōji*) which completes and fulfills it. "Although the Dharma is equally endowed to everyone, without practice it is not manifested, and without realization it is not attained. [The Dharma] is neither one nor many; release it and it fills your hands. It is neither up nor down; speak it and it fills your mouth."[51] The dialogue with the elderly monk stunned Dōgen into a self-imposed injunction to exert himself fully to bring forth the Way. No time could be wasted so long as it continually developed and prolonged the practice of awakening. Dōgen no longer saw time in terms of sorrow, unchanneled urgency, boredom or longing; he found that each and every and any moment could be an existential occasion to realize Buddha-nature.

Dōgen underwent one more significant experience that led to his breakthrough of the soteriological impasse concerning the relationship between impermanence and Buddha-nature — the occasion of his *satori* achieved under the guidance of master Ju-ching. It is noteworthy that Dōgen did not formulate his own philosophical understanding of the *Dharma* until after his enlightenment. One of his major contributions was to stress without question or compromise the absolute simultaneity of Buddha-nature and self-realization, which involves the identity of theory and practice, ontology and existence, philosophy and religion, original and acquired enlightenment. Philosophical reflection must derive from personal, practical experience and cannot precede it. "Concerning the [experiential] logic (*dōri*) of Buddha-nature, the Buddha-nature is not realized before Buddhahood (*jōbutsu*) is attained; nor is it realized after Buddhahood is attained. Rather, the Buddha-nature is invariably manifested simultaneously with the attainment of Buddhahood."[52]

Continuing his quest in China, Dōgen was eager to become the disciple of Ju-ching (J. Nyojō), who was widely respected for his tireless, deeply sincere and uncompromising approach to Zen meditation. Only a true and inspiring master, Dōgen felt at this point, could convey the meaning of the Way through an authentic face-to-face encounter between teacher and disciple. The decisive moment for Dōgen, as recorded in *Kenzeiki*, came during a session of intensive meditation when Ju-ching thunderously reprimanded another monk for falling asleep after countless hours of *zazen*: "In *zazen* it is imperative to cast off body and mind! How could you indulge in sleeping at such a critical point?" Dōgen was suddenly awakened upon hearing this remark. He told Ju-ching that his body and mind had indeed been cast off (*shinjin-datsuraku*), and the master confirmed the authenticity of his *satori*.[53] Dōgen had fully rid himself of bondage to passions and delusions — self-imposed volitional and conceptual fixations — and had spontaneously manifested the liberation of True Manhood.[54]

The impact of the incident was that Dōgen had crossed the fabricated boundary which heretofore separated two kinds of time — the eternal and instantaneous, awakened and mundane, *nirvāṇic* and transitory, purposeless and directional. It was the point where his urgency, striving, longing and despair met and were reconciled to ultimate meaninglessness, goallessness and non-attainability, no longer in terms of futility, but as the constant renewal of the Way through continually renewed self-exertion. Instead of trying to make *mujō* go away or regretting it, Dōgen saw that it offered the genuine risk which perpetually enhances enlightenment. Dōgen does not dissolve the polarities of time into a metaphysical synthesis of oppositions, an approach which is antithetical to his own, but stresses full and dynamic existential seizure of the totalistic moment, encompassing past, present and future as well as self and world, all beings and all Buddhas, life and death. To totally exert onself is to be totally released from bondage to oneself, to gain fully integrating immersion in the impermanence of self and phenomena. The difference between Dōgen's *zazen* before and after his breakthrough of the "gateless gate" (*mumonkan*) is that he has achieved a genuine experience of temporal reality beyond a particular attitude-response to time limited by perspective and situational context. It is full realization of the moment by virtue of the emptiness of the moment. Because nothing is expected or sought, everything is gained. As Dōgen has abandoned hesitation, reflection, and choice, he is free for immediate, spontaneous self-surrender and self-realization, profound awareness of the mystery and precarious beauty of ephemeral realities. "Right here," he later exults (echoing the historical Buddha's proclamation), "there is no second person!"[55]

On the basis of his awakening, Dōgen developed his philosophical understanding that *bussho* is fully rooted within, and not in contrast to temporal conditions and the mutability of *dharmic* factors because "time itself (*ji*) already is none other than being(s) (*u*); and being(s) are all none other than time." [56] The Way is a continuingly spontaneous dynamism (*zenki*) to be manifest right here-and-now (*genjōkōan*) through single-minded sitting (*shikan-taza*), the reciprocal spiritual communion between oneself and a Buddha, disciple and master (*kannō-dōkō*), and the inexhaustible possibilities of the active Buddha (*gyōbutsu*). Awakening does not happen once, but must be ever-continuing and ever-renewed. The identities Dōgen maintains between theory and practice, life and death, the three tenses, mind and body, self and others are based on the primordial unities of *mujō-bussho* and of *u-ji*, which represent two-fold perspectives of the selfsame, holistic, dynamically unfolding reality conceptually ungraspable yet experientially ever-manifest in each and every particularity.

Dōgen's vision had become so clear that he willingly revised and even grammatically altered previous Buddhist teachings and expressions to being the formulated or theoretical *Dharma* in accord with his realization of the ideal or attained *Dharma*.[57] Dōgen's philosophical writings are to be seen as the transmission of his full comprehension, appropriation and duplication of Śākymuni's awakening. When he says, for example, that the impermanence of Buddha-nature is seen in "walls, stones, tiles, grasses," this is not merely a cognitive claim or a non-conceptual metaphor, but a reflection of his existential liberation from, through and into time. "Each moment and each *dharma* is inseparable from the [temporal] process of life itself, and each thing and each mind is inseparable from the [temporal] process of life itself."[58]

Issues in Methodology

A central question to be explored here is whether there may be, in light of Dōgen's approach to Zen, anything philosophically problematic in Heidegger's emphasis on Dasein's factical decisions for deriving ontology and his suspension of the existential significance or of the soteriological meaning in his work. Does the unresolved tension in Heidegger's thought between ontology and existence, theory and practice reflect a limitation or lack of personal awareness which needs reevaluation? Does this very tension lead to the unfinished and unsettled nature of Heidegger's philosophical enterprise? The justification for considering these critical points is that Heidegger has admitted at the end of his philosophical career that his project remains unfinished, and that its conclusions are more questionable and problematic than ever. Furthermore, there seems to be a vacillation and uncertainty in Heidiegger's various approaches to Being and time from *Sein und Zeit* to the later works; and his critical reexamination and reinterpretation of previous thinkers from the standpoint of primordial time demands that his own thinking be analyzed and evaluated by the same relentlessly critical and challenging standard. At the same time, Heidegger's careful and thoughtful concern with hermeneutics and language — the non-traditional and non-substantive terminology and methodology of his creative questioning and dialogue — as well as his understanding of the convergence of the existential and ontological dimensions of temporality, serves to highlight and deepen an understanding of Dōgen, helping to clarify many doctrines and expressions that would remain ambiguous without the critical comparative context. Thus, meanings, implications and ramifications will be drawn out that are inherent in each thinker's work but perhaps not fully apparent without this critical juxtaposition, reconstruction and evaluation of their philosophies.

In any case, it is clear that Heidegger considers himself to be writing in *Sein und Zeit* from the standpoint of phenomenological neutrality. Although he asserts that phenomenology must be hermeneutic (that is, interpretive in terms of Dasein's circular understanding of Being rather than merely descriptive) and based on the existence of Dasein, whether authentically self-chosen or inauthentically neglected, he consistently denies any proposal of a "moral" difference between authenticity and inauthenticity. The former is not morally superior or prior to the latter; falling is not the loss of purity, but the way of Being which Dasein is in-the-world for the most part.[59] Heidegger's disclosure of Dasein's temporal freedom is not to be construed as an existential injunction, although it can be and frequently has been so interpreted. Dōgen, on the other hand, writes from the perspective of one who has "cast off body and mind of self and others," and who, on that basis, does exhort the Zen and lay practitioner. It is central to his task to deny any possible separation of theory and practice, and to think and philosophize only in terms of — and not through the suspension of — his personal attainment of True Manhood immediately and completely manifested and renewed in concrete situations. He insists in "Bendōwa," "You must realize that for a Buddhist practitioner, any debate concerning the superiority or inferiority of one teaching or another or the depth or superficiality of any doctrine is pointless; all that is essential is the authenticity [*shingi*] of practice."[60]

This disparity between Heidegger's and Dōgen's underlying methods and aims is reflective of fundamental differences in their respective views of primordial time. Although they seem to be in accord concerning the overcoming of linear sequential time and of false eternalism as well as in their disclosures of key elements which constitute genuine temporality, they disagree on the existential and ontological meanings of primordial time. For example, Heidegger considers time the "horizon" for understanding Being; there is a basic relatedness between time and Being in that temporality is the meaning of Dasein and thus the fundamental ground for an ontological discovery and interpretation of Being. Yet he admits that his interpretation is tentative and inconclusive. Dōgen, however, establishes a complete and harmoniously interpenetrating selfsameness of time, all beings, Buddha-nature and self-exertion at each and every totalistic moment. Also, Heidegger maintains that primordial — and authentic — time is futural, based on Dasein's anxious anticipation of its possibilities; he associates the present with fallenness, although this dimension too can be authentically transformed. Although Dōgen refutes the "now" that has been isolated from existence and from past and future, he ultimately affirms the dynamism and totality of the fully realized all-encompassing moment.

These disagreements are intensified because it seems likely that each thinker, if positioned in mutual philosophical encounter and dialogue, would strongly disagree with many of the other's conclusions about the meaning and structure of primordial time. Heidegger, for example, does consider the notion of an eternal moment, similar to Dōgen's view of the complete here-and-now (*nikon*), in light of Nietzsche's doctrine of the eternal recurrence of the same events by the will to power in the Moment, and he discounts it as unliberated metaphysics based on the static view of now-time. Dōgen, on the other hand, refutes the Senika view that enlightenment is to be futurally anticipated, recalling Heidegger's emphasis on anticipatory resoluteness, by affirming Buddha-nature spontaneously renewed each and every totalistic moment.

The points of controversy between Heidegger and Dōgen will be considered in light of the guidelines which both thinkers would set for discourse with other philosophical viewpoints, which seem to demand that these other doctrines be challenged, criticized and — if necessary — overcome from the standpoint of an uncompromisingly non-substantive disclosure of primordial time. In "Dialogue with a Japanese,"[61] Heidegger stresses his deep reluctance to impose uncritically and unreflectively traditional Western metaphysical categories, which are heavily laden with historically determined and self-limiting connotations, on East Asian thought, so that the dynamism and insubstantiality of East Asian notions would not be obscured. Yet, he does recognize the philosophical need for dialogue with East Asia from an original and creative — non-substantive or primordial — perspective. Thus, Heidegger's attempted disclosure of the unity of temporality — more primordial than the Western fixation with *ousia* — is uniquely fruitful for an exposition of and critical comparison with Dōgen in order not only to reconstruct each thinker's views, but to evaluate their conclusions about primordial time.

At the same time, the grounds and the need for a critical analysis of Heidegger in light of a thinker such as Dōgen are implicit in Heidegger's stated intention of overcoming Western misconceptions of Being derived from inauthentic time. In order to determine the success of Heidegger's project, his work must be examined in a universal setting; that is, not strictly from a Western standpoint which may presuppose the very deficiencies he tries to challenge, but from the perspective of comparison with an Eastern thinker who also claims to eliminate any trace of substantiality in his understanding of time as the preeminent philosophical task. The starting point of Dōgen's reflections is the universal encounter of man with the irrefutable and inescapable reality of impermanence. He maintains that his approach to the problematics of temporal existence is "of constant application" or "applicable to all" (*fukan*), or of universal significance and validity, and he would criticize any and all partial viewpoints, even those taken by Buddhists, which conceal the profound unity and insubstantiality of being-time. Without such a philosophical encounter, it would appear that Heidegger's notions are limited to his response to the Western tradition, which is precisely why Heidegger himself criticizes Nietzsche's will to power as the *reversal* rather than the surpassing of previous substance ontologies.

If, for example, Dōgen's conception of the fully realized moment, itself based on a critique of misguided eternalism, escapes the limitations which Heidegger finds with Western doctrines of eternity, there is then a serious challenge to Heidegger's view of futural temporality. The grounds for Dōgen's participation in a philosophical dialogue with — and his possible overcoming of — Heidegger's thinking is the standard set by both thinkers: any view which falls short in any subtle way of a full overcoming of derivative time must be exposed and de-structured. Thus, dialogue between Heidegger and Dōgen is not apologetic or statically standing still, but critical and progressive, pointing away from attachments to substantiality and toward a clear and consistent non-substantive view of primordial time justified in terms of and accounting for the multiple dimensions of existence. Heidegger suggests in *Was Heisst Denken?* that because no original thinker fully understands himself, the unthought and the unspoken in his expressions must be explored and rediscovered. Similarly, Dōgen takes an adamantly non-sectarian stance, insisting uncompromisingly on the realization of the true nature of impermanence and being-time. The philosophical encounter established here will continually question and probe as to whose philosophy of the existential and ontological dimensions of primordial time represents the most complete, radical and thoroughgoing breakthrough from the derivative or substantive view.

Any presentation and analysis of Heidegger must take into account the entire development and range of his thinking in terms of his fundamental aims as carried out in various stages from "Being and Time" to "On Time and Being." It is equally necessary to limit the account to the most pertinent materials. The focus in this analysis will be on Heidegger's *Sein und Zeit* for two interrelated reasons. First, because it offers the most systematic and the richest material for comparison with Dōgen's philosophy of time in terms of its complex intertwining of the ontological and existential dimensions. Also, much of the recent scholarship on Heidegger has tended to overlook the continuing significance of *Sein und Zeit*, preferring to take up Heidegger's suggestion that it be seen as a stage, however essential, which leads to and is superceded by his later works, the so-called "Heidegger II." Heidegger's later writings, particularly his reflections on *Ereignis* as the "event" which is not á particular occurrence but that which makes occurrence as such possible, will be examined in terms of their continuity with and extension of the notions in *Sein und Zeit*. Of Dōgen's works, the *Shōbōgenzō* is central due to its philosophical breadth and profundity. It evaluates and critically revises many prominent Buddhist and Zen doctrines in terms of Dōgen's radical reinterpretation of the Buddhist understanding of time. His autobiographical and explicitly exhortative works, particularly *Zuimonki*, are also cited in accord with his refusal to allow any gap between theory and practice, living and understanding, universal significance and personal experience.

The investigation of the affinities and disparities between Heidegger and Dōgen concerning time will concentrate on: 1) their analyses and attempted overcoming of derivative time, which is achieved through 2) the disclosure of radical contingency inescapably pervading existence (revealed in terms of the notions of finitude in Heidegger and impermanence in Dōgen), which points to 3) the dynamic existential and ontological unity of primordial or non-substantive temporality. The method includes both exegesis through a reconstruction of each thinker's arguments, and critical-comparison by the examination and evaluation of the disparities in the fundamental aims, approaches and accomplishments of the philosophical views of Heidegger and Dōgen as well as of the soteriological implications expressed therein.

Chapter 2

The Origin of Derivative Time

Problematics of Derivative Time

The analysis of the arising and persistence of the notion of derivative time, as presented by Heidegger and Dōgen, is essential to the disclosure of the possibilities for realizing primordial time. The deficiencies of the conventional fixation with linear sequence must be exposed and overcome in order to illuminate and establish the true nature and structure of unified and dynamic temporal existence. The twofold focus of the analysis of derivative time attempts to unravel the deeply-rooted and self-perpetuating entanglements between inauthentic existential understanding that gives rise to and is, in turn, reinforced by ontological misconceptions. Both thinkers investigate the views of the average man, whose unreflective attachment to the supposed constancy of now-time seeks to deny his temporally determined contingency, and so becomes the disguised basis for the metaphysician's false claims of an eternity detached from the vicissitudes of existence. Their examination of the origin of derivative time attempts to reverse this vicious cycle of ensnarement by showing that in the genuine ontological structure of history and continuity, the present is not static or a substance but thoroughly pervaded by past and future, which makes possible an authentic reinterpretation and reappropriation of the traditional deficient ontologies.

The focus of this chapter will be a critical reconstruction, comparison and evaluation in light of the fundamental philosophical aims of Heidegger and Dōgen of how each analyzes:

the derivative nature of sequential time's relationship with primordial time; the inauthentic connection between an obsession with now-time or fixation with substance and speculations about eternity; and the possible authentic link between a true understanding of past and history and the overcoming of previously transmitted ontologies within their respective traditions. The comparative section of the chapter will critically contrast their attempts at de-structuring derivative time by examining their approaches to the relationship between self, world and time; past, present and future; as well as between the conception of history and creative philosophical interpretation. It will be shown that whereas Heidegger's analysis of now-time leads to an emphasis on the priority of future and past and to an inability to disclose the temporality of entities, Dōgen overcomes the inauthentic static now-point through disclosure of the all-inclusive simultaneous passage (kyōryaku) of the three tenses encompassing all phenomena.

First, an introduction to the predominant concerns which guide each thinker's analysis. The central concern for Heidegger is to discover why the meaning of Being has been concealed in the history of Western metaphysics in that Being is conceived as the first and/or highest immutable and enduring being because the increasingly rigid and supposedly self-evident presupposition that beings are actually "now *in* time" has not been challenged. Being in the primordial sense of the presencing (Anwesenheit) which holds sway has been reduced, according to Heidegger, to the objectified status of some substantive entity (ousia) that is merely present-at-hand ((vorhanden); the emerging, arising or unconcealing process which illuminates Dasein's encounter with phenomena (and which Heidegger contends is the original meaning of *physis* and *aletheia*) is mistaken for that-(actual thing) which-emerges. In *Humanismusbrief* Heidegger charges that, "The oblivion of Being makes itself known indirectly through the fact that man always observes and handles only beings. Even so, because man cannot avoid having some notion of Being, it is explained merely as what is 'most general' and therefore as some being, or as the product of a finite subject. At the same time 'Being' (Sein) has long stood for 'beings' (*Seiendes*) and, inversely, the latter for the former, the two of them caught in a curious and still unraveled confusion."[1] Man always stands in the light of Being, but he tends to think only from beings back again to beings with merely a glance in passing toward Being as such. Just as genuine illumination is in every case a possibility for man, there are elements inherent in his existence which subvert or obstruct this potential, propelling him toward inauthenticity.

This existential-ontological deficiency is analyzed in *Sein und Zeit* in terms of the hermeneutic circularity of Dasein's ontico-ontological priority for the possibility of any and all ontologies, whereby its own specific state of Being remains concealed from it. Dasein is for the most part absorbed with or fallen in the world of its concern, so that it understands itself as a present-at-hand (*vorhanden*) being "in" a present-at-hand (*vorhanden*) world rather than as the transcendental structure and unified totality of care (Being-in-the-world thrown-projection). Consequently, "the primary understanding of Being has been diverted to Being as presence-at-hand — a diversion which is motivated by that [phenomenon] of falling itself."[2] Because Dasein is always in each case ontically already familiar with itself in that an average everyday self-understanding is for the most part idly and ambiguously presupposed, Being remains ontologically farthest from it in that its essential nature is rarely questioned. Nevertheless, pre-ontologically Dasein is surely no stranger to Being. The aim of fundamental ontology is to uncover on the basis of Dasein's factical-*existenziell* decisions the *existenzial*-ontological foundations of ecstatic temporality, and at the same time to see why an understanding of this ground is lost in ontically-oriented ontological interpretations based on now-time.

As Dasein falls back upon the world in which it finds itself, its misconceptions about time and history allow it to fall prey to the apparent dominance of the metaphysical tradition's preoccupation with infinitude. Thus, the analytic of Dasein's inauthenticity necessarily involves a destruction of the history of ontology since both everydayness and metaphysics derive from the common phenomenon of falling. This destruction is largely carried out in Heidegger's later works (Heidegger II).[3] The hermeneutic starting point is shifted there, however, from a phenomenologico-ontological analysis of Dasein's inauthentic falling and the possible repetition of its authentic potentialities, to an historical "step back" which re-thinks the self-concealment of Being itself that has led to the current destitute aftermath of metaphysics and the global dominance of willful technology.

Dōgen's primary interest is to eliminate any rift, however subtle, that may appear in Buddhist expressions of theory or techniques of meditation which violates the absolute inseparability and simultaneity of practice and realization, original and acquired enlightenment, Buddha-nature and the attainment of Buddhahood as spontaneously manifest here-and-now in every activity and expression of the True Man who has "cast off body and mind." In "Fukanzazengi,"Dōgen's first work after his enlightenment, in which he begins the task of transmitting the Right Law (shōbō) to Japan where he felt that it had until then been impossible to learn, he insists that "the slightest discrepancy [between practice and realization] makes the Way as distant as heaven and earth."4 But he also concedes that two powerful and pervasive doubt blocks — which he himself endured before his breakthrough under the instruction of Ju-ching — can create such a disparity and will, if not fully uprooted, become heretical views that ultimately obstruct awakening. "Indeed," he writes in that essay, "the Whole Body [of Buddha] is far beyond worldly dust, so why is there a need to brush it clean? It is never apart from one right where one is, so what is the purpose of training?"5 The first question refers to the Senika heresy that Buddha-nature is immutable and unchanging, seemingly beyond and not approachable through the "mundane" efforts of daily practice, yet only attainable in the future at the conclusion of practice. The second question cites the naturalistic heresy which unreflectively affirms the everyday world prior to authentication by the resolute and dedicated exertions of the True Man. Although apparently contradictory, the common impact of both heresies is to negate the necessity for the utmost and sustained yet ultimately purposeless and non-striving exertions here-and-now of the "skin, flesh, bones, and marrow." The heretical tendencies thereby perpetuate what Dōgen calls the restrictive and debilitating "bonds of seeking the Buddha external to oneself" (*butsu-baku*)[6] — an attachment to a static and contemplative enlighten-ment either artificially removed from or inauthentically accept-ant of the incessant transformations of the impermanent world.

Dōgen tries to overcome the insidious "bonds of the falsely externalized Buddha" which shackle the primordially and spon-taneously "active Buddha" (*gyōbutsu*) by analyzing in "Uji" why the average man's (*bonbu*) deep-seated delusions misconstrue the true nature of being-time. The average view of time mistakes the essential dynamism and unity of being-time for a fixed, isolated point within the external framework of time. The incessant fluc-tuations of the *dharma*'s dwelling-place (*jū-hōi*) are thus confused with the mere coming and going of horary sequence; and gen-uine passage of the three tenses is mistaken for "time flies." Because of these basic and generally undetected misconceptions, the primordial identity whereby all beings in the entire *Dharma*-realm are linked together as time's occurrence at each, every and any moment (*jiji*) is lost, and the totalistic here-and-now is either overlooked or confused with static constancy. Consequently, the supposed eternity of Buddha-nature is posited, and inauthentic-ally bifurcated into the aspects of potentiality and actuality, pres-ent practice and future attainment, and subjective pursuit of an objectified goal. "It is because," Dōgen writes, "this very time and this very being are learned as something other than the *Dharma* that the sixteen-foot golden body [symbolic of realiza-tion] is not recognized as myself. But even the evasion of [the truth] that I am the sixteen-foot golden body is a fragment of being-time."[7]

In "Uji" and other chapters of *Shōbōgenzō*, particularly "Busshō," Dōgen challenges and reinterprets, radically revises and even deliberately changes or intentionally misreads both philosophically and expressionally the words of Mahāyāna sū-tras and Zen masters which in any sense deny rather than fully and uncompromisingly reflect the profound existential significance of the transiency of being-time. Dōgen is unhesitatingly critical of what he considers misleading or obstructive scripture and authority. Yet he strongly disagrees with the orthodox Zen view of a "special transmission *outside* the scriptures without reliance on words and letters."[8] He insists on the continuing quest for creative expressions (*dōtoku*) which divulge the inexhaustible meanings of the Way as a matter of the spiritual "vines" or entwinements (*kattō*) by which Buddha (-master) and Buddha (-disciple) (*yuibutsu-yobutsu*) commune with, instruct and enlighten each other. Dōgen's emphasis on full and unimpeded realization of the Right Law concretely embodied in the True Man here-and-now diverges significantly from the doctrines of his contemporaries, Hōnen, Shinran and Nichiren, which derive from a firm belief in the hopelessness of self-power (*jiriki*) in the Age of Degenerate Law (*mappō*).

Heidegger's Analysis of Derivative Time

The question of Being is raised in *Sein und Zeit* in terms of how Dasein, the distinctive being for whom Being is the ownmost and determinative issue of its existence, comes to know itself in relation to — and by standing out amongst — entities in the world. The traditional metaphysical conception of man's relationship to the world presumes that Dasein is first of all a spiritual Thing which somehow gets placed "into" a space consisting of material things that it perceives, knows and manipulates. Knowledge is considered an act that transpires "between" and as a result of the *convenientia* of two supposedly constant things present-at-hand — the *subiectum* and *substantia*, which appear in Cartesian philosophy as *res cogitans* and *res extensa*. "But because [the primordial] structure of Being remains ontologically inaccessible, yet is experienced ontically as a 'relationship' between one entity (the world) and another (the soul)," Heidegger challenges the tradition, "and because one proximally understands Being by taking entities as entities within-the-world for one's ontological foothold, one tries to conceive the relationship between world and soul as grounded in these two entities themselves and in the meaning of their Being — namely, to conceive it as Being-present-at-hand."[9]

Heidegger maintains, however, that neither the self nor the world nor the relationship between them is simply present-at-hand because something like the world is always revealed to Dasein, which is never worldless or detached but in every case concernfully alongside entities and solicitously with Others. Heidegger seeks both to overcome and to analyze the origin of deficient representations of Dasein by uncovering the unified yet multi-dimensional phenomenon of Being-in-the-world (*In-der-Welt-sein*) prior to the distinctions of subject/object, theory/non-theory, spirit/matter, essence/existence, etc. "Ontologically," he suggests, " 'world' is not a way of characterizing those entities which Dasein essentially is *not*; it is rather a characteristic of Dasein itself."[10] Worldhood is not an ontical collection of material or natural things external to a subject, but the *a priori* basis and region of Dasein's de-severant and directional spatiality, and of the practical involvements by which Dasein discovers and makes use of references, signs and equipment as it encounters Others. Being-in connotes dwelling and residing, an implicit familiarity of Dasein more fundamental than knowledge and will, cognition and volition, assertion and disposition, illumined or self-disclosed in the three-fold totality of care: (1) understanding, the forestructure for the possibility of self-transparency and hermeneutic interpretation; (2) facticity, by which the determination and limitations — the "disclosive submissiveness" or thrownness — of Dasein are revealed in the states-of-mind or moods which assail it; and (3) falling, or absorption with entities as publicly interpreted which Dasein finds itself alongside.

Care itself is grounded in ecstatic temporality, which is not a succession of sequential nows, but the integral dynamic process of Dasein as ahead-of-itself (understanding as future or coming-towards, *Zu-kunft*) yet already found (facticity as past or having-been) in the world to which it is for the most part bound (falling as present or making-present). "The future is *not later* than having been, and having been is *not earlier* than the Present," Heidegger argues in a refutation of the conventional view of time as a linear sequence of three tenses. "Temporality temporalizes itself as a future which makes present in the process of having been."[11] The ecstatic temporality of care [to be examined more fully in the final chapter] is ontologically prior to and makes possible Dasein's transcendence, spatiality, metaphysical speculation, theoretical discovery and practical behavior as well as the dual existential possibilities of authenticity and inauthenticity, of Dasein's winning itself or its abandonment to the dictatorship of the they-self's public world.

For the most part, according to Heidegger, the unity and multi-dimensionality of temporality is ontologically concealed because Dasein is existentially preoccupied with deficient and indifferent modes of an evasive self-flight from the authentic possibilities of discourse, sight and interpretation, into the idle talk, curiosity and ambiguity of the they-self (*Man-selbst*). In falling (*Verfallen*), everything primordial and mysterious is considered obvious and self-evident, and the unique dynamism of temporality is reduced to the monotonous uniformity of "all one and the same." This everyday outlook takes the form of an obsession with the measurement of time through the use of clocks, calendars and statistics, which in turn reflects the sense that one can either take or lose time that is considered all the more precious as it forever slips away. Inauthentic Dasein is increasingly concerned with the apparent actuality of the present so that the past and historical facticity as well as the future and possibilities for transcendence, which are primordially and ecstatically interwoven with the present in the most essential and pervasive ways, get eclipsed and frequently seem to be entirely missing or appear in some derivative mode. Dasein is engaged in making-present in its relation to entities which it discovers and uses alongside itself in-the-world, an activity that is necessary for circumspective deliberation and scientific investigation, but which becomes problematic when this deficient interpretation is turned back upon Dasein so that "Dasein understands its ownmost Being in the sense of a certain 'factual' Being-present-at-hand."[12]

Dasein's everyday state is a "way to be," a "how" of existence which neither disappears nor is fully eradicated by authenticity, but constitutes an *existenzial* condition that can only be momentarily modified *existenzielly*. Falling is not the loss of a former moral purity nor is authenticity a free-floating isolation above the troubles of the world. Because it is an inherent possibility of Dasein's ecstatic existence, falling is grounded in — arising from even while concealing — temporality itself. "Temporality has different possibilities and different ways of *temporalizing* itself. The basic possibilities of existence, the authenticity and inauthenticity of Dasein, are grounded ontologically on possible temporalizations of temporality."[13] In contrast to Hegel,[14] who according to Heigegger's interpretation holds that the Absolute Spirit must necessarily and first of all by its very essence fall "into" time as an obstacle when it is not in itself complete in order to ultimately overcome time and realize itself, Heidegger maintains that falling is a mode of existence that belongs to temporality neither accidentally nor inevitably, but as an essential ever-present possibility that is never fully overcome.

By virtue of its facticity, Dasein prepares for itself a constant temptation for the alienating and tranquillizing acceptance of the public world. Only because Dasein is ecstatically stretched along *from* birth *to* death, traversing the time granted to it between these boundaries and maintaining itself throughout with a certain sameness, does it consider itself to be actual only in the present now — "within-time" — thereby forgetting its past and fearing its future so that its ecstatic movement appears to be stifled. As temporality, care reckons with time in a way already familiar to it in its planning, preventing and taking precautions concerning that which will take place "later on," or happens "now," or has occurred "earlier." There is in time-reckoning itself a recognition of the unified relational structure between the three times that is characterized both by datability and existential significance, but this remains for the most part unclarified and vague. Furthermore, Dasein is thrown into the world and surrendered to the seemingly arbitrary but maddeningly regular changes of day and night, light and dark which in certain foretold and unavoidable sequences take away the possibility of sight that is needed for social intercourse and practical endeavors. The sun already dates the time with which Dasein is concerned, so that something like a clock is discovered along with the world, and this readily translates into a publicly available measure for time.

Dasein's problems arise when it no longer regards the clock as an expedient tool created by and at the disposal of its concern, but looks at it and says "now" and measures how long this now lasts. It determines the frequency and duration of the now's presence in that stretch in terms of an unchanging standard. Dasein falls precisely when it says to itself that the present moment, however fleeting, is an enduring substance and that the endlessness of time, however lasting, seems to slip or fly by. The nows are present-at-hand along with entities. Although they are not *vorhanden* in exactly the same way as things, they are seen in the same general horizon, simply ranging themselves along one after another in succession. The nows pass away and those which are gone make up the past; the nows come along and those which are approaching define the future. The constancy of the now is common for all nows whether of past, present or future. Even though it is said to change so swiftly, this persistent and forbidding presentness of the now is always thought to prevail. The sequence itself is considered *vorhanden* in the same way as the now, but it has its own time which includes particular now-points, carrying them along without interruption, and perpetuating the existential gap Dasein has created between itself and time.

Once committed to ontological misconceptions derived from an existential deficiency that is supported though not necessarily dictated by its factical conditions and submission to the world, the datability, significance and interrelatedness of ecstatic temporality are forgotten. Time seems to be passing away "out there." Dasein feels that time must not be lost, and the more it tries to track and define time, the more time is controlling and determining Dasein. Surrender to now-time reflects the lurking anxiety which Dasein feels about its own passing toward its end, which is inauthentically transmuted into fear of something *vorhanden* though not-yet actual — a now which is constant and substantive that is approaching in the endless sequence. "*Dasein knows fugitive time in terms of its 'fugitive' knowledge about its death.*"[15] Rather than admit that it is perpetually in the process of dying as Being-towards-the-end and resolutely facing death, Dasein firmly and inauthentically believes that time in-itself is forever flying by. Dasein finds false comfort in the appearance of time as endless on both sides, receding ever-behind and advancing ever-forward, so that an end can never be found on either side. The more insistent Dasein is that something be done "now, at this instant!" expecting more time while realizing that there is less and less, the more it refuses to confront its finitude, taking refuge in the thought that time keeps coming along and going by — as if time does not let itself be halted. "Here it is not as if the finitude of time were getting understood," Heidegger writes, " . . . In the everyday way in which we are with one another, the levelled-off sequence of 'nows' remains completely unrecognizable as regards its origin in the temporality of the individual Dasein."[16]

Just as Dasein fearfully refuses to acknowledge its future which pervades the present as the imminence of death, it also obliterates its past, which is reduced to what is merely no longer present-at-hand. Heidegger distinguishes between two conceptions of the past, which lead to two radically different understandings of history. The derivative view of the past is that *vorhanden* time has vanished and is left behind (*Vergangenheit*) by Dasein, although it can still be carried along in the present as a *vorhanden* monument, ruin or artifact to be idly and curiously gazed at without authentic existential engagement or ontological reflection. "Lost in the making present of the 'today', [Dasein] understands the 'past' in terms of the 'Present'."[17] Scientific history (historiology) surveys and records the supposedly objective facts which are over and done with. In considering Dasein a substantive entity subjected to the events, circumstances and vicissitudes which befall it, historiology simply gathers information about the deeds Dasein has performed.

The primordial meaning of the past, Heidegger maintains, is the ecstatic having-been-there (*dagewesen*) of Dasein fully integrated with, and continuing to influence and permeate the present and future. Authentic Dasein hands down to itself and takes over afresh its past through *existenziell* repetition of what it has-been as its ownmost fate in light of its resolute freedom for death and the possibilities of what it can-be. Dasein *is* its past, not as a no-longer-there which follows limply along after it, but in the sense of thrownness going ahead of and coming towards it as thrown-projection that is never, in Heidegger's image, "caught" or "coming to a stop."[18] Dasein's past influences its futural projects which in turn generate the decisions it makes. Genuine historicality (*Geschichtlichkeit*) does not merely observe Dasein's behavior; it is rather Dasein itself fatefully recalling and renewing its choices, alive to the full multi-dimensional unity of its temporal foundations. "History (*Geschichte*) as happening (*Geschehen*)," Heidegger writes in *Einführung in die Metaphysik*, "is an acting and being acted upon which pass through the present, which are determined from out of the future, and which take over the past. It is precisely the present that vanishes (*verschwindet*) in happening."[19]

The derivative obfuscation of the ecstatic unity of Dasein's future and past lead directly, according to Heidegger, to the deficiencies of the metaphysical tradition. Out of time-reckoning — the phenomenal aspect of temporality which is closest to us — there "arises the ordinary everyday understanding of time. And this understanding evolves into the traditional conception of time."[20] Infinitude, an unwillingness to acknowledge the future out of fear of one's finite existence, is the hallmark of and the highest value-standard sought by metaphysics since its inception. The self-surrender by philosophers to the apparent but false mastery of the tradition itself, which claims self-evidence for the material it offers for a redundant reworking rather than a radical and repetitive reexamination, is due to the obliteration of the having-been and the consequent hardening and rigidifying of past thinking. An understanding of authentic historicality, however, makes possible the loosening of this sedimentation that conceals Being-as-presence through the ecstatically-grounded hermeneutic circularity of creative questioning and dialogue, which uncovers and clarifies the primordial foundations of previous thinkers' expressions of Being prior to their conscious or deliberate intentions.

A de-struction of the history of ontology based on the phenomenologico-ontological repetition of Dasein's ecstatic temporal-historical ground is imperative for two interrelated reasons: first, because fundamental ontology must probe deficient ontologies as exemplary expressions derived from everyday understanding; second, because Dasein as historical cannot regain its authenticity unless it appropriately takes over its past interpretations.

By de-struction, Heidegger does not mean something negative like shaking off the tradition, or the "vicious relativizing of ontological standpoints." Rather, he seeks to re-discover the tradition's "birth certificate" by the analysis which frees up Dasein's heretofore concealed phenomenal content. Nevertheless, such an ontological revision cannot help but "do violence" (*Gewaltsamkeit*) to the claims of the ordinary understanding of time, or to its complacent and tranquilized obviousness that is all-too-apparent in metaphysics itself.

The projected overcoming of traditional metaphysics remains in rudimentary form in *Sein und Zeit*, but is executed in Heidegger's later works, many of which consist of or include lengthy interpretations or "hermeneutic conversations" with past metaphysicians from Anaximander to Nietzsche, based on the view that while no thinker fully understands himself, each essential thinker does express a partial disclosure of Being.[21] In Heidegger II, however, the dilemmas of derivative metaphysics are no longer seen as a consequence of inauthentic, irresolute Dasein, but as the "error" or pervasive un-truth which permeates human ek-sistence due to the self-concealment of the destiny of Being as such (rather than any particular mistake made by man). The mysterious closure of Being precipitates a fateful decline in thinking inevitably consummated in the willful conceptualization and manipulation of beings by the triumphant human subject. History is the mission on which man has been sent by the epochal or eschatological clearing (*Lichtung*) of Being; and the errancy of wandering amidst beings to seek and never find Being is the fate man must endure due to Being's self-withdrawal. "Oblivion of Being belongs to the self-veiling essence of Being. . . . This means that the history of Being begins with the oblivion of Being, since Being — together with its essence, its distinction from beings — keeps to itself."[22] Being was disclosed to the earliest Greek thinkers as the illuminative event or presence of Dasein's encounter with beings, variously named as *logos* or *physis* — the process of self-emergence or bursting-forth into openness. The primordial difference between presence and things-present, however, has subsequently been forgotten and hypostatized through an "abundance of transformations" into Idea, Substance, God,

Cogito and finally the self-certifying and self-objectifying Will.[23]

The understanding common to both *Sein und Zeit* and the later Heideggerian approaches towards overcoming the tradition is that the fundamental and perdurant entanglements of metaphysics occur when infinitude is reified in Plato's notion that lived-time is an "image of eternity." The supposed constancy of now-time is thus elevated to a supreme though well-disguised position in that Being is conceptualized as an immutable supra-sensuous and supra-temporal realm over and beyond temporal-historical existence. Time is thus considered a self-limiting condition or negative attribute of cognition that prohibits man from full access to the eternal Truth removed from ecstacy and finitude. The insidious connection between now-time and eternity appears in Aristotle's conception of the endlessness of causally-connected now-points. It is also perpetuated by the medieval theological preoccupation with the *nunc stans*, timelessness represented as the "standing-now."

Heidegger considers Kant the first thinker for whom time becomes problematic in its ontological meaning. Kant does intend — although not explicitly, according to Heidegger's hermeneutic reconstruction — to put the time of the finite human subject at the synthesizing and creative center of the transcendental imagination as the universal condition for the possibility of encountering phenomena and as the origin of space. Yet Kant misrepresents finitude as an ontical limitation, Heidegger asserts, and the original Platonic bifurcation between eternity and temporality emerges in the Kantian separation of the noumenal and phenomenal realms. By holding back from a genuine disclosure of the temporal ground and constitution of existence, Kant further shows the poverty and entanglements of the traditional conception of time that binds his thought.

At the culmination and conclusion of metaphysics, an insatiable longing for infinity prevails in the modern dominance of the absolutized *subiectum*. Hegel, according to Heidegger's critical interpretation, seeks to fully and finally surpass finitude by elevating all phenomena to the status of eternal Being. "Hegel alone apparently succeeded in jumping over this shadow," Heidegger contends, "but only in such a way that he eliminated the shadow, i.e., the finiteness of man, and jumped into the sun itself. Hegel skipped over the shadow, but he did not, because of that, surpass the shadow."[24]

Although Nietzsche claims to undermine human fixations with the "fable" of a so-called eternal Reality that stands over and against the temporal world condemned as illusory appearance, he merely reverses, according to Heidegger, the traditional priorities by valuing now-time rather than eternity. Nietzsche's doctrine of the eternal recurrence of the self-same will to power attempts to preserve the constancy of the now through the monotonous uniformity of the redundancy of the will to will more will, the most unvarying perpetuation of that which is ceaselessly unvarying.[25] Nietzsche thus reduces Being to the level of the becoming of beings without penetrating to temporality which underlies this distinction, thus fully obfuscating the primordial in blurred indistinguishability with the derivative. The possible permutations of the links between now-time and eternity, according to Heidegger, are thereby fully exhausted, though by no means overcome.

Dōgen's Analysis of Derivative Time

Dōgen seeks to overcome any tendency to dichotomize Buddha-nature that obstructs the path to realization, by analyzing and uprooting the unenlightened views of the average man who fabricates separations between beings and time, self and time, time present and the time of past and future, t1 an t2 as well as between passage and that-which-passes, arrival and the process of coming, time and space. All such fabricated dichotomizations may continue to haunt and subvert the efforts of the Zen disciple. These existential and ontological rifts constitute the self-imposed and self-perpetuating barriers to a genuine understanding of the impermanent nature of *busshō* and the primordial unity of practice and realization in that they project enlightenment onto a supra-temporal realm severed from "daily being-time right within this very twenty-four hours."

In "Busshō" Dōgen presents his own interpretation of a Zen

parable concerning the fourteenth patriarch Nāgārjuna in order
to illustrate how subtle yet insidious misconceptions concerning
time impede the here-and-now realization and explanation of
Buddha-nature. In the legend, Nāgārjuna sat before a congregation and he "manifested a body of complete freedom while sitting, just like the appearance of a full moon . . . expressing
thereby the original body of buddhas."[26] Yet the members of the
congregation were unable to see or comprehend the master's
form, although his foremost disciple Aryadeva pointed out that
it was, indeed, right before them.

According to Dōgen's exegesis, Nāgārjuna did not literally
transform himself into the moon, but his dropping-off of body
and mind spontaneously manifested the illuminating power,
vastness and clarity of Buddha-nature. The disciples' dilemma
lay in their egocentric effort to look beyond the fully concrete,
active embodiment of bisshō in the personhood of Nāgārjuna,
in their futile pursuit of a symbolic vision of the self-limitation
or literal transformation of Eternity into a round moon. Because
of their self-centeredness, they thereby falsely bifurcated Buddha-
nature into the aspects of essence and manifestation, reality and
symbol, changelessness and apparent form — a self-entangling
and highly problematic stance that is for the most part supported
by traditional interpretations of the legend which misunderstand
the pedagogical nature of the Mahāyāna doctrine of three Buddha-
bodies (Trikāya)[27] as being distinct from the "majestic activities
of the active Buddha" (gyōbutsu-igi). Dōgen insists, however, that
"The form in which [Nāgārjuna] manifested his body is the same
form we all have sitting here right now. This very body we have
is manifesting a round moon shape. . . . There is not even one
Buddha who is not making this 'thereby expressing' his Buddha-
body. The Buddha-body is the manifesting body, and there is
always a body manifesting Buddha-nature."[28] Neither Nāgārjuna
nor any other Buddha "symbolizes" or represents bisshō; rather,
each single moment of his selfless activity is the immediate and
complete practice, penetration and expression of enlightenment.

In the "Uji" fascicle, Dōgen analyzes the source of the bifurcations of Buddha-nature by focusing on the self-deceptive and
egocentric preoccupations of the average man. Dōgen

distinguishes between derivative and primordial meanings of the term *uji* which can be deduced from an interpretation of the Zen saying: "Sometimes (*uji*) standing so high up on the mountain top/ Sometimes walking deep down on the bottom of sea/ Sometimes a three-headed eight-armed [demon or *Acala*]/ Sometimes a sixteen- or eight-foot [Buddha]. . . ."[29] In the literal or conventional usage of "sometimes" or "at a certain time," *uji* seems to refer to a fixed point in which events occur, an irreducible instantaneous sequential segment that is considered separable from existence and towards which man takes the attitude that it is either appropriate or unfavorable, either useful and fitting or unmanageable and untimely — in short, that it is either in the form of a Buddha or a demon at a particular point in time. If, in the derivative sense, *uji* takes one form at a certain time, it cannot for that time be said to take any other form. The two forms are considered mutually exclusive possibilities; one is previous and finished, the other is current, and they do not overlap.

Uji can, however, also be understood in the primordial sense that all beings and all times are originally, perpetually and without exception, partiality or interval — encompassing Buddha *and* demon simultaneously — inseparably linked together each and every moment. Beings are invariably temporal occurrences; time always presences *as* all beings. There is no being in the entire *Dharma*-realm outside this very moment of time. In "Kūge" Dōgen writes, "Just as flowers appear in many colors, colors are not limited to flowers. Rather, each and every moment appears in colors such as blue, yellow, red, or white. Spring gives rise to flowers, and flowers give rise to spring."[30] Although the average man is inauthentically or egocentrically attached to the supposedly self-evident coming along and going away of twenty-four regular and repetitive horary sequences, the truth of the selfsameness of being-time prevails whether or not it is ever realized. "Any false step taken is still being [-time]. Moreover, even before and after the misjudgement is shown, still there is found the dwelling-place of being [-time]."[31] Man's doubts about time, or even his lack of doubt, his understanding or misunderstanding, his realization or failure to realize its true meaning, show variation and inconsistency from one moment to the next and are themselves shaped and determined by the incessant fluctuations of being-time. Thus, even misconceptions about being-time are evidence of its pervasive nature and represent an opportunity — generally not taken — for creative re-investigation and re-reflection which may lead to genuine realization. As the Zen poem suggests, the primordial meaning of *uji* is embedded and always partially revealed as the true basis, even if disguised and not recognized, in the everyday expression, "sometimes," itself.

The initial and fundamental breach between beings and time necessarily and inescapably involves other delusory bifurcations between self and time, self and beings, $t1$ and $t2$, present and past/future, passage (*kyōryaku*) and that which passes, arrival and the process of coming, intention and expression, etc. All of these gaps, if not thoroughly uprooted and overcome, result in the heretical and ultimately obstructive conceptions of Buddha-nature, which is falsely separated in terms of eternal/transitory, supra-mundane/ twenty-four hours, potential/actual, end/means. Dōgen does not suggest that the breach between *u* and *ji* is first in an actual or chronological sense — that would violate his whole approach — but that all bifurcations occur at the same time any egocentric misjudgment is made; each is implicated in every other one. Thus, all the derivative views in their multiple variations and insidious consequences must be refuted in order to cast off the inauthentic self and spontaneously manifest Buddha-nature. Without such a radical analysis, the temporality and mutability of *busshō* remains unrealized. Buddha-nature is indeed beyond everyday twenty-four hours if conceived of as a linear sequence leading to an end-point, but it is, as are all experiential factors of existence, right here-and-now within the primordial nature of daily being-time.

Once the various inauthentic separations are accepted in their presumed self-evidence, however, the average person believes that time is passing by in-itself "out there" because he seeks to disassociate himself from his own temporal activity, longing for relief from responsibility for the exertion and dedication required by spiritual practice. The view that *uji* is "sometimes" a Buddha or "sometimes" a demon is likened by Dōgen to crossing a river and climbing a mountain. The *bonbu* inauthentically aspires for the attainment of a ruby palace at the summit, a remote pinnacle from which he could idly oversee the landscape, feeling secure and triumphant, without having to labor through the task of making his way in the "mud and water," symbolic of the *bodhisattva*'s compassionate vow to save all sentient beings. The palace symbolizes all the idle hopes and expectations which existentially fear or reject and ontologically deny through self-fixation here-and-now activity. Obsessed with the fabricated and romanticized future represented by the grandiose palace, which may or not exist or ever be reached, the past is considered to have vanished, and the present is overlooked or discounted so that the separation between self and mountain-river is as great as that between heaven and earth.

This self-deception, ontologically misleading and existentially foolhardy, is hardened by a deep-seated anxiety about impermanence and attachment to *ātman* , the ego's dread of being passed over by the flight of an external framework of time coming from the future and going through the present into the past without end. The ruby palace does not represent the attainment of a genuine selfless, holistic perspective, but an inauthentic attempt to remove oneself from the vicissitudes of the temporal setting with which one is directly and unavoidably involved. Attachment to the fabrication posited as a futural goal attainable only at the mountain peak aggravates the gulfs created between self and time, beings and time, and the three tenses so that they assume enormous and seemingly insurmountable proportions, obliterating the immediacy and comprehensive totality of the here-and-now (*nikon*). Dōgen insists, however, that in climbing the mountain and crossing the river, which are never left far behind, man exists through time so that in man there must be time. "I already am, and time cannot slip away."[32] Whether in the form of coming and going or not coming and going, being-time invariably transpires right now.

Furthermore, the Buddha (symbolic of today) and the demon (symbolic of yesterday) lie precisely in this very moment of climbing the mountain; they are like various peaks in the range of mountains that represent the interconnected manifestations of temporal occurrences as daily being-time. For Dōgen, the concrete activity of the time of the mountain and river has preeminence — it is altogether ontologically more real and existentially more significant — than the fabricated ruby palace. "Does or does not," he demands, "the very moment of ascending the mountain and crossing the river chew up and spit out the time of the palace made of rubies?"[33] *Nikon* at once encompasses and underlies ("chew up") and overcomes and refutes ("spit out") the conventional or derivative fixations and attachments.

Dōgen also seeks to eliminate the deceptive gap between arrival or attainment and the activity or movement of coming, in his interpretation of the Rinzai school's saying, "Sometimes the intended meaning gets there, but the expression does not get there . . . [sometimes the reverse, sometimes both get there concurrently, sometimes neither get there]."[34] In his exegesis of this verse, Dōgen radically shifts the emphasis from the question of getting there or not, to the temporality which is fundamentally the same at all stages of development. The important issue is not attainment *per se*, but the dynamic interrelated processes of getting there, not getting there, intended meaning and expression, all of which constitute unique momentary perspectives of being-time. "While the time of getting there is unfinished, the time of not getting there is already here."[35] Not getting there is of no lower status than getting there in that both manifest *uji*. Nothing slips away, no time is lost or to be considered more or less appropriate than any other interdependent moment, just as there is no "right" or "wrong" time for instruction, practice or realization of the *Dharma*. As Dōgen says elsewhere, "The occasion (*jisetsu*) is not in the past or the future but right here-and-now."[36]

Dōgen accentuates the dynamic nature of movement and continuity, which is no longer statically conceived as time-points "piled up on top of one another or lined up side by side" in a linear uni-directional fashion. Rather, movement is disclosed as the simultaneous interpenetration of all beings occurring right-now and throughout the unity of past, present and future. Dōgen distinguishes the genuine significance of passage (*kyōryaku*) from the derivative view that "time flies," which is conceived of as "something like the wind and rain moving from east to west."[37] The apparent "flight" of time is artificially separated from and considered an obstacle to existence, and it is thought to possess an inevitability and inviolability at once terribly remote and voraciously victimizing. Dōgen does not deny the reality of the past or history, which he claims is ironically the position taken by the average man who believes that the past has disappeared or dissolved, but he reorients and deepens the existential meaning of this temporal dimension by showing its ontological inseparability from the totalistic presencing of being-time encompassing all tenses in an ultimately equalizable and simultaneous realization. *Kyōryaku* is not merely passing away. Rather, it signifies the comprehensive asymmetrical process of the True Man's enlightened existential projection and ontological understanding right-now moving simultaneously in and through past, present and future, actively engaging the passenger and passageway as well as the full context of the experiential reality surrounding and permeating the movement. "There is passage from today to tomorrow, passage from today to yesterday, passage from yesterday to today, passage from today to today, and passage from tomorrow to tomorrow."[38] *Kyōryaku* at once extends through all dimensions and gathers the total weight of previous and futural activity into this very present moment. By virtue of *kyōryaku*, the lives of former Zen masters are not to be added up backwards in terms of chronological sequence, but are to be understood as interpenetrating occasions of the spontaneous manifestations and continuing transmission of being-time.

The derivative view of the past, according to Dōgen, gives rise to the grave misconception that the "selfsame mind-to-selfsame mind transmission" of Zen awakening to the Buddhist *Dharma*, as symbolized in Bodhidharma's coming from the West, was an event that merely took place at some former and distant time and at a remote place, as if removed from one's own immediately present temporal existence. ". . . the Dharma that makes passage is misundertood," he writes, "as moving eastward a hundred thousand worlds and a hundred thousand epochs away."[39] Such a misjudgement about being-time reduces the spontaneous Zen transmission to the mere transporting of doctrine from one country and one historical period to another, as represented by the moving of artifacts such as rare copies of sūtras and documents, and images and idols. Dōgen, however, unlike many of his contemporaries, proclaimed himself "empty-handed upon returning to his native land" (kūshu-genkyō) from his pilgrimage to China, having acquired nothing but a "soft and flexible mind" (nyūnan-shin). He insists that Dharmic transmission and realization is itself kyōryaku, and therefore all past enlightenments are fully and directly duplicated and recreated right-now and continually throughout all ages. No time is overlooked; every moment of exertion is a unique occasion at which "the bright star [symbolic of Śākyamuni's awakening] appears, the Tathāgata appears, the [Dharma-]eye appears, the uplifted flower [symbolic of the initial Zen transmission to Mahākāśyappa] appears,"[40] each aspect simultaneous with present realization.

Thus, Dōgen specifically and adamantly rejects the view emphasized in the Kamakura era Pure Land and Nichiren sects that the world since the times of Śākyamuni had become so degenerate and men so inferior that they could not hope to attain enlightenment through their own exertive power. In the era of mappō, according to the other Japanese doctrines, man must resort either to the recitation of nembutsu to remove sin and win the grace of Amida Buddha (in Hōnen), or to a life of naturalism (jinen-hōni) with simple faith in and utter reliance on the power of Amida (in Shinran), or to the chanting of the sacred title (daimoku) of the Lotus Sutra to gain salvation (in Nichiren). Belief in the sheer degeneracy of mappō, Dōgen feels, encourages one to postpone the spiritual quest in expectation of a later and perhaps more worthy and fruitful time. In light of his understanding of the continuity of being-time, however, Dōgen stresses, "All human beings are born with this potential [to successfully practice Buddhism]. . . . Students of the Way, do not wait until tomorrow. This very day, this very moment, practice in accordance with the teaching of the Buddha."[41] No one is condemned by the historical epoch to which he is born. Selfless action and strenuous yet purposeless effort alone make possible full emancipation here-and-now.

Furthermore, Dōgen's notion of *kyōryaku* leads him to diverge significantly from Rinzai Zen, which he feels overemphasizes the view that the *Dharma* cannot be communicated through words (the expressions of masters) or letters (sūtras and commentaries). Although Dōgen acknowledges the limitations of unedifying or distracting and indulgent discourse, he maintains that the simultaneous interrelatedness of past and present experiences of enlightenment demands that the *Dharma* be perpetually reexplored and renewed by the True Man through creative divulgences of the innumerable and inexhaustible dimensions and meanings of the Way. "During such practice no time must be wasted," Dōgen writes, ". . . Therefore, expressing the Way now contains no doubt or error. That is why present expression of the Way possesses past observation, and observation of the past possesses present expression of the Way. Therefore, right-now there is observation and expression. Present expression and past observation are [both inseparably] linked and [separated] by thousands of miles. Present practice is brought about by this very expression and observation of the Way."[42] Because the transmitted *Dharma* is nothing but this very being-time of the True Man, continuing appropriation and emulation must entail continuing observation and expressiveness. Sustained exertion (*gyōji*) necessarily involves creative speaking (*dōtoku*), seated meditation (*zazen*) invariably entails "explaining mind, explaining nature" (*sesshin sesshō*), and spiritual communion between master and disciple (*kannō-dōkō*) includes the "vines" (*kattō*) of Dharmic dialogue, in order to unfold and clarify the inexhaustible meanings of the temporal nature of *busshō*.

Similarly, the genuine passage of the *Dharma* does not allow for an arbitrary bifurcation into the aspects of its being "inside" or "outside" scripture.[43] Nor should there be an artificial hierarchy which distinguishes between superficial speech (symbolized by the Bodhidharma's "skin" in the traditional interpretation of a Zen legend) and profound silence (symbolized by his "marrow"), or between illusory expression and the reality of experience.[44] Dōgen reinterprets Zen notions such as *kūge* (false perception of seeing flowers in the sky), *gabei* (painted rice-cake), *muchū* (dream), and *kattō* (entwinements), which usually designate illusory states of mind and uses of language, to free them from any contrast between truth and falsity, reality and metaphor. For example, he maintains that *kūge* does not indicate "one who has eye disease," as it is traditionally understood, but the manifold blossoming petals (*ge*) of genuinely realized emptiness (*kū*, which also means "sky"). Yet Dōgen does not advocate idle preoccupation with mere words lest the practices of reading sūtras and composing commentaries take priority over active meditation. Rather, he accentuates the expressive reality fully manifest by the true form (*jissō*) of all temporal phenomena which comprise the "universal sūtras": "The trees, grasses, and land [involved in self-fulfilling *samadhi*] are ceaselessly emitting a radiant light and preaching the deep and mysterious Dharma."[45]

Dōgen's radical reinterpretation and reformulation of Buddhist expressions is justified in terms of his understanding of the true *kyōryaku* of the *Dharma*. Previous theories must be revised by a creative hermeneutic reading which can even involve grammatical "distortion" so that the expressions fully reflect and convey the perpetually renewed endeavors of the True Man of *shinjin-datsuraku*, which permits not the slightest ontological or existential discrepancy between self-realization, all beings, each moment, Buddha-nature and activity. The sham of the "ruby palace" which takes the form of the false eternalization of impermanence-Buddha-nature (*mujō-busshō*) that has infiltrated scripture, doctrine and practice must be radically uprooted and entirely de-structured.

In "Busshō," Dōgen exposes a variety of misconceptions permeating Mahāyāna and Zen theories and practices that stem from fundamentally derivative views of being-time. Buddha-nature, he suggests, is frequently posited as an eternal substance which is actual yet transcendent of moral causation and the life-death process, thereby reflecting an inauthentic attempt to deny the self. It is also represented as an original potentiality that can only be attained as a teleological end; or, either anthropocentrically as a human possession idealistically projected upon the world of phenomena or a cosmological absolute that embraces men. In all such views, the conventional understanding of *uji* as an enduring, fixed time-point is presupposed in disguised fashion and — out of existential-ontological blindness or ego-fixation — fabricated into the "ruby palace" of false transcendence and eternalism.

Dōgen seeks to de-structure these misconceptions, not in order to do away with the notion of Buddha-nature, but to restore to this central Mahāyāna doctrine the true meaning and significance of primordiality or originality as a dimension of experience inseparable from and simultaneous with total and immediate here-and-now realization. Although assertions about Buddha-nature in Mahāyāna literature are generally intended as provisional and pedagogical constructions which are not to be hypostatized as ultimately real, Dōgen is not satisfied with that rationale. He contends that any possible misleading implication in any doctrine betrays a deep-seated misunderstanding that must be challenged and overcome. If the expression is even slightly derivative, Dōgen suggests, then the ontological understanding and existential experience on which it is based must be inauthentic as well. After all, any subtle gap that is falsely created is, from the primordial standpoint, as great as that between heaven and earth.

In order to fully eliminate the "slightest discrepancy" between Buddha-nature and the totalistic moment, Dōgen radically reinterprets Huai-hai's Zen injunction which seems on the surface not to be problematic concerning time, but under careful inspection reveals how profoundly and insidiously disturbing are the permeations of derivative time. The Zen dictum (which may represent a paraphrase from the *Nirvāṇa Sūtra*) is: "If you wish to know the Buddha-nature's meaning, you should watch for temporal conditions. If the time arrives, the Buddha-nature will manifest itself."[46] Although these words appear to successfully relate Buddha-nature as inseparably connected to temporal conditions, Dōgen feels that they may reinforce both the Senika and naturalistic heresies unless appropriately interpreted. An inauthentic reading would assume that Buddha-nature is beyond daily being-time and yet comes about as a "matter of natural course." If the time is suitable, the Buddha-nature will arrive whether or not there is sustained exertion. But, "if the time does not come," Dōgen comments on the derivative view, "then whether you study with a teacher in search of the Dharma, or practice the Way in relentless pursuit, it is not manifested."[47]

All of the existential and ontological breaches the average man has generated in his understanding of being-time become apparent here in the implication that the time-in-itself can and will "arrive" as an independent process separable from the transiency of *uji*. "Should watch for," Dōgen maintains, however, does not imply a rift between watcher and the watched, or between "right" and "false" seeing. Rather, "it is just seeing" precisely what is here-and-now fully manifest as all temporal occasions — genuine ontological insight that does not gaze beyond itself to "find and see" time. "If the time arrives" (*jisetsu nyakushi*) is taken by Dōgen to mean "the time has already arrived" (*jisetsu kishi*), not in some futural realm to be anticipated and pursued like the "ruby palace," but right here-and-now. There is no "if" from the standpoint of *uji* because there is no time of the twenty-four hours that is not the "proper" time; not one moment that is separable from complete realization. The time already here is itself the full presencing of Buddha-nature, which does not have to "arrive" on the scene. "There is no time right-now that is not a time that has arrived. There is no Buddha-nature that is not Buddha-nature fully manifested right here-and-now."[48] The True Man, indeed, does *not* await the coming and going of temporal conditions, but must spontaneously penetrate all beings at all times through sustained exertion.

Comparative Examination

In contrast to the teleological orientation of their respective philosophical traditions, Heidegger and Dōgen attempt to radically reverse the deep-seated and perdurant tendency to pursue the attainment of a supra-temporal realm supposedly superior in origin and value to daily existence. Instead of gazing beyond time by separating reality from time or expecting to achieve a goal outside of the temporal context, they explore and clarify ontologically the meaning of time that is already within or inseparable from existence. Both thinkers disclose the temporal structures that prevail in spite of — by underlying and betraying — claims of infinitude. Heidegger's notion of ecstatic temporality and Dō-gen's notion of being-time constitute the foundations of existence itself. Whether or not it is ever realized or acknowledged, primordial temporality holds sway as the generally disguised basis for both a preoccupation with the measuring of time and speculative flights which attempt to surmount time. Although the unity of time may not be seen or may appear fragmented, it still prevails and is evident even in those inauthentic modes of being which tend to conceal it. Derivative time is neither to be disproved as a logical flaw or contradiction nor negated as mere illusion, but it is exposed by Heidegger and Dōgen as a limited and inauthentic standpoint that is obstructive to genuine understanding if taken as the sole approach to temporality.

Although both thinkers challenge the stranglehold of now-time, and the consequent loss of the authentic significance of past and future, central differences are apparent in the aims and scopes of their philosophical investigations, as reflected in their analyses of the origin of derivative time. The fundamental disparity between them is that whereas Heidegger tries to de-structure now-time by deepening an understanding of past and future on the basis of the temporal-historical constitution of Dasein, Dōgen deepens the existential and ontological meaning of the present by incorporating the past and future within the totalistic passage of all beings spontaneously appearing as all-times. Heidegger does maintain that the inauthentic now can be partially reclaimed as an authentic moment of vision. Yet, in his overcoming of derivative time, Heidegger clearly asserts the ontological priority of the future and transcendence constituting the primordial basis of the past and historicality. Falling, he maintains, is invariably related to a preoccupation with the present. Also, throughout the authentic temporal happening (*Geschehen*), the present "vanishes" (*verschwindet*) in relation to the preeminence of the past and future. Genuinely conceived as Dasein's repeatable having-been, history for Heidegger is never simply left behind, but neither is it in any sense fully identified with the present.

For Dōgen, however, the authentically realized right-now is nothing other than the complete spontaneous presencing of being-time extending simultaneously throughout past, present and future; the past is one inseparable dimension of the selfsame dwelling place at each and every occasion of being-time. From Dōgen's standpoint, Heidegger's analysis of temporal-historicality does not overcome the "ruby palace," which symbolizes the onto-logical fabrications and existential deceptions that insidiously lurk and dominate so long as the ultimate and complete unity of beings and the three tenses of time are obscured in any subtle way. If there is the slightest gap, Dōgen maintains, between temporal-ity and immediate realization here-and-now, the separation be-tween truth and existence remains as great as that between heaven and earth.

The distinction between Heidegger's conception of the cir-cular interrelatedness of past, present and future and Dōgen's notion of the simultaneity of the three tenses is, in turn, grounded in differences in their means of defining and reorienting the ensnarements of derivative time. Heidegger closely associates Dasein's falling with its preoccupation with the derivative pre-sent. Once this connection is drawn, Heidegger places himself in the position in which he must give priority to the future over the present as the true basis of the past, and to possibility over actuality. He is also unable to successfully relate human temporal-ity to the time of other beings.

Heidegger maintains that falling is inextricably related to exis-tence as an inherent component of the three-fold structure of care, which Dasein for the most part *is* so long as it exists alongside and uses entities. Falling can never be fully overcome, but only *existenziel*(ly) modified "for the moment." Inauthenticity is such a pervasive possibility of existence because Dasein's circumspec-tive making-present of entities present-at-hand, a necessary mode of comportment in both science and handiwork, is the condi-tion of temptation that leads to Dasein's deficient understanding of itself as one more *vorhanden* being amongst others. Heidegger writes that ". . . *falling* has its *existenzial* meaning in the *Pres-ent*. . . . As this making-present which gets entangled in itself, curiosity has an ecstatical unity with a corresponding [inauthen-tic] future and a corresponding [inauthentic] having been."[49]

Because falling is defined as a state intrinsic to Dasein's Being,

Heidegger is reluctant to existentially criticize derivative time or to offer injunctives for overcoming it (although he does offer an ontologically critical exposition and de-struction of its limitations), lest authenticity be misconstrued as an escape from world-concern and phenomenological neutrality be mistaken for moral exhortation. Although Heidegger claims that his analytical depiction of falling is not "disparaging" in a moral sense,[50] it seems that the very notion of hermeneutic phenomenology (as ek-sistentially interpretive rather than merely descriptive) does and should imply some criteria for evaluation — a hierarchical framework which relentlessly challenges and uproots various modes of existential and ontological deficiency. At the same time that Heidegger insists that he does not pass moral judgement on falling, however, he clearly suggests that man is necessarily bound to inauthenticity by the very conditions and nature of care as thrown-projection. Heidegger's later works accentuate the implication of an inescapable determinism of existence through the doctrine of the eschatological structure of Being's concealment-in-unconcealment, which is said to precipitate an inevitable decline in thinking. Heidegger seems to suggest that modern man is "condemned" to the current destitute era of willful technological dominance by the withdrawal of Being as the fundamental ground of history. Man cannot exist authentically without attending the futural advent of Being itself emerging from the past as Dasein's having-been and coming-towards Dasein.

Furthermore, Heidegger is not capable by his own admission of investigating the time of *vorhanden* entities because he associates Dasein's concern for things present-at-hand with the state of falling into now-time. Dasein loses itself in the static now precisely when it deals with entities which are thereby excluded from the true nature of ecstatic temporality that uniquely belongs to Dasein's multi-dimensional structural totality. Although Heidegger is not uninterested in disclosing the time of entities in-the-world (*Weltzeit*) whose being is distinct from that of Dasein, it seems that the framework of fundamental ontology prohibits a resolution of this matter. "Such entities," he writes, "can never be designated as 'temporal' in the strict sense. Like every entity with a character other than that of Dasein, they are non-temporal, whether they Really occur, arise and pass away, or subsist 'ideally.' "[51] Thus, Heidegger's Dasein-orientation in *Sein und Zeit*, which tends to overlook the temporality of other beings, functions to a large extent within the horizon of Kantian transcendental analysis, and it is not fully free of the elements of modern *subiectit*ät, which is an ontological inversion of rather than a liberation from substance ontology, of which Heidegger himself is critical of Kant as well as Descartes, Hegel and Nietzsche.

From Dōgen's (Buddhist) standpoint of non-ego or non-self (*muga*, the thoroughgoing impersonal and insubustantial nature of existence), Heidegger's exclusive focus on Dasein seems to perpetuate but not overcome or eliminate substance ontology, now disguised by a still derivative reversal, the limitations of which Heidegger has exposed in other modern thinkers and acknowledges at the conclusion of *Sein und Zeit* and in later essays (particularly *Humanismusbrief*). This dilemma embedded in Heidegger's hermeneutics — his inability to escape from the *subiectum* and therefore the *ousia* — is a key reason for his "turn" from *Daseinanalytik* to a more naturalistic and aesthetic access to "Being as such" (*Sein als solches*) in the investigations of art, poetry, spatiality and thinghood in Heidegger II. The consequent lessening of the significance of the existential dimension by abandoning a concentraton on Dasein, however, accentuates a sense of vacillation, uncertainty and imbalance in his approach, for which there is no resolve without a breakthrough from any conception of substantiality or its inversion, subjecticity.

Because Dōgen's definition and method of analyzing derivative time is different than Heidegger's, his conclusions are also quite distinct. In contrast to Heidegger, Dōgen does not presuppose the distinction between *existenzial* and *existenziell* levels which implies (in Heidegger's thought) that since falling is a necessary *existenzial* condition, it is never completely surpassed but merely altered in an *existenziell* mode for the moment if the time is right. Rather, Dōgen maintains that the conventional conception of time is only one possible and partial perspective which can and must be fully overcome through the absolute and inalterable inseparability of the sustained (*existen-ziell*) exertion of here-and-now realization which comprehends the (*existenzial*) interpenetration of all beings at all times.

Dōgen's emphasis on the importance of existential injunctive for ontological insight is illustrated in "Genjōkōan" by the example of someone who ventures out into the middle of a great sea and observes no other aspect than the circularity of the water, and thus assumes that the ocean is round. Because of a particular experience, a partial perspective which betrays a self-centeredness or ego-fixation is presupposed. The most obvious feature to observe and the easiest conclusion to draw becomes an ultimately debilitating fixation if never questioned or challenged. Like a fish out of water or a bird out of the sky, existential deficiency and misguided ontology, according to Dōgen, is an unnatural, debilitating and hopelessly self-destructive state. But the sea can be experienced in innumerable ways — to a fish it is a palace, to a *deva* it is a necklace of precious jewels. The partial and one-sided standpoint must be superceded by a holistic perspective which penetrates and realizes each and every phenomenon as the dwelling-place of being-time. "To understand the [true] nature of *dharmas*, you must realize that in addition to the apparent circularity or angularity of the mountains and seas, there are other dimensions and perspectives which are great and inexhaustible, as the world is manifest in all possible directions. You must realize that this holds true not only all around us, but right here and within even a single dewdrop."[52]

Heidegger maintains that the *Seinsfrage* is in each case "*je meine*" as something at stake in my existence, but Dōgen unhesitatingly stresses that existential awakening to non-self is necessarily coterminous with the overcoming of derivative ontologies based on an inauthentic self-fixation. Dōgen does acknowledge the limitations of language and instruction in conveying the ultimate meaning of being-time, for even someone, he says, who has been able to express the truth for a long time is "still groping in the darkness for his original face." But Dōgen repeatedly and uncompromisingly affirms the capacity for the simultaneous realization by the True Man of existential (encompassing Heidegger's *existenzial* and *existenziell* levels) and ontological truth at all moments of the passage of being-time. In his rejection of the notion of *mappō* and his radical reinterpretation of the dictum "if the time arrives," for example, Dōgen refutes any historical or metaphysical doctrine which tends to delay or impede full realization by separating truth from the present moment. The truth of being-time is not a matter of projection or recollection, or of the awaiting of an advency and the repetition of previous possibilities in which the present "vanishes." Rather, it is the immediate and complete realization of the totalistic now during which the past and future no longer disappear, but are encompassed and profoundly explored each moment.

Being-time, according to Dōgen, does not arrive on its own in any subtle sense, but is perpetually enacted, enhanced and renewed through the True Man's sustained exertions. "It is through the exertions of all Buddhas in the past, present and future that all the Buddhas of the past, present and future are spontaneously manifested."[53] Ontological truth (the presencing of being-time) and existential effort, primordiality and spontaneity, are coterminously realized here-and-now without expectation, hesitation or deliberation. The occasion of the truth of being-time lies precisely in this very present moment of exertion. Dōgen's position on the limitations inherent in language and instruction is, thus, far removed from Heidegger's tension about or inability to offer a moral or existential critique of inauthentic now-time since it is defined by him as the way Dasein *is* for the most part. "Teaching him to raise his eyebrows and blink his eyes [symbolic of realization] is a mistaken being-time," Dōgen concedes. But, he concludes, "Not teaching him to raise his eyebrows and blink his eyes is an even more misleading being-time."[54]

Similarly, because Dōgen does not associate now-time with the necessary and inevitable state of man's everyday concern with thing-like beings, he does not need to exclude the totality of phenomena from his notion of being-time. Primordial time, for Dōgen, is not the ground by which man comes to know the phenomenal world as a matter of finite transcendence or of standing out amongst entities. Rather, being-time is the absolute inseparability of time's spontaneous manifestation as all beings at any occasion, a comprehensive and pervasive self-sameness of all particular selves, beings and Buddhas manifest at each and every totalistic moment without distinction, partiality or any sense of barrier or exclusiveness.

Dōgen challenges what he considers the limitations of the heretical tendencies in the anthropocentric conception of Buddha-nature as a substantive human possession, the idealist view of it as a psychological projection upon beings, and the absolutist view of *busshō* as an abstract and infinite identity underlying phenomena and unaffected by their contingency. He eliminates any possible separation of any dimension, manifestation or stand-point of being-time by pointing directly to the temporal nature of the innumerable and inexhaustible appearances of the "true form of all *dharmas*" (*shohō-jissō*): "You must realize that it is by this very reason [of *uji*] that there are all the phenomena and all the many grasses in the world as well as each particular blade of grass and each particular phenomenon in its own place in the world. To survey the matter in this way is the initiation of prac-tice."[55] In "Sansuikyō," Dōgen insists that an understanding of the movement of mountains is not separate from — but is essen-tial for — an insight into the innate and unceasing dynamism of human activity.

There does seem to be an agreement between Heidegger and Dōgen about the essential role in philosophy of creative interpreta-tion founded on the recovery of a primordial existential realiza-tion and understanding of time. Because deficient ontology expresses, however partially or misleadingly, the true nature of time, both thinkers insist on taking license to radically revise previous ontological expressions, not arbitrarily or destructively, but in order to reduce the false separations created and perpetu-ated in philosophy between self, world and the three tenses. Heidegger's hermeneutically circular approach toward interpreta-tion is oriented in terms of the past and future in accord with the temporal-historical constitution of Dasein. "In working out the question of Being, we must heed this assignment, so that by positively making the past our own, we may bring ourselves into full possession of the ownmost possibilities of such inquiry. . . .

From the phenomena of handing down and repeating, which are rooted in the future, it has become plain why the historizing of authentic history lies preponderantly in having been."[56] The hermeneutic circle is grounded in the ecstatically dynamic interplay between the having-been which is authentically repeated through anticipation of the future. Recovery of the past is made possible because *logos* as the potentiality-for-discovery is always already involved in the forestructure of *Seinsverständnis*. The circle for Heidegger is a pathway of thought which can never be completed in that it perpetually falls into untruth in the present as it attempts to repetitively wrest authentic resolve and ontological transparency from out of the hiddenness of the future.

Dōgen's creative interpretation, however, is based on his understanding of the *kyōryaku* of *Dharma* and, thus, the totalistic presence of being-time, which encompasses in ultimate selfsameness all previous and forthcoming realizations and expressions. The total penetration and realization of any single practice, explanation or experience at this very time fully discloses the entire Dharma-realm because all beings, all selves and all Buddhas at each and every moment are harmoniously and simultaneously linked together. "To fully enlighten the sixteen-foot golden body [symbolic of the presencing of being-time] by means of the sixteen-foot golden body is to spontaneously manifest resolve, practice, *bodhi* and *nirvāṇa*; this itself is being, this itself is time. Ultimate and complete realization of all times as all beings is to have no left-over *dharma* because the left-over *dharma* is itself a *dharma* left-over."[57]

Creative speaking and explaining of the Way, according to Dōgen, reaches at one and the same time, without distinction or obstruction, "back" to recall Śākyamuni's original enlightenment and "forth" to project inexhaustible means of divulging its innumerable implications and dimensions. It extends simultaneously "upwards" to the universal awakening experience not limited to any particular time but continually presencing here-and-now, as well as "below" to unique expressions whose evocative power arises from and stimulates a specific temporal and historical context. In contrast to Heidegger I who expresses disinterest in *existenziell* awakening and Heidegger II who portrays modern man as primordially limited by the destruction of the current epoch, Dōgen uncompromisingly stresses direct and immediate realization that allows no gap between past, present and future or between possibility and actuality. In his reinterpretation of Huai-hai and his refutation of the notion of *mappō*, Dōgen discloses the various temporal dimensions as ultimately non-differentiable yet experientially ever-variable as discrete momentary perspectives of the totalistic passage of being-time.

The definition and analysis of derivative time carried out by Heidegger and Dōogen at once influences, reflects and is determined by conclusions concerning primordial time. The separations in Heidegger's thought between the "theoretical" (*existenzial* disclosure) and the "practical" (*existenziell* decision), self-as-temporality and the time of entities in-the-world, the primordial intertwining of past and future and the derivative present — all of which Dōgen insists must be fully and finally overcome without the slightest gap — derive from the fact that Heidegger has so closely associated the nature of derivative time with the present tense in the sense of Dasein's making-present that which is present-at-hand. Heidegger's analysis of the problematics of derivative time, which posits the inevitability of Dasein's falling into a fixation with the present as a necessary *existenzial* condition inherent in existence, involves certain presuppositions which tend to diminish the radical nature and universal significance of his projected overcoming of conventional conceptions of time as represented in traditional substance-oriented metaphysics. These basic differences between Heidegger and Dōgen will be further explored in the following chapter, which examines the nature of the future and its relation to past and present in light of the disclosure of the radical contingency of existence as portrayed in the notions of finitude (in Heidegger) and impermanence (in Dōgen).

Chapter 3

Finitude and Impermanence

Problematics of Finitude and Impermanence

The notion of finitude in Heidegger's understanding of Being and the interpretation of impermanence in Dōgen's approach to Zen have a parallel role for each thinker's project in terms of overcoming fixations with substance and attachments to eternalism, and in establishing the basis for a realization of the dynamism, unity and insubstantiality of primordial time. The disclosures of finitude in Heidegger and of impermanence in Dōgen have a profound and significant affinity in that they serve as the necessary and essential turning points that lead from the defi ciencies of derivative time to an understanding and realization of primordial time. Finitude and impermanence, while quite distinct in terms of many of the conclusions and implications drawn by each thinker, do commonly point to the radical contingency of existence ontologically revealed through nothingness which prevades man's existential encounters with vicissitude, anxiety, dying and loss.

The aim and function of these notions is twofold. In a negative-destructive sense, they dislodge and undermine misguided ontologies of constancy and infinity derived from man's inauthentic fixation with now-time by showing the underlying unified movement and contingent or insubstantial nature of the three tenses of temporal existence. The positive-constructive meaning of finitude and impermanence is to lay the foundation for the establishment of thoroughly non-substantive and non-static philosophies of temporal continuity, duration and change.

Thus, the central issue for the comparative examination is to evaluate how complete, thoroughgoing and radical is the break with and the overcoming of substance ontology achieved in Heidegger's notion of finitude or in Dōgen's interpretation of impermanence. The success of each thinker in this task very much determines their accomplishments in analyzing and disclosing primordial time.

The previous chapter was a critical reconstruction and evaluation of how Heidegger and Dōgen investigate the relationships between deficient existence or derivative notions of time and misconceived ontology as an hypostatizaiion of eternity. The focus here is on how they disclose the contingent nature of reality that is fundamentally and universally prior to any particular authentic or inauthentic human decision but which, if resolutely experienced and appropriately conceived, can lead to authentic existence and genuine ontological disclosure. This philosophical ordering or arrangement of the underlying structure of each thinker's arguments suggests that in order for Heigegger and Dōgen to make possible the transition from derivative time to primordial time, they must portray in an ontologically and existentially persuasive manner the profoundly meaningful permeations of radical contingency in the existence of the average man. The conventional fears of the apparent inescapability of death, of the future, and of "time flies," for example, are, from the primordial standpoint, an inauthentic acknowledgement and expression of a stifled awareness of the true evanescence of time. The ontological truth of radical contingency is thereby partially and inavoidably revealed, although man may be existentially incapable of fully disclosing it.

Both thinkers portray contingent reality as underlying and unaffected by any person's attitude, acceptance or understanding, yet intimately, directly and forcefully related to and perceived in terms of — because it continually influences and determines — one's ownmost concerns. Radical contingency must be ontologically ("objectively" and non-evaluatively, universally and impartially) clarified on the basis of an authentic existential ("subjective" and concrete) response. In addition, Heidegger and Dōgen attempt to overcome previous doctrines in their respective philosophical traditions which tend to overlook or betray the full ontological and existential significance of radical contingency. They maintain that because contingency has not been understood from a sufficiently radical or fundamental standpoint, but in a derivative way as a realm in contrast to and of inferior status than eternity, the meanings of finitude in Western metaphysics and of impermanence in Buddhist thought have for the most part been misrepresented. Thus, both thinkers expose the deficiencies involved in previous *limited* ways, Western and Buddhist respectively, of tackling the problem by stressing how it is important to restate the question of contingency without already presupposing derivative conceptions of time.

Heidegger and Dōgen uncover contingency neither as a human condition in contrast to an eternal power, nor as a partial and temporary drawback of man or an unfortunate yet correctible flaw, nor as a psychological or factual emotional problem. Rather, contingency is the universal and undeniable, ultimate and all-pervasive basis, nature and structure of existence. The critical comparison of the efforts of Heidegger and Dōgen to surpass the problematics of substance ontology will explore their respective approaches toward the issues of death and dying, non-existence and nothingness as the existential pointer to an impartial or neutral disclosure of the ontological nature of radical contingency. Heidegger's futural orientation in terms of viewing Dasein as Being-towards-the-end, already indicated by his analysis of derivative time, will be contrasted with Dōgen's emphasis on the impermanent and insubstantial totality of life/death here-and-now.

Heidegger maintains that the essential meaning of finitude has been overlooked in the Western metaphysical tradition because it has been conceived of as an ontical collection of finite *vorhanden* entities either created by or of a lesser realm than the Eternal. Although Heidegger is critical of Christian theology (which he believes remains a part of and determined by the Western onto-theo-logical forgetfulness of Being), he attempts to surpass substance ontology by integrating fundamental ontology with anti-metaphysical Christian eschatology. The Christian standpoint reveals a more primordial relationship with time and temporality in terms of man's standing-out toward a future not at one's disposal, for which dying, dread, guilt, and the call of conscience are the formative experiences. By introducing religious doctrines in this philosophical context, however, Heidegger does not merely attempt a new synthesis between speculative metaphysics and theology. Rather, he seeks to highlight and deepen the original significance of the Greek notions of *aletheia* and *logos* which, according to his understanding of pre-Socratic thought, suggest the inherent limitation, concealment or hiddenness that comes-to-pass in all presencing or disclosure.

Although Heidegger's approach is greatly influenced by Aristotle's philosophy of causality and Augustine's religious doctrine of life experience, the main influences on his disclosure of finitude seem to be two modern thinkers — Kant, whose "metaphysics of metaphysics" or critique of the tradition from within it is based on the finite nature of the possibility of human knowledge, and Kierkegaard, whose Christian psychological studies of dread, sin and despair show human choices about one's ultimate limitations to be the basis of religious freedom. Heidegger seeks to overcome Kant, however, by grounding epistemology in the phenomenologico-ontological analysis of Dasein's everydayness (*Alltäglichkeit*), which thereby provides the *existenzial* foundations for Kierkegaardian dogmatic psychology (which in itself remains restricted to the *existenziell* level of inquiry). Heidegger philosophically moves, for example, from an analysis of Dasein's *existenziell* encounters with death to the *existenzial* disclosure of finitude as Being-thrown-unto-death or Being-towards-the-end.

The central task of fundamental ontology, Heidegger maintains — unlike the apparently similar disciplines of Scheler's philosophical anthropology and Kantian epistemology — is to investigate the finitude (*Endlichkeit*) of Dasein, which is not an end that comes as the termination of life, but the unavoidable limit which Dasein perpetually *is* as existing. Such an inquiry into finitude is no arbitrary exploration of the properties or the imperfections of man. Because the possibility of *Seinsverständnis* is intrinsically rooted in the finitude of Dasein, the task of laying the foundation of metaphysics is itself founded on the question of finitude, in such a way that this finitude can first become a problem that is appropriately unfolded, explicated and interpreted. In *Vom Wesen des Grundes*, Heidegger writes that Dasein's power of freedom or potentiality-for-Being is inherently limited and bound by its thrownness amidst beings, and it is thus pervaded by a non-power. As Dasein's freedom for understanding is permeated by the unfreedom of its concrete circumstances, so is truth permeated by untruth and authenticity by inauthenticity. "This sort of powerlessness (thrownness)," he asserts, "is not due to the fact that beings infect Dasein; rather it defines the very Being of Dasein. Every project of world (*Weltenwurf*), then, is *thrown* (*geworfener*). We must clarify the *essence of finitude* of Dasein in terms of the constitutive features of its Being before proceeding to any 'self-evident' definition of the finite 'nature' of man, any description of those characteristics which follow from finitude alone, and certainly any hasty 'explanation' of the ontical heritage of finitude."[1]

The intrinsic powerlessness of existence is analyzed in *Sein und Zeit* in terms of the "boundary situations" (*Grenzsituationen*) of anxiety, guilt and death which bring Dasein face to face with the nullity (*Nichtigkeit*) or null ground and conclusive end that permeates everydayness. The totality of Dasein is always an outstanding issue still to be settled which Dasein is continually moving towards in the time allotted to it between birth and death. In his later works, Heidegger explores the mysterious concealment of Being's illuminative mission which demarcates the temporal-historical boundaries of the finite epochal regions holding sway over the inevitably needful yet forgetful course of human destiny.

Dōgen maintains that the fundamental significance of impermanence is directly and inseparably related to an ontological/existential realization of the Buddhist truth of non-self (*muga*, the thoroughgoing insubstantiality of human and phenomenal existence). To overlook, deny or betray impermanence is to necessarily miss the essential meaning of non-self. He is critical of previous doctrines in the development of Buddhist philosophy which tend to violate the ultimate and complete selfsameness of *mujō* and *muga* by portraying impermanence in terms of some

trace of substantiality and by associating non-self with a realm
that transcends contingency. For example, Abhidharma speculation concerning the duration of the momentary *dharma* in terms
of the stages of arising, abiding, desistence and cessation as well
as the eternity of past, present and future presupposes both an
enduring substratum that can be analyzed into reducible yet persistent segments and the permanence of *nirvāṇa*.

Dōgen also suggests, however, in a more stunning, original
and forceful critique, that a misconception of *mujō* (and therefore
of *muga*) may haunt Hui-neng's Zen doctrine of *kenshō* ("seeing
into [one's own-]nature"), or at least prevalent interpretations
which fail to realize the essence of impermanence in its most
radical dimensions. Hui-neng himself is generally hailed for his
sensitivity to the issue of non-substantiality. Yet, Dōgen contends
in "Busshō" that the sixth patriarch's utterance, "men have
norths and souths, Buddha-nature does not," may be misunderstood to mean that man has a substance (or permanent self which
possesses directions, attributes and markings) but that Buddha-
nature is eternally transcendent of impermenence, devoid of substance and all-pervading. Such a view recreates the Senika heresy
by implying that Buddha-nature is an attainable goal reached
at the end of linear sequence through inauthentic self-denial
rather than genuine realization of non-self. It thereby perpetuates
derivative bifurcations between a substantive self and the impermanent movement it undergoes, and between the contingency
of unenlightenment and the eternity of enlightenment.

Dōgen insists that the problem of life and death (*shōji*) and
of the swift changes of impermanence is the "one great matter"
of Buddhism which requires the diligent and authentic attention of all practitioners of the Way who seek to selflessly cast
off body and mind of self and others. The true nature of the
universal and continual processes of arising-desistence and
generation-destruction consuming all insubstantial phenomena
must be thoroughly clarified, ontologically penetrated and existentially realized. A profound and deeply-moving awareness of
impermanence stimulates the mind's resolve (*hosshin*) to seek
enlightenment with the necessary sense of urgency, determination and continually renewed exertive effort. Dōgen maintains,

"When the transient nature of the world is recognized, the ordinary selfish mind does not arise. . . . Reflecting on the transient nature of body and life, exert yourself just as the Buddha Śākyamuni did when he raised his foot [symbolic of sustained effort]."[2] Furthermore, impermanence is not merely one issue amongst others, nor a question to be logically resolved or removed through trance, but the preeminent existential and ontological concern leading to the truth of non-self. "This realization [of impermanence] is not achieved by some temporary method of contemplation. It is not creating something out of nothing and then thinking about it. Impermanence is a fact before our eyes. Do no wait for the teachings from others, the words of the scriptures, and for the principles of enlightenment."[3]

Dōgen's understanding of impermanence is shaped by a confluence of factors, including the doctrinal-metaphysical (Buddhist concepts of dependent origination, *anātman* and *karma* which depict the universal insubstantial flux); the poetic-emotional (the Japanese aesthetic category of *mono no aware*, poignant sadness about the passing of things naturalistically symbolized by the morning dew or scattering leaves); and the historical-cultural (social upheavals and natural disasters in Kamakura Japan leading to the commonly-held belief in epochal degeneracy). These influences are at once distilled in terms of Dōgen's intensely personal experiences of suffering and lamentation, which are uniquely reflective of the all-pervasive ephemeral nature of momentary existence, and transcended through his "casting off" any subtle attachment to self. Dōgen explicates and interprets the inexhaustible meanings of impermanence as a means of exhortation and edification concerning the directness and immediacy of the spiritual quest through the use of poetic and naturalistic metaphors as well as ontological analyses of the totalistic, insubstantial dwelling-place of being-time and the radical impermanence of Buddha-nature.

Heidegger's Disclosure of Finitude

Heidegger maintains that finitude must be recognized as the primordial basis of ontology in that the possibility for the comprehension of Being is itself the innermost essence of finitude. "As a mode of Being, existence is in itself finitude and, as such, is only possible on the basis of the comprehension of Being. There is and must be such as Being only where finitude has become existent."[4] Heidegger concedes that in Aristotelean metaphysics, there would seem to be no significant relationship between ontology and finitude. But Heidegger's thinking is greatly influenced by — even as it attempts to reinterpret and overcome — Kant's analysis of finitude as a fundamental condition of transcendental knowledge. Kant, the one and only philosopher in the Western tradition who genuinely explores the meaning of finitude, according to Heidegger, does not establish the finitude of *vorhanden* entities by showing, ontically, that they have been created by an infinite God. Rather, he explains their finitude by pointing out that they are things only insofar as they are possible objects of finite knowledge. Knowledge, in turn, is finite because it is essentially receptive; it must be solicited and affected by those entities which announce themselves to it. Thus, finitude for Kant is the very necessity of reason to objectify entities which it represents by forming concepts. Finitude manifests itself as the uncreative, receptive basis of an otherwise creative act — knowledge.

In Heidegger's critical reading, however, there is an even deeper meaning of finitude implied, though not fully articulated by Kant. Heidegger notes in *Kant und das Problem der Metaphysik* that Kant grounds his three primary philosophical inquiries (the cosmological, what can I know?; the psychological, what ought I to do?; and the theological, what may I hope?) in a fourth and more fundamental question, What is Man? According to Heidegger, the relationship between the first three questions and the fourth one is not merely accidental because the three are nothing other than the fourth query and must be reducible to it. The full significance of finitude does not merely pertain to the problem of knowledge, as Kant asserts. Rather, as Heidegger creatively interprets Kant, finitude lies in the very Being and total factical structure of man who has been thrown and is stretched-along in the midst of beings on which he is dependent, such that he can never fully be master of himself.

"It follows that human reason is not finite only because it propounds these [first] three questions," Heidegger observes, "but, on the contrary, it propounds these three questions because it is finite and so radically finite, indeed, that in its rationality this finitude itself is at stake."[5] If man were an infinite power, he would not have to question the nature and meaning of his Being. The questioning process itself indicates that man's power-of-Being (*Seinkönnen*) is pervaded by a non-power (*Nicht-Können*); his freedom is restricted by a transcendental need (*transzendentale Bedürftigkeit*). In choosing any particular possibility, countless others must be overlooked, discounted, or left unknown or unacknowledged.

In *Sein und Zeit*, Heidegger investigates the powerlessness and precariousness of Dasein's Being in terms of the null ground permeating the three-fold structure of care. *"Care itself, in its very essence, is permeated with nullity through and through."*[6] As Being-in-the-world, Dasein occupies an open yet bounded realm defined and delineated by inherent limitations. Dasein has not been granted absolute presence but exists on an always problematic borderline. The ultimate conditions under which it can act are not at its disposal and are constantly being taken away from it. The primordial "Not" or nothingness at the very base of Dasein is not a mere privation in the sense of a lack, flaw or imperfection. It does not signify a state which Dasein at one time possessed but has since lost or surrendered, or which it has not yet had but could still achieve. Nullity is not something that has happened to Dasein once or that may occasionally happen and from which it can seek reprieve; nor is it an obscure quality that attaches itself to Dasein and which might be eliminated through sufficient progress. Rather, this nullity is the perpetually encountered borders of Dasein's finite existence.

A central aim of hermeneutic phenomenology is to uncompromisingly portray the essential and all-pervasive character of Dasein's nullity as the best means of overcoming substantive/ eternalist ontology, which derivatively attempts to leap beyond finitude to attain a supra-temporal and supra-historical truth. The genuine meaning of the "Not" has remained obscure in traditional ontology and logic, Heidegger maintains, because of the inauthentic fixation with constant actuality which confuses the multiple and profound dimensions of nothingness with privation. Heidegger's procedure is to analyze the *existenziell* origins of the deficient understanding of finitude in order to authentically disclose its underlying and universal *existenzial* structure. Finitude haunts Dasein even in the most innocuous circumstances that are seemingly protected from its permeation by the tranquilizing shell of the they-self's commitment to substance and eternity. In the extreme *Grenzsituationen* of anxiety, guilt and death, finitude is revealed, whether authentically or inauthentically encountered, as the eerie and indefinite yet forbidding and overbearing horizons of Dasein's intrinsic confinements that can strip bare all attachments to infinitude.

Anxiety, according to Heidegger's analysis, continually pursues and threatens everyday Dasein which is for the most part submissive to the public interpretation of self and world as the two interacting substantive or present-at-hand (*vorhanden*) entities of subject and object. In falling, Dasein flees from the true nature of its unified yet multidimensional and contingent selfhood into the deceptive ensnarements and temptations of feeling constantly "at-home" in the public world. Anxiety, the feeling of uncanniness or not-being-at-home (*das Nicht-zuhause-sein*), brings Dasein face to face with the "nothing and nowhere" of worldhood — its eminently non-*vorhanden* and interdependent status — which is so disturbing to the obstinate self-assurance and seemingly obvious familiarity of *das Man*. Uncanniness does not come from a definite direction, but is already "there" with Dasein's clearing (*Lichtung*). It is so close and potentially oppressive that it stifles the breath and creates an overwhelming claustrophobia, and yet it is nowhere at all. The nothingness revealed in anxiety does not come from an absence, denial or elimination of entities, but from the finitude which Dasein suddenly realizes in itself as the pervasive basis of thrown-projection. Anxiety individualizes Dasein, bringing it back from its absorption in the public world, and making it aware that the possibilities of inauthenticity and authenticity are matters of its ownmost choosing.

Anxiety discloses Dasein's freedom precisely because it exposes Dasein's finite dependence on the world no longer conceived as a random gathering of *vorhanden* entities. Finitude is further revealed as Dasein's Being-guilty in that Dasein has in every case already been thrown and abandoned to a particular set of conditions and contexts which limit and determine its choices. Dasein's potential for self-illumination is perpetually clouded by the lurking and disturbing unknown and unseen — that which is concealed and cannot be brought forth by any amount of decisive volition. "In being a basis — that is, in existing as thrown — Dasein constantly lags behind its possibilities. It is never existent *before* its basis, but only *from* it and *as this basis*. Thus 'Being-a-basis' means never to have power over one's ownmost Being from the ground up."[7]

Primordial Being-guilty is inauthentically experienced or ontically conceived, Heidegger observes, as an indebtedness pertaining to a particular misdeed, debt or unfulfilled responsibility, a failure to satisfy some requirement incurred in a broad range of values and standards, from the loftily moral to the strictly legal, for which some form of punishment is required. The genuine ontological meaning of guilt as the nullity of thrownness, however, is prior to and makes possible first of all any notion of indebtedness or of moral failures and omissions, and not the other way around.

Hurled into the world of definite circumstances and environment, Dasein projects itself upon possibilities largely determined by the conditions of its facticity, including its imminent and inevitable end as the final and unmistakable factor. The totality of Dasein is continually permeated by the possibility of its ultimate and inavoidable impossibility. This end is neither a point at which Dasein just stops nor a condition added on at the conclusion of life, but the nullity of care as the thrown basis of death. Death is perhaps the fullest and most overwhelming reflection of finitude. Even the everyday Dasein concedes a sense of certainty about the fact that it is forever passing away. The they-self, however, attempts to *existenziel*(ly) avoid, escape or ignore the *existenzial* and ontological significance of its end by ascribing to it the quality of remoteness — that endless time is flying by on its own. The end of Dasein is inauthentically considered an actual state when man will no-longer-be-there, something which will invariably happen in the future but has not yet taken place, and which is fearfully awaited rather than resolutely anticipated. Certainty of the end is objectified on empirical grounds alone: death has been observed, there is ample evidence for it, and its occurrence cannot be denied.

The inauthentic view of end as mere demise is reflected in various ontically-oriented approaches to death which gather information about particular ways dying has been dealt with at different points in history by various individuals or social groups. Heidegger's *existenzial* analysis, which uncovers the universal meaning and structure of the being for whom the inevitable possibility of its end is the central concern of its Being, is more primordial than and takes precedence over derivative approaches. Heidegger includes among these: science (biology, medicine and physiology which obtain data and statistics about the longevity of living organisms, including man, that reach a point of demise); social science (psychology, biography and ethnology which are concerned with the emotional reactions of someone who is about to die); as well as the quasi-scientific outlook of theology and theodicy (which are preoccupied with the possibility of an afterlife or immortality, and with reconciling human suffering in terms of the unfailing justness of an omniscient divinity).

The primordial meaning of the end as a continuing process which is nothing other than Dasein's thrown-projection can be understood, Heidegger maintains, when death is no longer misrepresented as a one-time event which happens to Dasein as a culmination or even conclusion. Rather, dying is the way to be which Dasein authentically takes over as soon as and so long as it dwells *towards* its end (not *at* its end). "In death, Dasein has not been fulfilled nor has it simply disappeared; it has not become finished nor is it wholly at one's disposal as something ready-to-hand. On the contrary, just as Dasein *is* already its 'not-yet,' and is its 'not-yet' constantly as long as it is, it *is* already its end too. The 'ending' which we have in view when we speak of death does not signify Dasein's Being-at-end, but a *Being-towards-the-end* of this entity."[8] Thus, death is the ownmost and non-relational possibility which is in each case uniquely mine and is never to be taken over and experienced by anyone else. Death is also the uttermost possibility of existence because it is the inescapable, ultimate and unsurpassable impossibility of Dasein, and therefore the possibility which is purest and furthest removed from actuality.

As Being-thrown-towards-its-end, Dasein is permeated by nothingness from top to bottom and from beginning to end as the "null basis of its null projection."[9] Death discloses the potential nothingness of Dasein as projectively ahead-of-itself, and guilt reveals the nullity of Dasein at its very ground as two-fold aspects of the selfsame care. Thus, Heidegger argues, there can be no substantive now-point isolated from the totally null structure of finitude. The question of the relationship between finitude and infinitude is not one of how the derived infinite time somehow lessens itself to become primordial finite temporality. "The problem is rather that of how *inauthentic* temporality, as *inauthentic*, temporalizes an *infinite* time out of the finite. Only because primordial time is *finite* can the 'derived' time temporalize itself as *infinite*."[10] Once finitude is genuinely disclosed, Heidegger maintains, the derivative nature of "endless" time is clarified, and the basis for the establishment of the primordial features of finite temporality has been lain.

The central element of continuity throughout Heidegger's collected works is its relentless ontological concern with the essential nature of finitude, so that "it is no longer thought," as is noted in *Zur Sache des Denkens*, "in terms of the relation to infinity, but rather as finitude in itself: finitude, end, limit, one's own — to be secure in one's own. The new concept of finitude is thought in this manner. . . ."[11] In his later writings, Heidegger explores "finitude in itself" from the standpoint of the nothingness of Being which is prior to Dasein's *existenziell* encounters with and decisions concerning its *existenzial* boundary-situations (*Grenzsituationen*). Finitude is the inherent powerlessness of Dasein, the primordial and universal condition which comes to pass independent of the authenticity or inauthenticity of man's approach or attitude. Therefore, it is necessary for Heidegger II to portray the ontological nature and structure of the boundaries of existence from the standpoint of "finitude in itself" rather than from the Dasein-oriented perspective of *Sein und Zeit*; or, from the standpoint of the Nothingness of Being's self-concealment rather than in terms of man's resolve or lack of resolve in confronting his nullity in *existenziell* situations. Heidegger writes in *Was ist Metaphysik?* that "Being itself is essentially finite and reveals itself only in the transcendence of Dasein which is held out into the nothing. . . . We are so finite that we cannot even bring ourselves originally before the nothing through our own decision and will."[12] Finitude is the essential nature of Being's self-concealment from man who experiences it as no-thing, a process which is intrinsic to the unconcealment or presencing of Being in manifold beings, and precedes all human volition and cognition.

The shift of emphasis in Heidegger's hermeneutics from an existentialist orientation to a "more primordial" (*mehr ursprüngliche*) access to the ontological disclosure of finitude is evident in the essay "Das Ding," in which Heidegger explicitly ontologizes the meaning of death as "the shrine of Nothing, that is, of that which in every respect is never something that merely exists, but which nevertheless presences, even as the mystery of Being itself. As the shrine of Nothing, death harbors within itself the presencing of Being. As the shrine of Nothing, death is the shelter of Being."[13] Death-as-finitude, experienced by man as his imminent end, remains ontologically significant in Heidegger's thinking, but is now disclosed as the mysterious realm of Nothingness which simultaneously conceals/reveals Being and thus makes possible all human limitations and boundaries.

In *Vom Wesen der Wahrheit*, Heidegger investigates finitude as the concealment which invariably comes to pass in and pervades the ek-sistent freedom of Dasein. The inner possibility of propositional truth as correctness, Heidegger maintains, is derivatively founded on Dasein's freedom to "let beings be" (*Seinlassen von Seiendem*) — the primordial attunement or openness which disclosively and poetically illuminates the emerging or unfolding presencing of phenomena prior to the management, preservation and planning of beings encountered or sought out. Permeating truth, however, is the possibility of the indefinite and indeterminable, the puzzling and unexplained, the undecided and questionable, which constitutes the mystery of Being and creates the needful condition of Dasein's intrinsic constraints. "Precisely because letting be always lets beings be in a particular comportment which relates to them and thus discloses them, it conceals beings as a whole. Letting-be is intrinsically at the same time a concealing. In the ek-sistent freedom of Dasein a concealing of being as a whole comes to pass (*ereignet sich*)."[14]

The mysterious concealment of Being conceals even itself in the process so that a forgetfulness (*Seinsvergessenheit*) of the mystery takes precedence in Dasein's comportment. Perpetually turning to and fro amidst beings which turn towards and away from it, Dasein clings to the readily available and controllable, taking itself as the subjective standard for the evaluation and manipulation of all other supposedly substantive beings. Finitude is manifest in the inevitable insistence of Dasein's relation to beings which accompanies and pervades ek-sistent freedom because of the primordial concealment of the presence of Being. "Even in insistent existence the mystery holds sway, but as the forgotten and hence 'inessential' essence of truth."[15] The space-time Dasein inhabits is bound by the non-appearance of Being which comes to pass in all that is illuminated, compelling Dasein to increasingly abandon its freedom for truth.

Thus, errancy or untruth, according to the later Heidegger, dominates man through and through. Errancy is not a particular mistake, but the ground and open site of any error, which makes possible the history of those entanglements in which all kinds of erring get interwoven. Primordial errancy is paradoxically at once the richest and most prodigious historical event in that it is the source of history which opens up all possibilities for creative questioning, reflection, dialogue and speculation, and also the most tragic occurrence because it inevitably involves the insistent forgetfulness of its mysterious essence. Since history is something human and finite it necessarily entails a fateful going-astray. Without this factor of error there could be no relation from one fate to the next, and thus no possibility of history. Errancy is the very nature and structure of history because Dasein as a finite being has untruth due to the concealment of Being in the very constitution of its clearing. Finitude, from the standpoint of Heidegger II, is therefore the primordial ground of Dasein's "turning into need" (*Wendung in die Not*); the source of the various intertwining temporal-historical epochs which it fatefully traverses; and the basis of the forgetfulness of Being as its overriding destiny permeating these epochal realms.

Dōgen's Disclosure of Impermanence

Dōgen maintains that the complete penetration and clarification of the meaning of impermanence is essential for the comprehension and realization of the thoroughgoing mutability and insubstantiality of Buddha-nature. He criticizes the "heretical" or non-Buddhistic tendencies of those who presuppose a separation between the incessant vicissitudes of all phenomena, symbolized by the blooming of flowers and the falling of leaves, and the true form (*jissō*) or essential nature of the *dharmic* factors of experience (*hōsshō*). "It is non-Buddhist to think that the mind moves and nature remains stable," he asserts, "or that nature remains pure and still while form changes."[16] Any subtle clinging to the notion of an enduring substantive substratum or fixation with a permanent self either existentially or ontologically underlying impermanence must be challenged and overcome to achieve a breakthrough to full, unimpeded realization of non-self. Dōgen argues that his radical understanding of impermanence is quite distinct from the derivative concept of "impermanence deduced by non-Buddhists and Hinayānists" (and by implication some Zen Buddhists as well). The derivative view results in a debate concerning the length, content and appearance of the transient moment, carefully distinguished from an unchanging eternity, by those who are apparently "suspicious, surprised, and frightened"[17] by truly disclosed impermanence as the clear pointer to an existential and ontological realization of non-self. The true nature of impermanence directly threatens their subtle and disguised ego-fixations.

Dōgen's initial and most formative experience of impermanence — the death and funeral of his mother at age seven — preceded his study of Buddhist doctrines pertaining to the universal flux or any significant contact with Japanese cultural attitudes about the sadness of "the fleeting world." Dōgen was at once painfully distressed by his personal suffering and sorrow, and aware of the unavoidable and all-pervasive conditions of transiency beyond particular experiences and yet most directly and despairingly realized through them. Even as a youth, Dōgen's mind was deeply stirred by the dual longing for soteriological deliverance from the anguish of suffering through ontological understanding of the true nature of impermanence. He pursued the Way with an uncommon and uncompromising attentiveness of spirit and selfless power of concentration and insight. He resolved that any view about impermanence which negated, overlooked, trivialized or fell short of authentically reflecting the ontological truth of the radical momentariness and unimpeded insubstantiality of reality permeating his profound existential experience of suffering needed to be radically revised.

In encountering the cultural outlook of Kamakura Japan, Dōgen was struck by its pervasive emotional and aesthetic sensitivity to the fleeting beauty and evanescent poignancy of the world. As a legacy from the Heian era, there was a heightened and almost ritualistically refined awareness amongst aristocratic poets and writers of the uncertain, unenduring and unstable quality of things (*hakanashi*) metaphorically represented by the change of the seasons, and of the fragility and frustration of human emotions involved in tragic love affairs as symbolized by the bird's winter flight or the falling of spring blossoms. Prevalent social attitudes about impermanence were at once greatly influenced by and yet a grave distortion of central Buddhist doctrines which analyzed the roots and perpetuation of suffering in terms of the relative, interdependent and insubstantial nature of transient existence. The Buddhist concept of *karma* (inescapable moral causation), however, was apparently inauthentically used as a psychological crutch to explain away loneliness and longing, and to rationalize the sense of the hollowness and unfulfillment of ephemeral and illusory phenomena, circumstances or human endeavors. Such misconceptions seemed to betray a deep-seated attachment to a fixated self or ego which was inauthentically believed to persist through and endure troubling and unsettling changes of emotion and circumstance.

The potentially genuine need for profound ontological reflection stimulated by an existential attunement to the unavoidable changes of life was unfortunately dissipated, Dōgen observed, either into pessimism, stoicism, resignation and fatalism as an attempt to withdraw from impermanence and escape into the false eternalism of the "ruby palace," or into an idle and even hedonistic self-indulgence in the aesthetically conceived and inauthentically affirmed substantive moment. Furthermore, widespread natural and social disasters had led to the belief in an apocalyptic crisis being consummated in the current degenerate age of utter human strickenness and helplessness, thereby placing responsibility for suffering in the hands of an uncontrollable and ineluctable "destiny," rather than lack of genuine existential awakening to and ontological insight into the ultimate selfsameness of impermanence/non-self.

Dōgen entered the monkhood precisely because of his overwhelming concern — as the ultimate matter of life and death, enlightenment or unenlightenment — to comprehend impermanence-*as*-impermanence. That is, he sought the most profound realization of non-self beyond an ego-fixated sentimental attitude or resignation to fate, and unbound by any arbitrary and inauthentic decision to accept and enjoy or to flee and escape from incessant change. In the Japanese monasteries, however, he found that Śākyamuni's dispassionate philosophical analysis of conditioned (impermanent and insubstantial or dependently originated) existence without reference to an eternal substratum or persistent self had been rendered almost inapplicable to serious practice in the quest for authentic attainment. The romanticized nostalgia and/or nihilism of the aristocracy had infiltrated Buddhist practices so that the essence of impermanence was mistaken for the mere coming and going of things, and insight into the universal nature and structure of non-self was reduced to the question of an individual's response to dying, loss or unhappiness. The misleading approaches to the flux were manifested in what Dōgen considered heretical tendencies to seek to transcend contingency (*sennigedō*) or to celebrate a shallow affirmation of transient reality (*jinen-gedō*), ego-oriented standpoints not necessarily overcome by Hui-neng's doctrine of "seeing into [one's own-]

nature." On the other hand, Dōgen was positively influenced by the aesthetic-naturalistic concern with impermanence of the poets, which helped to offset an overly speculative preoccupation with the issue of the duration of momentariness that had long haunted Buddhist scholasticism, by directing attention toward the depth of existential and ontological meaning in one's personal encounter with and overcoming of the deception of an enduring ego.

Dōgen's breakthrough to a genuine understanding of impermanence was largely inspired by two experiences as a Zen disciple which enabled him to penetrate beyond the appearance of change into the essence of the impermanent and insubstantial moment itself. A passage in *Zuimonki* records the tremendous impact Zen master Myōzen, a famous disciple of Rinzai whom Dōgen accompanied to China, exerted on Dōgen shortly before their departure. At the time of their scheduled pilgrimage, one of Myōzen's beloved teachers on Mt. Hiei, Myōyū, became seriously ill and lay on his deathbed, imploring his student to put off the journey until after his death. Myōzen, acknowledging his great indebtedness to his mentor, queried the other monks for advice. Dōgen, supporting his colleagues, counselled Myōzen to delay the voyage: " 'If you feel that your Buddhist enlightenment is adequate now, it would be better to put off your trip.' "[18] Myōzen, however, refused to be deterred in his quest because he realized that the great question of impermanence was not merely a matter of how or when one dies. He reoriented the problem of the individual's passing away in terms of the more fundamental issue of the universal and insubstantial nature of generation-destruction, which is too urgent for any ego-preoccupied sentimental hesitation or regretful deliberation. " 'You all seem to agree.' " Myōzen lectured the monks, " 'that I should stay, but my view differs. Even if I were to stay now, it would not prolong the life of a dying man. Even if I were to stay now, and take care of him, I could not stop his suffering. Even if I were to comfort him in his final hours, it would not have anything to do with his [freedom] from the cycle of birth and death. . . . It would be of absolutely no use in [detaching] from the world and gaining the Way.' "[19]

Myōzen's clear observation and rugged determination to abandon any subtle clinging to ego-fixation illustrated the profound and universal permeation of impermanence throughout all aspects of experience as an issue more urgent and demanding than any particular individual's demise. Ju-ching, however, taught Dōgen that impermanence was nothing other than the self-generating and self-renewing momentariness of existence unobstructed by desirous expectation and ego-centric longing. Upon his *satori*, Dōgen no longer viewed impermanence from the standpoint of a spectator self overseeing a continuing process of change moving from one point in time to the next — the derivative view which presupposes a substantive substratum enduring throughout multiple transformations. Rather, he realized impermanence from the liberated perspective of *shinjin-datsuraku* (having spontaneously cast off or abandoned any fixation, obsession or preoccupation with an enduring ego in "self" or phenomena). He fully and spontaneously penetrated into *mujō* as the purposeless and selfless totality of each and every moment encompassing before and after, past and future, life and death and yet "cut off" (*saidan*) from before and after, life and death in that it is absolutely without substratum. There is no-thing/no-self which changes. Impermanence is no more or less than the impermanently innate and unceasing dynamism of non-self without reference to or contrast with any other supposedly stable thing or process outside it. Dōgen writes in "Genjōkōan," "To study the self is to forget the self . . . [by] cast(ing) off body and mind of self and others."

In "Busshō," Dōgen maintains that the "preaching, practicing, and realizing of impermanence by the impermanent themselves is nothing other than impermanent."[20] Impermanence is not relative to anything beyond or underlying it which is not impermanent. If both saints and ignorant men were not thoroughly and radically impermanent, there could be no possibility for transformation. Dōgen discloses impermanence in its most essential nature as the insubstantial foundation and constitution of all aspects and dimensions of existence. Therefore, Buddha-nature is the very impermanency of "grass and tree, thicket and forest, men and things, nations and lands, mountains and rivers"[21] and every other of the innumerable human and naturalistic phenomena. All impermanent phenomena are Buddha-nature because they are impermanent; the Buddha-nature, because it is impermanent, is nothing other than all impermanent phenomena.

Busshō does not in any sense limit or lessen itself to "become" impermanence. Rather, Buddha-nature (*busshō*) and impermanence (*mujō*) are the primordially selfsame *mujō-busshō*. In order to stress that impermanence is not to be contrasted with permanence in a subtle way, Dōgen acknowledges that there is an authentic meaning of "permanence" if it is understood in the sense of " 'prior-to-turning' (*mi-ten*) [that] is beyond the traces of coming and going."[22] The genuine conception of permanence, which is ultimately indistinguishable from the genuine meaning of impermanence, points to the vigorously dynamic and nonsubstantive totalistic present moment beyond the mere appearance of change, or unbound by the dichotomy of permanence/impermanence.

Although Dōgen disdains unedifying aesthetic indulgence, he is an accomplished poet who harnesses lyrical metaphor and seasonal imagery to emotionally evoke the ontological significance of existentially realized impermanence, as in the following *waka* entitled "Impermanence" ("Mujō"):

Yo no naka wa	To what shall
Nani ni tatoen	I liken the world?
Mizudori no	Moonlight, reflected
Hashi furu tsuyu ni	In dewdrops,
Yadoru tsukikage.	Shaken from the crane's bill.[23]

According to this verse, the entire world, represented by the moon, is fully contained in each and every of the manifold dewdrops symbolic of the inexhaustible contents of all impermanent moments. For this very occasion, the breadth and vastness of moonlight comes to rest in each single waterdrop, and every drop of dew reflects the whole illuminative panoramic display. Dōgen's *waka* at once suggests the beauty and sadness of the natural setting and the complete calmness and tranquility of the True Man of *shinjin-datsuraku* who has cast off all ego-fixated emotions of longing and regret. Dōgen does not point to an abstract synthe-

sis of universality and particularity, but divulges the ever-varying
and ever-renewable possibilities of each impermanent and insubstantial totalistic moment. The duration of the moment is a matter
of existential penetration and exertion, and is thoroughly incal-
culable. As Dōgen observes in a passage in "Genjōkōan" which
further explores the metaphor of moonlight reflected in water,
"The depths of the one correspond to the heights of the other.
As for the length or brevity of time, you must investigate the
breadth or smallness of the water and determine the dimensions
of the moon and the sky."[24] There is no measure for impermanence because it is not relative to anything else which does not
partake of impermanence. It lasts so long as total dynamism is
fully exerted by every insubstantial and interpenetrating experiential factor.

The dimensions of Dōgen's interpretation of impermanence
throughout his works include the exhortative, poetic-naturalistic
and ontological. First, in his autobiographical works, Dōgen offers
numerous parables, anecdotes and homiletic injunctions to inspire
his disciples with a sense of immediacy and urgency in the soteriological quest for the Way of non-self so that they will train
as if their lives were directly at stake with each decision and
effort. He tries to recreate Myōzen's dedicated and selfless spirit
which penetrates past the coming and going of things into the
great matter of *mujō* itself. In *Zuimonki*, Dōgen stresses the inseparability of the meaning of impermanence and the arousing of
the *Bodhi*-seeking mind (*hotsu-bodaishin*) which pursues existential and ontological realization of *muga*. "Think only of this day
and this hour, for tomorrow is an uncertain thing; and no one
knows what the future will bring. Make up your mind to follow
Buddhism as if you had only this day to live. To follow Buddhism
means, on all occasions and at the risk of your life, to make it
flourish and bring benefit to all beings."[25]

Secondly, in *Shōbōgenzō* Dōgen frequently uses naturalistic
metaphors, such as falling blossoms and the withered plum tree
(*baige*) which blooms ever anew, to illustrate the interpenetration of life and death, arising and desistence in each impermanent and insubstantial self-generating moment. Aging, dying and
destruction, according to Dōgen, do not indicate some negative
condition — as it is understood in the derivative view of imperma-

nence — but point to the ever-renewable and selfless possibilities of evanescence. He refers to Ju-ching's words, " 'Reuin attained enlightenment upon seeing the peach blossoms bloom, but I attained it when I saw them falling.' "[26] Dōgen also observes that the old plum tree endures and withstands various conditions — strong winds, harsh storms, the vicissitudes of sunlight and other elements — but it invariably returns anew, reflecting, stimulating and containing (through the law of interpenetration) the awakening of all other phenomena. Withering represents the total detachment and selfless imperturbability of existential and ontological realization of *muga*, which is fully and profoundly integrated with and revealed by the radical transiency of momentary existence. "When the old plum tree blooms, the entire world arises. When the entire world arises spring arrives. . . . Each and every moment of past, present and future without exception or limit is renewed. This 'renewal' is beyond newness [in the conventional sense]."[27] The idea of "renewal" thereby expressed is not novelty contrasted with antiquity, but the vigorous and insubstantial activity inherent in both living and dying.

The exhortative-soteriological and naturalistic-aesthetic dimensions of Dōgen's understanding of impermanence are grounded in his ontological analysis of the totalistic moment or *dharma*-stage (*jū-hōi*) that "is possessed of before and after . . . and cut off from before and after," encompassing simultaneously the interpenetration and independence of life and death. In "Genjōkōan" he writes:

> Firewood is reduced to ash and cannot become firewood again. So, one should not hold the view that ash is succeeding and firewood is preceding. One must know that firewood dwells in the *dharma*-position of firewood [of which] there is preceding and succeeding. Although there is before and after, it is cut off from before and after. Ashes are in the *dharma*-position of ashes [of which] there is preceding and succeeding. Just as firewood does not become firewood again after it has been reduced to ashes, so man does not resume life after death. . . . Life is a complete manifestation of time and death is a complete manifestation of time. Take, for example, the relationship between winter and spring. Winter does not become spring; nor does spring become summer.[28]

In this and related passages, Dōgen maintains first of all that life and death are not separable, but occur simultaneously within each moment. Life and death appear every moment instantaneously, naturally and thoughtlessly. There can be neither life nor death without the other at the very same time. Life and death together constitute the total dynamic activity (zenki) of the dharma-stage. Consequently, life should not be clung to and affirmed nor death feared and negated. Also, life and death together should not be hated and escaped from nor should nirvāṇa, conceived of as the resolution to the problem of life and death, be greedily desired outside of impermanence itself. In "Shōji" Dōgen asserts, "This present life and death itself is the life of Buddha."[29] If life and death (shōji) is rejected with distaste or abided in with attachment, the life of Buddha is lost and one is left only with the appearance of the Buddha. Total detachment and selfless freedom from the dilemmas of life and death demands full immersion in life and death non-obstructively realized through each impermanent and insubstantial moment. "Clinging in attachment to life, shrinking in abhorrence from death, is not Buddhist. Realizing that both life and death are a combination of various conditions being manifested before your eyes, you utilize a way of complete and unrestricted freedom."[30]

The first dimension of jū-hōi refers to the aspect "possessed of before and after," encompassing the totality of simultaneous possibilities. The second dimension is the directness, immediacy, and spontaneity "cut off from before and after," without endurance or substance. Dōgen paradoxically maintains that while life and death are harmoniously interpenetrative, "life is life itself and death is death itself." These two elements are independently impermanent and insubstantial in and of themselves, and stand alone without requiring any outside existence or reference. "Life is not obstructed by death, death is not obstructed by life. . . . Life is the manifestation of the total activity of life, and death is the manifestation of the total activity of death."[31] From the standpoint of each element, life and death are unimpeding and independent stages which contain the totality and insubstantiality of temporal events in the entire Dharma-realm. Life is the total stage of the dynamic working (kikan) of zenki encompassing multitudinous *dharmas* manifesting their unique dynamism. Life and death are not consecutive transformations of an essentially constant entity. Life does not turn into death, just as the ash must be considered a completely different manifestation of *jū-hōi* than the firewood; nor does death turn back into life, just as the ash does not once again become firewood.

The conception of life and death as sequentially related occurrences would imply that the entity which contains them consists of a stable or enduring substratum. Ordinary people, Dōgen notes, think that life is like a tree which begins with a seed, grows, then perishes, and that death is the tree which is no longer alive, as if life were the first activity and death the second. This view actually harbors a dichotomy between life and death as well as between the object and the life-death process it undergoes. Dōgen maintains, "Life is the manifestation of the total dynamic working; death is the manifestation of the total dynamic working." When there is life, there is nothing but life. When there is death, there is nothing but death. In maintaining that life is life itself (although it depends upon death) and that death is death itself (although it depends upon life), Dōgen does not contradict his emphasis on the simultaneity of life and death, but enhances it so that it is not understood in an average or derivative way. Life and death each possess before and after in that they are determined by the influences they simultaneously receive and project. Yet they are cut off from past and future because they manifest absolute and insubstantial presence without reference to any other tense or relative phase of time. Examining impermanence from the perspective of impermanence itself directly, clearly and profoundly discloses no-self, of which death is a unique and complete manifestation in itself, just as is life.

Finally, Dōgen suggests that from the standpoint of radical impermanence, the activity of each *dharma*-stage is neither life nor death, which suggests freedom *from* life-death in terms of (without trying to escape) life-death. The time of no-life and no-death is the spontaneous and perpetually vigorous impermanent and insubstantial motion of *jū-hōi* "prior-to-turning," which cannot be categorized in terms of going or coming, eternity or momentariness, permanence or impermanence, being or non-being, life or death. "Though [life and death] is not uniformity, it is not variablility; though it is not variability, it is not sameness; though it is not sameness, it is not multiplicity. . . . And the manifestation of their total dynamic working exists within what is neither life nor death."[32] At this very impermanent moment which is both uniquely manifest and universally insubstantial there is at once life and death and therefore the life of Buddha; life itself and death itself; and the life of no-life and the death of no-death. All represent shifting perspectives of the multiple dimensions of full realization of no-self. Furthermore, Dōgen emphasizes that the total dynamism is itself nothing but impermanence. To say that *zenki* is inseparable from the impermanent *dharma*-stage does not mean that there was no previous manifestation of *zenki*. The previous manifestation is contained within, but is likewise independent of the present manifestation. No manifestations of total dynamism, regardless of when or where they occur, impede any other manifestation; each impermanent and insubstantial moment is continually and expansively renewed.

Comparative Examination

The notions of finitude and impermanence seem to share a common starting point in that they disclose the profound and complex interrelatedness between the existential and ontological dimensions of primordial time which, if appropriately conceived, overcomes the inauthentic entanglements of derivative time. The analysis of the origin of derivative time, examined in the previous chapter, uncovers the direct link between deficient existence and misguided ontology. With the disclosure of radical contingency, Heidegger and Dōgen attempt to fully and clearly undermine attachments to now-time by illuminating the non-substantiality of existence overwhelmingly and inescapably manifest through each individual's encounter with death, anxiety and suffering. Radical contingency is the ultimate ontological condition independent of existential choice. Yet it becomes visible only through the resolve of someone willing to face it, which in turn makes possible the continuing cultivation of authenticity. Because contingency is universal, it is of utmost significance to the individual; only when the individual sees contingency in its universality can there be existential transformation. Heidegger's notion of the hermeneutic circle seems to be an appropriate explication of the dynamics of overcoming deficient existence through ontological disclosure, which is made on the basis of and simultaneously lays the foundation for existential authenticity.

Heidegger and Dōgen share a concentration on death and dying as the extreme experiential point for the convergence of the dimensions of existential decision and ontological disclosure concerning radical contingency. Death is the preeminent transcendental matter always pointing beyond the particular experience of loss and forcing one to come to terms existentially with the underlying ontological meaning of contingent existence. Both thinkers are in accord in their refutation of basic misconceptions concerning death. They maintain that death is not an end to existence which arrives as a termination or culmination, or as a passage to another existence. Death is not merely a psychological concern to be investigated only at the time when someone is about to die. Nor should it be approached as a speculative issue in order to justify the apparent arbitrariness of its occurrence or to rationalize the suffering it creates in terms of certain metaphysical or theological presuppositions about eternity. Rather, death penetrates every moment and aspect of life, so that the ways one encounters his dying become normative for his approach toward living. Underlying the self-flight and self-deceptiveness of "time flies," there is expressed the understanding that death is always being confronted — even if in a derivative mode of fear as one possible and perhaps the most prevalent approach. Not only can death take place at any time; it pervades each and every moment. Death frames existence to such an inevitable and all-pervasive extent that it must be taken into account in all one's affairs.

Despite these similarities of viewpoint, however, key differences in the analysis of death by Heidegger and Dōgen reflect fundamental disparities in their approaches to the central issue involved in uncovering finitude and impermanence: that is, the overcoming of substance and eternalist ontology derived from now-time through the neutral or non-evaluative disclosure of the universal nature of radical contingency. The central aim of Heidegger's thought is the de-struction of traditional substance ontology through a "fundamental ontology" of finite Dasein as Being-towards-the-end. Heidegger shows the permeation of death-as-end throughout life (in *Sein und Zeit*) and death-as-Nothingness pervading unconcealment (in Heidegger II), such that existence itself is a continuing response to the end because the end itself is essential to existence. By emphasizing the imminence of Dasein's end as the ultimate and unsurpassable limitation of its presence, Heidegger shifts the focus of ontology from the derivatively conceived actual present to the anticipation of futural possibilities which become historically repeatable as Dasein's having-been. "[Dasein's] finitude," he writes, "does not amount primarily to a stopping, but is a characteristic of temporalization itself. The primordial and authentic future is the towards-oneself existing as the possibility of nullity, the possibility which is not to be outstripped."[33]

Heidegger does not, however, really diverge from the presupposition that life exists or is stretched along *from* beginning *towards* the end in a particular span of time allotted to it. Thus, his emphasis on death heightens the view that life is to be evaluated in terms of accomplishments achieved before the span runs out. In the later works, this quasi-substantive framework is not dissolved, but is expanded to encompass the finite historical epochs whose spans are greater than the life of any particular Dasein which is, in turn, limited, determined and bound by the unfolding of the fateful consequences of these eras. Heidegger's attempted reversal of the orientation of metaphysics from actuality to potentiality, now-time to the future, everydayness to the end does not necessarily overcome substance ontology or the presupposition of an enduring substratum.

Dōgen however, seems to more clearly surpass any subtle clinging to a concept of a substratum of a supposedly constant entity which is thought to undergo death as well as other transformations. Dōgen's analysis goes beyond an accentuation of the interweaving of life and death, existence and non-existence, presence and absence, by focusing on the total activity of the duration-less and selfless yet inexhaustible stages of life itself and death itself as independent, non-relative and complete manifestations of impermanence. He writes, "The total activity of life and death holds sway imperceptibly. You should learn of going and coming that there is life and death in going, there is life and death in coming, there is going and coming in life, there is going and coming in death . . . throughout all the realms of the world."[34] Impermanence, according to Dōgen, is not generated by a specific outside cause, but it arises by itself as each and every present moment. It is dynamic, indivisible and insubstantial and cannot be segmented into parts, so that non-existence is not said to follow upon existence as if they were two distinguishable and separable states of an essentially constant entity. Rather, death or non-existence is the impermanent present completely fulfilled in and of itself. In death, there is nothing other than death itself in all its impermanent and insubstantial multi-dimensional dyna-mism — possessed of before and after yet cut off from before and after — just as in life there is nothing but life itself.

Both thinkers emphasize human encounter with death and dying, contingency and vicissitude, non-existence and nothing-ness to undermine and overcome fixations with substance and attachments to eternalism and teleology, yet they reach different conclusions in terms of the radicalness and depth of their respective breakthroughs from derivative time. Heidegger's approaches — his investigation of Dasein's *existenziell* confronta-tion with dying and guilt in terms of the *existenzial* condition of finitude in *Sein und Zeit*, and the disclosure of the pervasive boundaries of Nothingness in Heidegger II — do not seem to be free of all traces or elements of substance ontology and do not point to the thorough and unobstructedly insubstantial nature of all phenomena. Dōgen, on the other hand, uses the meaning of impermanence to deepen and rediscover the existential, onto-logical and soteriological dimensions of non-self, which is the basis for his analysis of being-time (*uji*).

The central differences between Heidegger and Dōgen are highlighted by one of the most intriguing and suggestive passages from the *Shōbōgenzō*:

> To study the Buddha Way is to study the self. To study the self is to forget the self. To forget the self is to be authenticated by all *dharmas.* To be authenticated by all *dharmas* is to cast off body and mind of self and others. The traces of enlightenment disappear, and traceless enlightenment is ceaselessly renewed.[35]

First, Dōgen insists upon the total inseparability of what Heidegger calls the *existenziell* and *existenzial* levels of inquiry and dimensions of realization. To learn the Buddha Way, that is, to ontologically clarify the ultimate selfsameness of *mujō/muga* in terms of life-death, the incessant falling of flowers, and the complex inner dynamism of the *dharma*-stage, is necessarily to existentially explore the responses and feelings of the self's (in a non-fixated sense) poignant and tragic awareness of impermanence. There can be no avoidance of personal reflection, insight and experience at every stage and level of clarification. The Way and the self are inseparably interrelated, each determined by the other and realized only *upon* realization of the other; neither dimension is penetrated either before or after the other. Heidegger's distinction between the *existenziell* levels may indeed be philosophically useful, but from Dōgen's standpoint it is significant only if understood as entirely provisional (for the sake of analysis) and ultimately discardable (for the sake of true realization).

Second, Dōgen maintains that the unity of Way and self necessarily leads to and is simultaneously based on genuine self-forgetfulness, or immediate and complete existential/ontological/soteriological realization of non-self. To learn the self is to spontaneously leave it behind without a trace. "To forget the self" does not mean, for Dōgen, to merely set it aside for the time being, as Heidegger phenomenologically brackets the *existenziell* level for the sake of *existenzial* disclosure. Nor is it to replace the self with a new concept or substratum, which only betrays a fixation with substance and subject in however a subtle or disguised fashion. Rather, genuine self-forgetfulness is to "cast off" all delusory or inauthentic bifurcations between mind/body, self/other, self/non-self as well as between enlightenment/unenlightenment and impermanence/permanence. All such distinctions are spontaneously released without residue, compromise, or the slightest attachment when the ultimate identity of *mujō* and *muja* is clarified and penetrated. From Dōgen's standpoint of non-self, Heidegger falls short of overcoming substance ontology. For example, Heidegger is critical of Kant for continuing to define the Self in terms of the traditional inappropriate ontology as the selfsameness and steadiness of something that is always present-at-hand, a view of the *subiectum* which revises but still derivatively presupposes and perpetuates an inauthentic fixation with the apparent constancy of *ousia*. Although Heidegger reorients the meaning of Self-constancy in terms of Dasein's anticipatory resoluteness in confronting its nullity, he does not fully abandon the concept of the endurance of the self or of any subtle distinction between finite/infinite. Heidegger's notion of finitude is not sufficiently radical to uncover the complete existential and ontological insubstantiality of self and world that is disclosed by Dōgen through spontaneous forgetfulness which penetrates impermanence at once possessed of and yet cut off from life and death.

Finally, Dōgen's phrase, "to forget one's self is to be authenticated by all *dharmas*" (as well as his analysis of the *dharma*-stages of firewood and ash and of spring and winter, and his poetry), shows that his understanding of contingency in terms of impermanence has a more naturalistic and holistic orientation than Heidegger's notion of finitude. In contrast to Heidegger's existential focus on Dasein in *Sein und Zeit* and to his attempted trans-anthropocentrism in later writings, Dōgen shows that the identity of *mujō/muga* is realized when and only when *all* phenomena, encompassing the human and the natural, totality and particularity, simultaneously cast off self-fixations, each dimension experientially realized in and through all other ones. Dōgen thus seems to overcome the subtle gaps Heidegger presupposes between *existenziell* and *existenzial* levels, potentiality and actuality, future and present, finitude and infinitude, anthropocentrism and a realm beyond man, all of which prohibit a breakthrough to realization of non-self.

In light of these critical differences between the two thinkers, it seems that any claim to universal applicability, meaning or relevance for Heidegger's disclosure of contingency is similarly

limited. Unless Heidegger's fundamental ontology has a significance that is universal and unbound by the particular epoch from
which its observations and conclusions are drawn, then his enterprise represents a philosophical anthropology of "modern"
Western man's sense of alienation from the curious anonymity
of the public world. In *Sein und Zeit*, Heidegger attempts to
universalize the condition of finitude through the *existenzial*
analysis of Dasein as anxiously Being-thrown-towards-the-end,
an approach to the problem of dying which still views death as
an end that is arriving from the future. Although death is not
merely *in* the future, according to Heidegger, it is not said to be
fully coterminous with the present moment. In his later writings,
especially *Was Heisst Denken?*, Heidegger maintains that the
finitude of Being in its epochal unfolding pertains only to the
temporal-historical development of the Western metaphysical
tradition. This position seems to be a consequence of the fact that
Heidegger's understanding of finitude is itself a reinterpretation
or attempted ontologization of Western theological doctrines concerning death and dying, guilt and consicence, which presuppose the prior incapability of man to fully attain truth in terms
of metaphysical doctrines which posit the necessity of historical-
epochal developments. Heidegger draws an intimate relationship
between man's finitude and his submissiveness to fate. Although
he denies an Eternal power which controls man, Heidegger does
hold that finitude itself makes it impossible for man to become
fully free from the historical consequences his inherent limitations fatefully generate. Thus, Heidegger's issue — death-as-end —
is not universally disclosed because his method of analysis is based
on Christian eschatological notions that he inherits in a partially
unacknowledged or unclarified manner.

For Dōgen, on the other hand, impermanence is more fundamentally, universally, naturalistically and insubstantially conceived than as an end which is perpetually approaching or as
a history which encompasses and determines man's fateful decisions. Impermanence accounts for the transiency and inevitable
decline of any and every historical epoch; nations and lands, as
much as grasses and trees and all other phenomena, are primordially nothing other than *mujō-busshō*. But Dōgen rejects any

attempt to identify impermanence itself with Japanese or Buddhist history. He clearly refutes the doctrine of *mappō*, for example, which assumes a necessary link between the aggravation of human suffering and the epochal decay of Buddhist *Dharma*. "Do not think," he writes in "Bendōwa," to adherents of *mappō*, "because ours is [currently] not a land of benevolence and insight, or because the people have a meager understanding, that the Buddhist *Dharma* cannot be comprehended here. Although all people possess in abundance the seed of wisdom, it seems that our people have not yet realized and lived it."[36]

Furthermore, Heidegger's notion of finitude is not neutral or value-free in that it does imply the inability of man to fully liberate himself from the deficiencies of the existence in which he is thrown, a problem also exposed in the previous chapter in the case of Heidegger's associating derivative now-time and the present with falling. Heidegger connects finitude with the inherent limitations, dependency and errancy of man which necessitates his inauthenticity. "The finitude of Dasein — the comprehension of Being — *lies in* forgetfulness. This forgetfulness is nothing accidental and temporary but is constantly and necessarily renewed."[37] The later Heidegger attempts to clarify the universality of finitude by asserting that falling or forgetfulness is not due to man's responsibility or lack of it, but to finitude in itself as the primordial condition which inevitably leads to *Seinsvergessenheit* (oblivion of Being). He thus puts himself in the problematic position of at once indirectly and confusedly criticizing finitude because it invariably involves inauthenticity, and yet refraining from any existential injunction to overcome forgetfulness since as part of finitude, it is proximally and for the most part *the way* of human existence.

Dōgen does not cast a negative judgement on the condition of impermanence itself, but he criticizes the deep-seated ignorance of the average man which prevents him from penetrating the truly dynamic and selfless nature of the present moment. He thus exhorts Zen disciples neither to submit to nor to transcend impermanence, but to realize its genuine meaning beyond the mere appearance of change which is bound by the concept of an enduring substantive entity, through the simultaneous fulfillment of existential and ontological understanding each and every impermanent, insubstantial moment. Dōgen's analysis of impermanence accentuates the depth and totality of the totalistic present. Heidegger's view, however, seems to suggest that man in his finitude must necessarily undergo repeated forgetfulness even as one gazes towards and anticipates the futural end. His definition of the dilemmas — and therefore his attempted overcoming — of metaphysics that arises from an inauthentic approach to finitude, is bound by the very pitfalls of substance ontology and Christian eschatology he seeks to expose and overcome.

In the following chapter, the gaps created in Heidegger's analysis between the derivative present (now-time) and the primordial future (disclosed in terms of finitude) as well as the primordial past (disclosed in terms of historicality) will be examined. They seem to lead to a subtle yet problematic separation between the ontological and existential dimensions of temporality that appears to be overcome by Dōgen's notion of the total simultaneous exertion of all beings as the here-and-now "perpetuation of the Way" (gyōji-dōkan).

Chapter 4

Primordial Time

Problematics of Primordial Time

The aim of the exposition of primordial time by Heidegger and Dōgen is to show that true temporality does not merely stand in some ontical connection with that which exists, but it is fundamentally and essentially interrelated with and inseparable from existence, holding sway throughout the multiple dimensions and by means of existence itself. Primordial time is neither an eternal realm beyond existence nor another attribute of existence which could be logically or ontologically added onto it either before or after existence is described; nor does existence, conceived of substantively, persist "in" objectified time. Temporality is neither a cause of existence that chronologically or cosmologically precedes it nor a product that is teleologically attained at the conclusion of linear sequence; nor is it a statically conceived evolution working its way into existence. Such conceptions unacknowledgedly assume and unreflectively betray fixations with substantiality and actuality characteristic of derivative time.

In their analysis of the origin of derivative time in the inauthentic tendencies of the average man, and in their refutation of the apparent legitimation and perpetuation of the conventional view that appears in their respective philosophical traditions, Heidegger and Dōgen both presuppose an underlying temporal unity and inner dynamism. The dynamic unity of primordial time prevails even if concealed and seemingly stagnated, and undermines deficient attachments to now-time and eternalism and the consequent surrender of the genuine significance of the past and future. According to the derivative view, the present is considered to be a fleeting yet substantive time-unit which is severed from existence and endures while the future approaches and forever recedes into the past. As man feels that he is continually losing his grasp on time, truth is posited as an eternal realm transcendent of and unaffected by temporal vicissitudes, thus disguising and reinforcing an attachment to objectified time. On the basis of a non-substantive disclosure of radical contingency, however, primordial time is uncovered by Heidegger and Dōgen in terms of a unique convergence of authentic existential response to change and loss and the ontological clarification of the non-objectifiable, temporal meaning of self, world, language, space, the three tenses, transcendence, and truth.

In order to offer an authentically non-substantive philosophy of primordial time, Heidegger and Dōgen must highlight the dynamic interrelatedness of the three tenses with the multiple dimensions of existence to overcome the most obvious as well as the most subtle and insidiously veiled deficiencies they have challenged in the many varieties of derivative time. They must account for the true nature and structure of both the present moment (deeper than or underlying now-time) and of change and continuity (deeper than "time flies"). Also, they need to illustrate the non-substantive temporal foundations of truth (in contrast to the false eternalism traditionally accepted in Western metaphysical approaches to the question of Being or in Mahāyāna Buddhist interpretations of Buddha-nature). That is, for Heidegger and Dōgen to clearly resolve the issues which are central to their respective philosophical projects, it is necessary for them to successfully overcome the inadequacies in both the conventional everyday and the traditional speculative views of time, which they have exposed for their common derivative basis.

The following elements of a doctrine of primordial time seem to be essential for the fulfillment of this task:

1. *Non-substantialism* — time must be freed of all traces of objectification so that it is no longer conceived of as an hypostatized framework apart from activity, but as the inherent dyna-

mism and fluidity of movement that characterizes both the immediate present and the continuity of duration; time must be de-objectified so that the truth of Being or of Buddha-nature can be so liberated.

2. *Non-reductionism* — the temporal unity of all phases of existence — selfhood, authenticity and inauthenticity, language, space, history, etc. — must be shown in a way that is at once true to experience yet unbound by conventional fixations, without reducing the multiple dimensions of existence to a monolithically conceived of time or merely equating them with time; time is not a first cause beyond existence nor is existence in all its aspects uniformly in time.

3. *Non-anthropocentrism* — although the existential dimension is stressed as essential for the disclosure of primordial time, true temporality is not limited to human experience (such a view would be a new form of reductionism), but must be shown to have universal breadth and significance in terms of its naturalistic dimensions; this point is a continual source of tension in Heidegger's thought and is crucial to the contrast between Heidegger and Dōgen.

4. *Non-differentiation* — primordial time must be disclosed as a unity of existential and ontological dimensions to eliminate any possible gap between time and existence or between truth and time, lest time be misconstrued as an independent realm somehow separable from or beyond existence or as an impasse to be surmounted for the attainment of truth.

In the concluding sections of this chapter, the approaches of Heidegger and Dōgen will be evaluated for their effectiveness both in overcoming their own philosophical traditions and in formulating a universally applicable doctrine of the true nature of time. A five-fold hierarchical schema will be developed to highlight and contrast the relation between their respective views of primordial time and those conceptions they have refuted as derivative. Heidegger's notions of the authentic present (*Augen-*

blick) and historicality (*Geschichtlichkeit*) will be contrasted with Dōgen's notions of the here-and-now (nikon) and passage (*kyōryaku*), as will Heidegger's notion of the self-same (*Ereignis*) and related notions in Dōgen, such as *zenki* (total dynamism), to discern the fundamental points of philosophical controversy between the two thinkers. For example, the apparent gaps or separations in Heidegger's understanding of primordial time be-tween theory and practice, present and past/future, Dasein and world-time will be considered in light of Dōgen's emphasis on the absolute simultaneity of all manifestations of being-time directly realized by the True Man's selfless exertion at each and every impermanent moment. Dōgen argues that, "The Way which is called 'now' does not precede exertion; 'now' is itself the immediate and complete realization of exertion (*gyōji-genjō*)."[1] Finally, the divergent soteriological (practical and experiential) implications in Heidegger's futural temporality will be contrasted with Dōgen's view of the totalistic present moment, in terms of how this reflects differences in their respective attempts at over-coming substance ontology.

For Heidegger, time as presencing is the "first name" of Being. Together in their essential underlying unity, Being and time constitute the great unthought matter at the basis of and propel-ling — yet for the most part derivatively veiled by — Western metaphysics. The uncovering of Being as such demands the gen-uine disclosure of time which is, in turn, to be thought in terms of its Being. The complex interrelation between Being and time is that time must be disclosed *as* time in its Being or un-*vorhanden* essence so that Being can be shown *as* non-objectifiable and non-substantial in light of its temporal pres-encing. Thus, the key to liberating Being from the thing-like or substantive status to which it has been derivatively reduced by traditional metaphysics is to demonstrate its primordial relation to time, which requires that time be disclosed in an appropriately non-ousiological manner. Time is not something which stands alongside Being to be superceded so that Being itself can be understood and expressed; nor does it stand in connection with existence. Rather, it is the fundamental and essential horizon that determines the truth of Being as the basis of self, world, and space.

But in order to reveal the Being of time as the access to the truth of Being as such, Being must be already in view through the forestructure of projective understanding. Furthermore, time itself is not the answer to the question of Being, nor is Being merely time. In one of his last works, *Zur Sache des Denkens*, Heidegger reflects on the hermeneutically circular nature of his philosophical undertaking as well as on the problematics of interpretation embedded therein: "Being and time determine each other reciprocally, but in such a manner that neither can the former — Being — be addressed as something temporal nor can the latter — time — be addressed as a being . . . . Time — a matter, presumably *the* matter of thinking, if indeed something like time speaks as presence. Being *and* time, time *and* Being, name the relation of both issues, the matter at stake which holds both issues toward each other and endures their relation."[2]

In *Sein und Zeit*, the profound hermeneutic reciprocity between Being and time is investigated and provisionally disclosed in terms of Dasein's anticipatory resoluteness as authentically Being *towards* one's ownmost, distinctive potentiality-for-Being no longer closed off by curious expectation, which reveals the futural nature and ecstatic-horizonal structure of temporality. On the basis of Dasein's *existenziell* encounters with the inherent limitations of the *existenzial* condition of finitude, the unity and primordial movement of temporality is shown as that which ontologically makes possible the interrelation of the three tenses and the priority of the future; temporality is the foundation for Dasein's transcendence, fateful self-repetition, spatial encounters, capacity for discourse as well as the average everydayness of falling.

Whereas in *Sein und Zeit* Heidegger seeks to restate, reorient, and re-solve (or solve anew) the traditional metaphysical questions of self, space and transcendence in terms of their basis in Dasein's temporal structure, Heidegger II claims to attempt a more radical project. In the later works, Heidegger does not try to answer the old questions in a new way, but to explore the unity of the three tenses of time from a trans-anthropocentric, trans-metaphysical perspective in terms of the selfsame event (*Ereignis*) or belonging-together of Being and time. By virtue of its "nearness" (*Nahheit*) as the true fourth dimension of time underlying the other three, *Ereignis* allows for the historical-epochal possibilities of thinking and for the naturalistic configuration of the four-fold (*Geviert*) of earth and sky, gods and mortals.

Dōgen's aim is to show that Buddha-nature is not an objectifiable transcendent realm or an eternal absolute which somehow manifests itself in the relative and transitory world of appearance. This is accomplished through a reorientation of Zen enlightenment in terms of a radical rediscovery and reaffirmation of the totality of the present moment, or the ultimate non-differentiability of ontological penetration or transparency (*tōdatsu*) and existential realization (*shō*) by means of fully dynamic activity at each and every occasion of being-time. Through one instant of the selfless exertion of *shinjin-datsuraku*, all interpenetrating phenomena appear and harmoniously permeate past, present and future.

The creative multi-dimensional unity of the three tenses, all beings and elements, and all possibilities and aspects of insight and experience is expressed metaphorically in "Zenki" by the parable of a man (symbolic of each particularity of exertive endeavor and selfless detachment) riding a boat (symbolic of the holistic manifestation of being-time). Aboard the craft, the man turns the rudder, sets the sail, and poles the boat along, his leverage providing its aim and direction. The boat carries the man, giving sustenance and support to his efforts, but without the man riding in and maneuvering it, the boat cannot be what it is or fulfill its course — an image which conveys the unimpeded inseparability of manifestation and practice, each dimension making possible, enhancing and continually renewing the other. "At such a time," Dōgen writes, "there is nothing else but the world of the boat. The heavens, the water, and the shore are all in all engaged in the time of the boat, and they are not the same as that which is not the boat's time. Therefore, life lives through me and I am me because of life. In boarding the boat, the true interdependence of body and mind is the dynamic working of the boat; both the whole earth and vast space are the dynamic working of the boat."[3]

In "Uji," Dōgen analyzes the structure of the totalistic moment in terms of the interrelated notions of right-now (*nikon*), spontaneous presencing cut off from before and after, and passage (*kyōryaku*), the dynamic continuity possessed of before and after. His emphasis on the continuity of passage indicates that *nikon* does not represent a new and subtly disguised form of eternalism, but the unity and insubstantiality of the existential and onto-logical foundations of the manifestations of being-time. Dōgen's disclosure of *nikon* and *kyōryaku* lays the basis for his radical reinterpretation of Mahāyāna ontological doctrines and of Zen existentialist imperatives. First, he reorients central notions such as *busshō* (original Buddha-nature), and *juki* (prediction of future Buddhahood) to free them from any trace of objectification by emphasizing the inseparability of primordiality and immediacy, and of attainment and present activity. Second, Dōgen accentuates the unified arising of the three stages of existential awakening — the spontaneity of resolve, the simultaneity of practice, and the renewal of realization — as an essentially temporal process that at once mirrors and contains the innate, unceasing and complex dynamism of *uji*.

Heidegger's Understanding of Primordial Time

Heidegger's hermeneutic procedure for establishing the truth of primordial time involves two interrelated dimensions of the "productive logic" of circular interpretation. The ontological dis-closure of the dynamic process of temporality is achieved on the basis of the existential possibility of authenticity, by which Dasein is liberated from the stranglehold of now-time through direct experience of the unity of time and of its own un-*vorhanden* nature. "The ontological 'truth' of the *existenzial* analysis, " Hei-degger writes, "is developed on the ground of the primordial *existenziell* truth. However, the latter does not necessarily need the former."[4] Authenticity is essential for the disclosure of tem-porality, but primordial time holds sway regardless of whether it is realized or not by encompassing both authenticity and inau-thenticity. Similarly, authentic existence does not necessarily depend upon or result in ontological understanding. Nor does an ontologically appropriate interpretation guarantee the attainment of authenticity. Heidegger acknowledges that he is forced by the very nature of his hermeneutic approach to grant that there may be a definite ontical way or a factical ideal underlying ontological interpretation. Yet he refrains from, and expresses a disinterest in exploring such an implication. That is, *existenzial* truth is grounded in and justified on the basis of the *existenziell* level, but it does not in turn propose any particular *existenziell* behavior that must be accepted as binding.

Nevertheless, the second level of hermeneutic circularity requires a concrete factical basis for uncovering authenticity. Just as ontology needs to be disclosed on the basis of authentic existence, authenticity itself must be appropriately grounded in terms of the definite *existenziell* determinations of Dasein's thrownness. Authenticity is not a "free-floating" behavior detached or withdrawn from or soaring above existence; nor is it a seclusion from the world. Rather, authenticity is the sober anxiety of individualized Dasein fully founded within and realized on the basis of its finitude. "Anticipatory resoluteness is not a way of escape, fabricated for the 'overcoming' of death; it is rather that understanding which follows the call of conscience and which frees for death the possibility of acquiring *power* over Dasein's *existence* and of basically dispersing all fugitive Self-concealments."[5]

The two-fold nature of anticipatory resoluteness reflects Dasein's authentic appropriation or self-retrieval of its thrownness-unto-death by means of its perpetual and meaningful encounters with its inescapable and pervasive nullity. Dasein's authentic response to its finitude or non-power is precisely the power of its freedom. Anticipation of death, which brings Dasein face to face with its imminent impossibility, shatters the bondage of the they-self to a fixation with actuality that closes off genuine possibilities. Inauthentic Dasein derivatively transforms its anxious certainty that death can, does and invariably will befall each person into the fear of something actual which is deterred to a later time, such that "the possible is drawn into the actual, arising out of the actual and returning to it."[6] In saying "one dies too, sometime, but not right away," everydayness concedes something like a certainty of death, but in an altogether ambiguous manner in order to weaken that certainty and to alleviate anxiety by covering up the abyss of dying. Freedom towards death, on the other hand, first makes futural projection possible *as* possibility by reclaiming the forestructure of care from its submission to the future derivatively conceived as the not-yet-now.

Dasein's resolute response to guilt is aroused by the call of conscience which awakens Dasein with the momentum of an abrupt push, stirring it from its *existenziell* deficiency by revealing the nothingness of finitude. Conscience bypasses or cuts through the illusions of *das Man*, which has abandoned itself to the apparent unchanging persistence of actual circumstances. The call of conscience penetrates to the genuine Self which is thrown into possibilities that are limited and defined but never completely staticized. "The appeal calls back by calling forth: it calls Dasein forth to the possibility of taking over, in existing, that thrown entity which it is; it calls Dasein *back* to its thrownness so as to understand this thrownness as the null basis which it has to take up into existence."[7]

Conscience exposes the deceptions of the they-self, rooting them out of their most insidious hiding places by disclosing their null ground. The call must not be conceived as a *vorhanden* entity which reports events, puts the self up for "trial" and passes judgements as if Dasein were an object, or offers soliloquies in which causes get pleaded. The conventional view holds that conscience performs an essentially critical function concerning problems of good and evil by reproving and warning in the sense of a disinterested spectator which surveys a person's behavior and offers practical injunctions as well as threats of punishment. According to Heidegger, the message of conscience is so clear, forceful and unequivocal, and its impact so profound and uncompromising because in calling Dasein back to the nullity of guilt, it says "no-thing." Conscience communicates the meaning of nothingness by keeping silent. "What does the conscience call to him to whom it appeals? Taken strictly, nothing. The call asserts nothing, gives no information about world-events, has nothing to tell. . . . 'Nothing' gets called to this Self, but it has been *summoned* to itself — that is, to its ownmost potentiality-for-Being."[8] Conscience appeals to one who wants to be brought back from falling into the public world. It comes from the resources of Dasein itself to recall Dasein itself, forcing the collapse of *das Man*.

Anticipatory resoluteness reveals primordial time as the meaning of care, which is not an entity outside of or an objectifiable cause of existence. Rather, care is nothing other than the inner dynamism and complex unified processes of thrown-projection, expressed tautologically by Heidegger as the "temporalization of temporality": "The meaning of Dasein's Being is not something free-floating which is other than and 'outside of' itself, but is the self-understanding of Dasein itself. . . . Temporality 'is' not an *entity* at all. It is not, but it *temporalizes* itself."⁹ The essential features of primordial time are futurity, ecstacy and finitude, in contrast to the derivative preoccupation with the constant now separated from the approaching not-yet-now that is continually subsumed by the no-longer-now. Heidegger repeatedly stresses that he is interested in the phenomenon of anticipatory resoluteness as authentic Being-towards-the-end not for the sake of moral judgement or to offer any practical proposal, but to discover the *existenzial*-ontological foundations which make possible the multiple variations and dimensions of existence. That is, his concern is not with anticipatory resoluteness as such, but with the primordial structure it reveals and which, in turn, underlies authenticity as one possible *existenziell* mode.

Heidegger maintains that anticipatory resoluteness is made possible only because Dasein lets itself "come towards" (*Zu-kunft*) itself in Being-towards-death as the ownmost potentiality of its nullity. Anticipation discloses the priority of the future in that the future is the true basis for the possibility of Dasein's authentic self-approach as well as its inauthentic expectation of the not-yet-now. The future is not the endless passing by of objectified time, but the self-generating movement of Dasein's forestructure of understanding, always projecting ahead-of-itself into novel and creative possibilities of knowledge, activity and expression. The primordiality of the future is demonstrated in three interrelated aspects: it is the basis of temporal existence, of the possibility of authenticity, and of the possibility of inauthenticity.

First, the future is the true ground of the three-fold struc-

ture of care, allowing Dasein to project ahead-of-itself towards
the end (future), to take into itself what it already is or has been
as Being-guilty (past), and to make present *vorhanden* entities
it finds itself alongside (present). The past as having-been
(*Gewesenheit*) and the present as making-present (*Gegenwärtigen*)
arise fundamentally from the future. Thus the designations about
care — that it is "ahead-of" or "already-in" — do not by any means
refer to now-points in actual time, but must be understood in
terms of their essential temporal meaning and structure. Just as
the future is not something "out there" hypostatically in front
of Dasein, but is inherent in the care-structure as its self-
approaching process, the past is not simply left behind but is
fully carried along as the thrown determinations of Dasein. "This
phenomenon has the unity of a future which makes present in
the process of having been; we designate it as *'temporality.'* "[10]

Second, the primordiality of the future makes possible
authenticity, not by causing Dasein to avoid or escape from its
factical conditions, but precisely by allowing it to resolutely come
to terms with the conditions. This is achieved by Dasein through
a profound acceptance and selective repetition (and not mere
toleration) of its having been that is continually projected as
futural possibilities. The authentic future and past coalesce as
the anxious rapture of a present moment of vision (*Augenblick*)
in a concrete yet eminently active situation (embracing the
passivity of resistance). In the authentic *existenzial* moment of
vision, resolute having been and anticipatory self-approach *come-
towards* and meet each other as the clearing or openness (*Da*)
of Dasein.

Finally, the future, when falsely objectified, is the basis of
inauthentic modes of expecting or awaiting the not-yet, forgetting the no-longer, and making present a substantive now-point
that arises and fades away in hypostatized time. Although
hermeneutically disclosed by Heidegger through Dasein's potentiality for authenticity, temporality is equiprimordially the
ground of inauthentic everydayness, whereby futural possibilities
are closed off and merely expected to arrive on their own in the
derivative not-yet now-point, while the past remains forgotten.
Dasein's self-entanglements and self-deceptions as well as its defi-

cient moods of indifference and carelessness are fundamentally temporal in the same way as the joy of anticipation and the equanimity of resolution.

Heidegger stresses that the present must be appropriately recovered along with the future and past in the mode of authenticity; resolute*ness* is not an empty ideal of existence, but necessarily takes the concrete and definite form of a resolu*tion* determined by what is factically possible in the situational (temporal-spatial) context encountered at the time. Nevertheless, the present clearly has a subsidiary role in Heidegger's notion of temporality. The authentic moment of vision is in every case based on the authenticity of futural projection; *Augenblick* is a consequence of anticipation, and not the other way around. Also, Heidegger pays more attention to the essential role played by the *in*authentic present in theoretical discovery and scientific investigation. According to Heidegger, theory and practice are not separable; one is not the absence of the other. Theory is not the suspension of concernful manipulation of entities, nor is practice merely sightless preoccupied concern; both are founded primordially in temporality. Dasein is for the most part engaged in a circumspective deliberation with, or the use of, ready-to-hand equipment. Theorizing and thematizing take place when these things are objectified as *vorhanden* entities to be investigated, analyzed, and categorized — that is, when a sudden change in perspective is brought about such that the entities are not altered, but are seen in a new way as objects of a distinctive mode of making present. Such objective investigation is not inauthentic in the sense of the they-self, however; the awaiting of discoveredness has its *existenziell* basis in a particular type of resoluteness.

Primordial coming-towards (future), having-been (past) and making-present (present) are neither ontically connected together nor collapsed into a monotonous or uniform identity, which would suggest the derivative view of successive now-points. Rather, they are intertwining and inseparable horizons which allow Dasein to stand ecstatically "outside-of-itself." Dasein exists both in and for itself and out amongst beings it concernfully uses and theoretically interprets. Temporality is the *ekstatikon* pure and simple by which Dasein views itself as a temporal-historical unity and individualized continuity of finite transcendence, rather than as a collection of isolated yet serially-connected time units. Ecstatic unity clears or illuminates thrown-projection such that "in every ecstasis, temporality temporalizes itself as a whole . . . that is, the unity of care-structure."[11] Primordial past, present and future are not independent realms but are fully implicated in each other at all times in that each ecstasis has its own horizon and the unity of the ecstases presences in each horizon. Futural understanding, for example, is always present in the process of having-been, and thrownness temporalizes itself as a future which is making-present.

The ecstatic-horizonal unity of temporality is the primordial condition of the "there" or openness of Dasein, the entity which understands Being, and thus constitutes the clearedness or lighting (*Gelichtetheit*) that makes Dasein bright and overt for itself and its projects. The illuminative power is not a *vorhanden* capacity implanted in or possessed by Dasein, but the temporal basis of its sight and understanding by which all possible and diversified dimensions of existence arise, including spatiality, discourse, transcendence and historicality. Thus, for Heidegger, in contrast to the onto-theo-logical tradition he seeks to overcome, time is not a gap to be surpassed to attain the truth of Being nor is Being simply the first and/or highest *vorhanden* being. Heidegger neither posits Being as an eternally transcendent realm (as in Plato or Aristotle) nor does he attempt to reduce Being to the totality of present-at-hand beings (Nietzsche) or elevate beings to the status of Absolute Spirit (Hegel). That is, Heidegger does not justify or eliminate (in a derivative fashion) the presupposed gulf between Being and time, but he discloses the non-*ousiological* temporality of un-*vorhanden* Dasein as the transcendental horizon of Being. Transcendence, according to Heidegger, is neither the speculatively claimed a-temporal or supra-temporal objectified realm beyond self and world nor the epistemologically analyzed perception of objects by a *vorhanden* subject. Rather, it represents the repetitive coming-towards of the thrownness or having-been of Being-in-the-world, that either loses itself in making entities present (inauthenticity) or resolutely encounters them in an active moment of vision (authenticity).

The temporality of Dasein is also the foundation for spatiality, discourse and historicality. Dasein is never a *vorhanden* thing or item "in" an externalized and objectified space that is defined in terms of its measurable boundaries. Only as projectively and ecstatically temporal can Dasein discover, break into and occupy space, making room for itself and the equipment it uses — bringing it close, handling it or keeping it at a distance — in a factical region. The discourse of Dasein does not merely refer to time in passing as one topic among many, but each utterance necessarily and fundamentally reveals its temporal basis. Each expression of language is in every case structured, regulated and determined by reference to one tense or a combination of tenses; even to say "is" in any form is essentially a temporal disclosure. Furthermore, languages themselves are temporally and historically determined. Languages can die, and particular uses and contexts within them are based on and gain their expressive power from the temporal structure — whether authentically or inauthentically modified — of Dasein which underlies any concern with the logical principles of grammatical construction.

The continuity of Dasein — the basis of the fact that it is stretched-along from beginning to end or between birth and death both individually and communally — is ontologically interpreted by Heidegger in terms of the phenomenon of historicality (*Geschictlichkeit*). The true basis of all historically significant events as well as the scientific study of history, historicality is grounded in the finite transcendence of care. Historicality is not an extra dimension added on to temporality, but is essentially interrelated with and inseparable from primordial time. Historicality has two levels of meaning. First, it allows occurrences, people, equipment, spatial sites, and epochs (or historical ages) to stand out in significance for current Dasein. This is not due to the fact that they are obsolete curiosities of the past, but arises because they constitute the having-been continually and projectively carried along as temporality. Historicality is the reason why Dasein may feel closer in understanding or attitude to a previous or even remote epochal period than to the present one. It also accounts for why an idea or expression may seem more meaningful and appropriate to a later historical era than to its own, as if it were awaiting the proper temporal conditions for its true arrival. Truth is determined not by arbitrary standards of "right" or "wrong," but by temporal-historical disclosiveness based on Dasein's coming-towards itself, which selectively chooses and repeats its having-been.

The second and deeper meaning of historicality is thus its essentially self-critical function, by which Dasein projectively selects through creative questioning, dialogue and interpretation what is currently relevant and important from its having-been. True history, according to Heidegger, is neither a random collection of human occurrences nor an external Plan which manifests itself in or "happens to" the human realm; it is neither the sum of the momentary actualities of experiences which come along successively and disappear nor a framework which this succession gradually fills up. Heidegger seeks to overcome traditional dichotomizations of history in terms of freedom vs. determinism, realism vs. idealism, original purity or impurity vs. teleological attainment, personalism vs. impersonalism, the natural realm of non-human beings vs. the historical realm of humans — all of which presuppose some derivatively objectified understanding of history. Rather, he maintains that historicality is based on Dasein's "reciprocative [self-critical, self-dialogical] rejoinder [selective negation, rejection or disavowal]" concerning the fateful repetition or handing-down to itself of its historical possibilities. Fate (*Schicksals*) is in turn founded on the equiprimordiality of death, guilt, conscience and freedom, and guided in advance by futural projection. It thus constitutes the paradoxical "powerless superior power" by which Dasein acknowledges the conditions of its finitude or powerlessness, and on this basis alone resolutely projects its factically realizable potentialities. Destiny (*Geschick*) refers to the co-historizing of fateful communicating and struggling with other Dasein.

In the context of emphasizing historicality as self-criticism, Heidegger reorients the three kinds of historiology — the monumental, the antiquarian, and the critical — that were distinguished in Nietzsche's philosophy of history. Nietzsche, Heidegger argues, never "explicitly point[ed] out the necessity of this triad or the ground of its unity. *The threefold character of historiology is adumbrated in the historicality of Dasein.* At the same time, this historicality enables us to understand to what extent these three possibilities must be united factically and concretely in any historiology which is authentic."[12] Monumental history, according to Heidegger's interpretation of Nietzsche, reveals futural possibilities, conditioned by and profoundly acceptant of the past, and no longer overlooked by a fixated and confused present. Once this potentiality is opened up, history done in the present is essentially a critique (and not merely detached scientific observation) of the past and how it is currently being handed down and taken over. Dasein's care about what it is depends on what it has been in light of what it can and will be. Antiquarian history is neither a restitution of the past out of curious nostalgia nor the tying of the present onto the obsolete, but Dasein's anticipatory self-choices. For example, in choosing a hero, Dasein is making an *existenziell* decision grounded in the three-fold historicality and therefore the tripartite *existenzial* structure of temporality.

At the conclusion of *Sein und Zeit*, Heidegger questions the success of using a phenomenologico-ontological disclosure of temporality as the necessary and essential access to the meaning of Being itself. Although he has shown temporality to be the meaning of Dasein, the relationship between primordial time and Being remains vague, elusive and problematic. Heidegger writes of his perplexity that "our way of exhibiting the constitution of Dasein's Being remains only *one way* which we may take. Our *aim* is to work out the question of Being in general. . . . Is there a way which leads from primordial time to the meaning of Being? Does *time* itself manifest itself as the horizon of *Being*?"[13] Heidegger's concern is that an over-concentration on the analysis of Dasein in his first major work bears and perpetuates the difficulties of the modern metaphysics of *subiectität*, which he has already exposed in Descartes, Kant and Nietzsche as an inversion rather than the overcoming of substance ontology.

This results in a three-fold dilemma for Heidegger that leaves the nature of Being more questionable than ever. The ontological problem which Heidegger acknowledges in *Sein und Zeit* is his inability within the framework of *existenzial* analysis to disclose and interpret the time of entities-in-the-world, which Dasein finds itself alongside and frequently uses as ready-to-hand equipment. That is, the ecstatic temporality of Dasein reveals that Being is not a *vorhanden* being, but it is not necessarily helpful in showing how Being is invariably the Being or presencing *of* beings which, like Dasein, need to be disclosed in terms of their non-substantive temporal foundations. Secondly, he is uneasy about a possible misreading of the analysis of anticipatory resoluteness as an existentialist imperative which advocates human willfulness or voluntarism and thereby overshadows the priority of the ontological dimension (the truth of Being as such) unfolded in terms of the hermeneutic circle. Thirdly, Heidegger believes that it is no longer possible to reestablish the basis of metaphysics, or to disclose Being within the context and framework of its traditional questions and issues, because metaphysical thinking is from its inception and by its essence preoccupied with substantive present actuality.

Heidegger does not intend to abandon his focus on the dynamism and inner unity of temporality or on the priority of the future as the "first name" of Being, but to reorient the questions of Being, time and their profound interrelation in a more primordial fashion. He attempts to free the matter of Being and time from any traces of subjectivistic (and therefore objectifying) re-presentational thinking by means of a "step back" to the realm of presencing (*physis* or *Anwesenheit*), which he maintains comes-to-pass prior to the traditional metaphysical fixation with absolute presentness (*ousia* or *vorhanden*). In his later writings, Heidegger tries to overcome the hermeneutic difficulties he exposes at the end of *Sein und Zeit* by approaching time from a perspective of disclosure that seeks "to raise the question how there can be presence as such."[14] This standpoint seems to be threefold: trans-anthropocentric (focusing on Being rather than Dasein); trans-metaphysical (without trying to resolve the old questions); and, therefore, frequently naturalistic-aesthetic (concerned with beings in and of themselves rather than only in terms of their usefulness to man).

Heidegger shifts his emphasis on human affairs from the notion of anticipatory resoluteness, by which Dasein decisively and selectively chooses its factical possibilities, to acquiescent releasement (*Gelassenheit*), a poetic thanksgiving or homecoming which unobstructively lets Being unfold. In that context, he asks if "the name for the task of thinking [should] then read instead of *Being and Time:* Opening and Presence (*Lichtung und Anwesenheit*)?"[15] In this light, Heidegger suggests the notion of the belonging-together or mutual appropriating event (*Ereignis*) of Being and time, Being and man, time and man, and Being and beings as a means of divulging the primordial source or selfsameness (*das Selbe*) which determines these relations by giving and taking, granting and withdrawing presencing as such. "Time," he argues, "is not the product of man, man is not the product of time. There is no production here. There is only giving in the sense of extending which opens up time-space."[16]

Ereignis,[17] Heidegger insists, is not meant to simply replace Being as an over-generalized metaphysical category. It is neither an all-encompassing concept under which Being and time could be subsumed nor a relation retroactively superimposed upon the two. Such views, he maintains, would be the result of trying "to derive the source from the river."[18] *Ereignis* is not a third entity attached to the other two, but a genuinely temporal designation of that which makes possible occurrence as such or Being as the presencing of time. Heidegger thus reorients the unity of primordial time in terms of what he now calls its "true fourth-dimension" — the nearing of nearness (*Nahheit*) — which is essentially the first dimension that gives, determines and enhances all the others. Nearness, from this standpoint, is the basis of the three tenses as well as space, language and history. Nearness preserves what has been or the past by denying its advent as present, and keeps open the approach coming from the future by withholding the present such that all dimensions are gathered in a threefold simultaneity. From the intimacy of the still center of nearness, all movement flows — time temporalizes and space spatializes. In his reflections on language, Heidegger writes, "Time's removing and bringing to us, the space's throwing open, admitting and releasing — they all belong in the Same, the play of stillness, something to which we cannot here give further thought."[19] Thus nearness, a notion which suggests the unity of time and space without implying conventional bifurcations between proximity and distance, is for Heidegger II the most meaningful temporal disclosure of Being as the basis of human and phenomenal existence.

Heidegger portrays the nearness of *Ereignis* in two inter-related dimensions — the historical-epochal and the naturalistic — which are largely continuous of and consistent with thematic developments in *Sein und Zeit*. First, in works such as *Holzwege* and *Nietzsche* (two volumes), Heidegger reflects on the history of metaphysics as the history of the self-withdrawal of Being itself from its beginning with Anaximander and the pre-Socratics to its completion with Nietzsche. The granting of nearness is the basis of the eschatological unfolding of the belonging-together of Being and man which, because of finitude or inherent con-cealment, has led through a gradual but inevitable decline to a progressive oblivion or forgetfulness of Being. Time and space are reduced by metaphysical thinking and consequent global technological dominance to the mere parameters for human measurement, calculation and exploitation. "Metaphysics is in all its forms and historical stages a unique, but perhaps necessary, fate of the West and the presupposition of its planetary dominance. The will of that planetary dominance is now in turn affecting the center of the West."[20] The current age as the destitute aftermath of metaphysics is, from Heidegger's eschatological standpoint, the threshhold point which can either lead toward further oblivion or to a genuine recovery of Being through man's poetic thanksgiving of the nearness of time-space.

The second dimension, developed in Heidegger II's reflections on art, language, thinking and thinghood (continuing *Sein und Zeit*'s analysis of discourse, transcendence, worldhood and spatiality) seems to be posited as a possible resolution to the oblivion of Being.[21] Heidegger naturalistically-aesthetically characterizes the authentic occurrence of true time as an ongoing and mutually appropriative interplay, or an illuminating and self-reflective yet purposeless "dance" (*das ereignende Spiegel-Spiel*). The interplay extends throughout time-space and gathers into simple oneness the unity of the four-fold (*Geviert*) of earth (the serving bearer), sky (the home of light and dark), gods (the messengers of Being), and mortals (those capable of dying and awaiting the divinities). Nearness, which preserves farness, is at work in each useful *Ding* (thing), such as a bridge or jug, or a profoundly poetic artwork, such as Van Gogh's peasant shoes, at once bringing into harmony and allowing the individuality of all members at play. As soon as one of the four is spoken, each of the others comes to mind.

Ereignis occurs as two inseparably interrelated movements — the one-fold which unites and appropriates, and the fouring which expropriates the unique ec-static dynamism of each element. "The fouring presences the worlding of world. The mirror-play of world is the round dance of appropriating. Therefore, the round dance is the ring that joins while it plays as mirroring. Appropriating, it lightens the four into the radiance of their simple oneness."[22] The polarity of mutual configuration of the human, divine and natural is, thus, at once held apart by differentiating its full multiplicity and borne together in the splendid simplicity of selfsameness. Each of the four is set out into its own in that none of the four insists on its separate particularity. The interplay is neither exhausted self-destructively nor expanded indefinitely, but it continually advances and renews, builds and preserves, enables and sustains all at once and one in light of all.

The doctrine of the round dance of *Ereignis* is perhaps the closest Heidegger comes to an ontology (surpassing traditional onto-theo-logy) which attempts to include the pervasive totality and non-substantive unity of temporal events of the world. The existential dimension, however, is thereby lessened in significance in that human resolve (now understood negatively as subjective willfullness) is denied priority in the intricate movement of the dance. At the same time, an emphasis on the futural-orientation of *Sein und Zeit* is heightened because Heidegger counsels that man can "do nothing but wait,"[23] not for a specific happening, but to be released from all traces of will into the temporal-historical coming-to-pass of the open realm of *Ereignis*. Man can neither initiate nor accomplish the harmonious interplay of the four-fold. He can only endure the current destitution and innate destructiveness of technology that is due to the self-concealment of Being-as-*Ereignis*. Furthermore, according to Heidegger's posthumously-cited statement,[24] man only has the capacity to "prepare to be ready" or to cultivate the "expecting of expectation" should Being epochally reappear to a new way of thinking of time and Being that is non-objectifying, non-conceptualizing, beyond will and the negation of will as well as the dichotomy of activity and passivity.

Dōgen's Understanding of Primordial Time

Dōgen stresses the total convergence of ontological truth and understanding and existential injunction and practice as full manifestations of the pervasive unity of being-time. Although the presencing of *uji* prevails regardless of whether or not its true nature is comprehended, primordial time ultimately depends upon and is fulfilled only by means of each being's fully sustained and perpetually renewed selfless exertive power. Since all beings are, ontologically, nothing other than the exertion of *uji* at each, every and any moment, Dōgen insists on the individual's utmost existential effort of *shinjin-datsuraku* at all times. He writes in "Gyōji" that the blossoming flower and falling leaf, the brightened and the broken mirror — images which symbolize the dual possibilities of enlightenment and unenlightenment — are equally the manifestations of sustained exertion. Since "everything is exertion," he maintains, "To attempt to avoid exertion is an impossible and unrighteous evasion of exertion [because] the avoidance of exertion depends upon exertion itself."[25] Therefore, it is imperative that exertion be authenticated through existential realization of non-self that makes possible an ontological understanding of the insubstantiality and dynamism of being-time. Philosophical insight and clarification is necessarily and ultimately grounded in personal experience, acceptance and affirmation of impermanence as the direct pointer to *muga* beyond relative attitudes of optimism and pessimism.

The total unity of all possible dimensions of reality and experience realized at every moment of being-time is expressed in "Uji":

The configuration of my-self makes up the entire [Dharma]-realm as time's occurrence at each, every and any moment. The mutual non-obstruction of things and things is the same as the mutual non-obstruction amongst all times. Therefore, the arousing of aspiration [in different] minds at the self-same time is the arousing [at different] times of the self-same mind. It is just the same with practice and attainment of the [Buddhist] Way.[26]

Dōgen thereby conveys the ontological inseparability and mutual non-obstruction arising spontaneously and simultaneously of all beings and all times, my-self and time, my-self and all beings in the entire Dharma-realm, each being and all beings, and one time and every time. He also divulges the existential unity of resolve and realization, practice and attainment, individual and universal awakening manifested right-now and throughout past, present and future. The configuration, display and activity of the insubstantial self is fully coterminous, contiguous and harmonious with that of all other insubstantial beings at each and every moment. Similarly, time and minds are at once the selfsame in that the awakening of spiritual intentions in one mind at one time arouses all minds at all times, and different because each mind is a unique occurrence and perspective of uji at any time. Thus, the unity of being-time does not merely allow for, but necessarily encompasses complete diversity and multiplicity in all realms, directions, standpoints and manifestations. Difference is by no means reduced to a monolithic equality by Dōgen. Rather, the totality and unity of all beings manifested as all times makes possible and is realized through the full array of experiential factors.

The central elements of Dōgen's philosophy of being-time are suggested by his interpretation of a traditional Zen poem at the beginning of the "Uji" fascicle:

Sometimes (uji) standing so high up on the mountain top;
Sometimes walking deep down on the bottom of the sea;
Sometimes a three-headed eight-armed [demon or Acala];
Sometimes a sixteen- or eight-foot [Buddha]. . .[27]

From the conventional standpoint which understands uji merely as "sometimes," time appears fragmented into deep-rooted and seemingly irreconciliable oppositions between now and then, appropriate or inappropriate, authentic or inauthentic. From the primordial standpoint, however, the unity of being-time expressed by this passage is seen in its multiple dimensions: *universal* (encompassing human and natural, sameness and difference, enlightened and unenlightened without obstruction or dichotomization); *insubstantial* (as the trans-personal basis of all activity without reference to ego or subject, substance or object, but only to ebb and flow of movement itself); and yet eminently *existential* (through the implicit imperative to realize Buddhahood in terms of the holistic presencing of naturalistic activity). For Dōgen, all talk of "nature" (*shō*), whether an all-pervasive Buddha-nature or an internal own-nature, that works its way into linear time or is realized teleologically through the suspension of time is unedifying and removes one from realizing non-self at this very insubstantial yet totalistic moment. *Uji* (as *muga*) is fully detached from the daily time of twenty-four hours derivatively conceived as sequential, and yet is found nowhere else but right within daily time when penetrated as the insubstantiality and impermanence of all factors of experience here-and-now and at all occasions. "The sixteen-foot golden body itself is time, and just because it is time there is the luminous glow of the radiance (*kōmyō*) of time, and you must study the matter right within this twenty-four hours."[28]

The ultimately non-differentiable existential and ontological dimensions of being-time, however, are provisionally analyzed by Dōgen in order to distinguish his doctrines from the reductionist views of idealistic monism (*sennigedō*) and naturalistic pantheism (*jinen-gedō*). Ontologically, the dharma-stage, or non-obstructive impermanent totality of life/death beyond life/death, is heuristically divided into the two aspects of immediate presencing right-now (*nikon*, cut off from life/death, before/after) and continuous passage (*kyōryaku*, possessed of life/death, before/after) extending throughout all times. First, the *dharma-stage* is manifest as a discrete, non-sequential particularity that is self-generating, self-contained and self-renewing. *Nikon* is not the self-imposed limitation of a supposedly absolute Buddha-nature, but an eternity and totality complete in and of itself as a holistic and dynamic situational context. The directness and completeness of the present moment is independent of anticipation or expectation because it is not coming from or going anywhere and nothing is left out of it. Nor can the absolutely immediate present be evaluated as appearing too little and too late or as premature and over-extended. The present moment is never lost or slipping away. Each and every instant must be esteemed and valued as the multi-dimensional impermanent/ insubstantial unity it constitutes. "Heaven is not before and earth is not after. . . The full manifestation of heaven and earth is here-and-now."[29] When the practicitioner of the Way attains one single *dharma* by casting off body and mind, Dōgen maintains, he permeates fully and freely that one *dharma* for that one eternal moment unbound by hesitation or deliberation.

Freedom from entangling attachments to the conventional conception of time as mere coming and going, Dōgen asserts, is to see "the time which has not-yet come" (*mi-tō*), fully disclosed right-now and free from arbitrary distinctions between arrival and movement, getting there and not getting there. Being-time appears precisely at this very moment without partiality or limitation, impediment or boundary. Each being non-obstructively penetrates in and through each moment, and in thereby realizing itself, it discloses the totality of beings at all times. "[The average man tends to think] that obstruction can be used by other *dharmas*, but there has never been any obstruction that obstructs other *dharmas*. I meet people, people meet people, I meet myself, meeting meets meeting."[30] At such a totalistic moment, all elements are simultaneously initiated and fulfilled. Dōgen concretely expresses the Kegonian notion of the harmonious interpenetration of particularity and universality, universality and universality, and particularity and particularity by emphasizing the purely dynamic activity of the unobstructed unfolding of the non-substantive temporal process — "meeting meets meeting" — in and of itself.

Thus, the *nikon* of *uji* represents for Dōgen the most effective way of expressing the innate and unceasing dynamism and insubstantiality of the Buddhist truth of non-self in its inseparability with impermanence, avoiding traditional bifurcations between time and space, conditioned and unconditioned, eternity and transiency, absolute and manifestation. Dōgen's notion avoids an attachment to eternalism either beyond man, as in the doctrine of an absolute and unchanging Buddha-nature, or within man, as in Hui-neng's doctrine of *kenshō*, both of which presuppose (from Dōgen's standpoint) a fixation with substance. Dōgen is not satisfied with the Mahāyāna preoccupation with the cosmology and teleology of *busshō*, nor does he accept the traditional Zen emphasis on human activity which still does not challenge and fully overcome the derivative notion of time. Rather, he accentuates the truly temporal foundations of both Buddha-nature and man, of the ontological and the experiential, through a creative rediscovery of the holistic and impersonal presencing of the dynamically immedate moment of being-time.

Dōgen stresses that the totality of the present moment is not to be considered a metaphor for eternity, but the full discovery, realization and affirmation of being-time just as it is. In "Tsuki" Dōgen maintains, for example, that tonight's moon demands our complete attention as an immediate and complete manifestation without regard for beginning or end, oldness or novelty. Furthermore, each quarter of the moon is complete within itself just as each and every form or existence is, as it is, the "true form of Buddha." Dōgen insists that his reference to moonlight is not merely a figure of speech which symbolizes the luminosity of being-time. " 'As it is' does not indicate likeness but 'this is it' "[31] as the true form of existence. Each aspect of the moon, and therefore each and every occasion of being-time, is in itself a complete manifestation without reference to anything outside it.

Dōgen further avoids any confusion of *nikon* with a newly derivative eternalism by stressing the temporal depth and experiential breadth of the right-now in terms of the notion of experiential continuity or totalistic passage (*kyōryaku*). Passage at once engages all aspects and dimensions of the selfsameness and simultaneity of past, present and future here-and-now as well as allowing for their full diversity, variety and differentiation.

The second element of the *dharma*-stage — *kyōryaku* — refers to the continuously creative and regenerating dimension of being-time. *Nikon* and *kyōryaku* are two inseparable, interpenetrating and ultimately selfsame, although provisionally distinguishable standpoints for understanding *uji*. Neither has priority; the difference between them is a matter of viewing either the surface (*nikon*) or the cross-section (*kyōryaku*) of a total temporal phenomenon. In Dōgen's metaphor of climbing the mountain, for example, *nikon* designates the particular and immediate activity that occurs as nothing other than the present occasion of ascent. *Kyōryaku* suggests the entire context and background of events of man and universe by which "life lives through me and I am me because of life." *Kyōryaku* encompasses all personal, social and natural history, conditioning and recollection as well as all futural projection, outlook and striving that both make possible and are contained within the concrete circumstances invariably and fully manifested right here-and-now. Each moment is complete as it is because it includes the full range of multiple perspectives and situations extending simultaneously and reverberating non-obstructively throughout the three tenses. Past, present and future themselves are merely provisional terms for conveying the totality of dimensions which appear at each and every moment.

Dōgen distinguishes five extensive motions of passage to refute the conventional view of serial progression, and to convey the complexity and insubstantiality, intricacy and fluidity, flexibility and multi-directionality of the dynamism of being-time. "Passage from today to tomorrow, passage from today to yesterday, and passage from yesterday to today" refutes the concept of chronology or linear sequence as appropriate for primordial time. "Passage from today to today" destroys a fabricated separation on any level of the essentially unified three phases of time since "today," which encompasses past, present and future, is said to move simultaneously backwards and forwards, advancing and retreating within itself. Finally, "passage from tomorrow to tomorrow" surpasses any view which gives sole priority to the derivative present tense because each of the unified dimensions is complete only through its ultimate identity with every other one.

Genuine passage, in contrast to the inauthentic conception

of time's passing forever away, contains the inexhaustible contents and innumerable manifestations of being-time continually emerging anew without substratum or duration. "Passage is like spring in that all the various manifestations of spring themselves are passage. . . Passage is not [just] spring; however, since it is the passage of spring, passage now completes the Way at the very time spring appears."[32] As one aspect of spring emerges, spring unfolds everywhere at all times. With each situation, appearance, fragrance, atmosphere and hue of this very spring, all previously experienced and forthcoming possibilities of spring are spontaneously realized right here-and-now.

The notion of *kyōryaku* establishes the basis for Dōgen's radical reorientation and reinterpretation of traditional Mahāyāna ontological doctrines, especially the notion of Buddha-nature, and of the Zen understanding of the existential path to realization. *Kyōryaku* is intimately connected to Dōgen's view of Buddha-nature in two interrelated ways: first, the simultaneity of past, present and future is the reason why Dōgen takes license to drastically revise and even alter previous Buddhist expressions of *Dharma* in accord with his own current experience of *genjōkōan*; second, Dōgen shows how Buddha-nature can be reunderstood and reexpressed in terms of its full integration with *kyōryaku* and *nikon*, or the ultimate selfsameness of this very moment with the holistic presencing of being-time. For Dōgen, *uji* does not necessarily replace *busshō* as the central doctrine to convey the existential-ontological realization of the Buddhist truth of non-self. He does not merely discard *busshō*; rather, he attempts to fully revitalize and restore its genuinely temporal significance through his creative interpretation of *busshō*-as-*kyōryaku*. There is no being-time that is not Buddha-nature; on the other hand, Buddha-nature is not manifested unless and until — or, more positively, only *upon* — one's realization of *uji* as the insubstantiality of all phenomena.

In the first section of "Busshō," for example, Dōgen seeks to clarify the temporal meaning of the well-known and widely-accepted passage from the *Nirvāṇa Sūtra*, "All sentient beings without exception have the Buddha-nature. Tathāgata abides forever without change." He creatively reads — or, rather, inten-

tionally misreads on the basis of his understanding of the
kyōryaku of *Dharma* — the first phrase of the passage, *shitsu-u-
bussho*, as "whole-being-Buddha-nature," in that to "have (*u*)
bussho can mean in a deeper sense to "be" *bussho*. The being
of *bussho* is not a fixed ontological substratum underlying all
phenomena. It is neither an entity possessed by all beings nor
a greater power which possesses or encompasses beings, but an
expression of suchness immediately and completely manifest as
each and every being-time both "within and without sentient
beings." Whole-being-Buddha-nature is not emergent being that
began at a certain time because it is manifest right-now as everyday mind; nor is it original or timeless being in that it fills the
past right up through the present. It does not subsist before practice and it is not attained after practice.

Thus, being-Buddha-nature must not be conceived of as
something hidden that is awaiting realization or as a potential
from the past which will come to the fore in the future that is
approaching. The traditional interpretation of the second sentence
of the cited passage implies that *bussho* is a constant essence
which when nourished by the "rain" of *Dharma* gives forth
branches, leaves, flowers, and fruits with new seed-potentials,
and it thereby presupposes a direct yet unacknowledged and self-
deceptive reliance on derivative time. It assumes that the past,
present and future are three separable and independent realms
through which existence passes, leading inevitably toward some
destination. Dōgen reappropriates the final phrase of the passage,
"without change" (*mu u hennyaku*), in the following way: *Tathāgata* is "non-existentent (*mu*), existent (*u*) and *is* change (*hennyaku*)." The ontological and existential significance of such a
reformulation, regardless of whether or not it is strictly grammatically "correct," is that "[Buddha-nature] is not a matter of what
is within or outside of the tree. It is always realized at each
moment of the past or present . . . root, stem, branch, and leaf
live the selfsame life and die the selfsame death and are Buddha-
nature as the selfsame whole-being."[33] In contrast to the derivative
conception of a Buddha-nature that is attainable at some later
time, all manifestations and elements at each and every time
(*kyōryaku*) are the spontaneous here-and-now presencing (*nikon*)
of this very being-time of *bussho*.

In other sections of the "Busshō" fascicle, Dōgen highlights and deepens the temporal significance of Buddha-nature by showing that it is inseparable and coterminous with impermanence (*mujō*), *karmic* consciousness (*gōshiki*), life-and-death (*shōji*), everyday activity (*gyō*), the manifesting body of the five aggregates (*shingen*), the occasion already arrived (*jisetsu kishi*), and a single instant (*ji*).[34] Elsewhere in the *Shōbōgenzō*, Dōgen reinterprets Zen notions which symbolize enlightenment to free them from a static representation or expression which implies a bifurcation between immutable and ephemeral time. He emphasizes that "one bright pearl" (*ikkya-myōju*), for example, contains all the changes of life of the inexhaustible past existing through time and emerging ever anew in the present. Similarly, "radiant light" (*kōmyō*) glows amongst all the harmoniously interpenetrating functions of temporal phenomena. Also, "original Buddha-mind" (*kobusshin*) is in no way separable from the spontaneous here-and-now presencing of *uji*. "The unfolding blossoms and manifold trees and grasses are none other than the unlimited realization of the original Buddha[-mind]."[35] From the standpoint of the *kyōryaku* of *Dharma*, not the slightest separation exists between primordiality and spontaneity.

As Dōgen's disclosure of the incessantly vigorous activity of the *dharma*-stage of being-time through his analysis and overcoming of conventional fixations is the basis for his reinterpretation of ontological doctrines, it also allows for his reorientation and restatement of the genuine temporal meaning of the stages of Zen awakening. Dōgen specifically refutes Rinzai Zen's over-reliance on *kōan* practice, which presumes that enlightenment can be suddenly acquired through the quick solution of a puzzle. He claims that the *kōan* may be answered and yet the insight remains bankrupt unless the authentic *kyōryaku* of realization is experienced at all occasions of being-time.[36]

Dōgen's analysis of the inseparable spontaneity of resolve (beginning or past in conventional terms), simultaneity and totality of practice (middle or present), and continually renewed development of realization (end or future) based on *genjōkōan* (here-and-now realization encompassing *nikon* and *kyōryaku*) seems to constitute the complete resolution of his initial "great doubt" concerning the relationship between original and acquired enlightenment. Dōgen was deeply troubled by the question why, if Buddha-nature is original and all-pervasive, there is any need for practice. His conclusion is that resolve, practice and realization are, like the three tenses of time, absolutely interpenetrating and inseparably fulfilled by virtue of the unified yet multi-dimensional *kyōryaku* of *Dharma* which reflects the *genjō-kōan* of non-self here-and-now. To cast off body and mind and to spontaneously forget the self is to fully manifest all levels and dimensions of experience right-now. Dōgen does not seek to reduce resolve-practice-realization to a monolithic uniformity, but to highlight the selfsameness underlying the creative tension between them, each phase interpenetrating and enhancing, fulfilling and renewing the others.

An understanding of the true nature of time thus breaks down any linear or sequential conception of Buddhist realization. Resolve and practice do not lead to or necessarily result in realization, but the three inseparable dimensions are fully realized at one and the same being-time. When one dimension appears in one mind at one time, it permeates all levels of each mind at every time without distinction, obstruction or partiality. "Because of this, when even a single person performs *zazen* for just a single moment, he penetrates all *dharmas*, and permeates all time, so that throughout past, present, and future in the unlimited universe, he is ceaselessly guiding beings to enlightenment. For each and every thing, this act is the selfsame practice, and the selfsame realization."[37]

The three "stages" of awakening are mutually contained and ultimately equalizable, though experientially distinguishable. "Perpetuating the Way unceasingly, resolve, practice, *bodhi* and *nirvāṇa* co-exist all the while without any interval; such is the perpetuation of the Way through sustained exertion."[38] Resolve, or awakening to the Buddha-seeking mind, is spontaneous in that it arises neither beginninglessly nor recently, neither innately nor through universal conditioning, neither before nor after effort. Rather, resolve constitutes an instantaneous stirring of the authentic spiritual intention and determination of a particular heart-mind which extends throughout all beings at all times. "Therefore, do not think that awakening is awakened only once . . . ," Dōgen writes. "Countless awakenings arise from the initial resolve to seek enlightenment. The resolve of innumerable persons started with the initial awakening of a single person . . . The initial awakening and *zazen* are neither the same nor different, neither added together nor separable."[39] Resolve itself is continually renewed through practice and sustained in realization; at the same time, it is resolve which unceasingly motivates practice and inspires realization. "[The resolve for enlightenment and attainment of the Way] are interconnected from beginning to end."[40]

Just as initial resolve constantly fuels practice, the sustained practice of *shinjin-datsuraku* enhances and affirms the dedication and conviction of resolve. Similarly, neither practice nor resolve can cease at realization. Enlightenment is not an attainable goal but a renewable insight and experience accentuated by diligent practice. In "Bendōwa" Dōgen answers the query as to why those who have already realized the *Dharma* must still practice, by insisting that "practice and realization are not two [separable] stages." The merits of unabated practice extend simultaneously to all beings throughout all times. "Because present practice is practice in realization, the initial discrimination of the Way in itself is the full manifestation of original realization. Thus, even while focused on practice, realization must not be anticipated apart from practice, because practice is nothing other than original realization. As practice is already involved in realization, realization is endless; as realization is involved in practice, practice is beginningless."[41]

The "beginninglessness" and "endlessness" or the spontaneity and renewal of originally and continuously unified practice-in-realization is the immediate manifestation and passage of this very moment of being-time. Because realization takes place nowhere else than here-and-now, which encompasses the totality of interpenetrating tenses, dimensions and elements, it necessarily involves the perpetual renewal of "continuous development beyond the attainment of Buddha" (*butsukōjōji*), which "is to see more and more Buddhas after becoming a Buddha." Realization continues no longer than the resolve which kindles it and the practice which sustains it. "When Buddhas are genuinely buddhas, they do not think of themselves as 'Buddhas'. Yet, this is the Buddha-realization which they continue to realize [as] Buddhas. . . . The traces of enlightenment disappear, and traceless enlightenment is ceaselessly renewed."[42] Forever renewed by the resolute engagement of sustained effort, realization reciprocally and continually enhances the aspirations and inspires the practices which perpetuate it.

Dōgen's emphasis on the temporal unity of practice and realization also seems to suggest that the presencing of being-time itself is made possible by virtue of the selfless here-and-now activity which realizes itself as primordial time. No aspect or realm of temporal existence is independent of the individual's exertive effort to cast off body and mind. The being-time of every single thing in "this" world and in "that" world, Dōgen maintains in "Uji" — the right and left domains of the heavenly universe and the multitudes on land and water — are all in all the spontaneous manifestation and the passage of one's own utmost yet purposeless exertion. "You should realize that without the passage of my utmost exertion at this very moment, there would be neither the manifestation of one single *dharma* or one single phenomenon."[43]

In highlighting the particularity of exertion, however, Dōgen does not appear to be making a solipsistic claim because he argues in "Gyōji" that it is the sustained exertion of *all* beings at *all* times "which is neither self-imposed nor imposed by others, but without condition or defilement" that makes possible, sustains and upholds the entire universe. Exertion is the ceaseless, all-encompassing and all-pervasive reverberating power which is the basis for the "perpetuation of the Way" (*gyōji-dōkan*). This constitutes a perfectly complete and harmoniously interpenetrating equilibrium brought forth without end by the activity generated by oneself and all other phenomena in the universe. "The merit of this sustained exertion upholds my-self and upholds others. The truth is that manifold beings circulating in heaven and on earth throughout the ten directions [of the universe] all in all partake of the merit of my sustained exertion. Others may not know of it, and even I may not realize it, but it is the case. Because of this, my spontaneous realization of sustained exertion and mastery of the Great Way is made possible by the sustained

exertion of all Buddhas and all patriarchs. All the Buddhas' spontaneous realizations of sustained exertion and mastery of the Great
Way are made possible by my sustained exertion."[44]

According to Dōgen's interpretation of the Buddhist *Dharma*,
gyōji[45] is more fundamental than dependent origination. "It
should be examined and understood thoroughly that dependent
origination is *gyōji*, but *gyōji* is not dependent origination."[46] Existential activity (selfless and purposeless yet utmost and sustained)
is thus the ontological basis of the temporal existence of all possible universes. Ultimately, time appears only through the total
activity engaged in the impermanent/insubstantial present. All
beings at all times emerge spontaneously and continuously by
means of their exertive power. Without such selfless activity,
there is neither time nor world. The full convergence of the existential activity of self and others as the ontological ground for
the perpetuation of the Way occurs at this very present moment.

Therefore, the totalistic moment embraces and realizes, and
is sustained and upheld by fully involved exertive effort. "The
exertion that brings the exertion of others into realization is
precisely our exertion right here-and-now. The right-now of exertion is not innately or inherently within us; the right-now of exertion does not come and go, arriving and departing. The Way
which is called 'now' does not precede exertion; 'now' is itself
the immediate and complete realization of exertion (*gyōji-genjō*)."[47]
All three tenses, life and death, all beings and all Buddhas, self
and world. particular effort and entire existence, practice and
attainment, living and understanding, Dōgen's insight and experience and the universal meaning of his expressions, the True Man
of no-self and the full temporal context of his surroundings all
in all living through one another are the spontaneous here-and-
now realization of the *kōan* (*genjō-kōan*) reverberating throughout the simultaneous and totalistic manifestations of the present
occasion of being-time.

Comparative Examination

Heidegger and Dōgen both illustrate the profound and intimate connection between an overcoming of the deficient average

view that time can be lost since it is believed to be endlessly slipping away, and the formulation of genuine ontological understanding of the unified dimensions of primordial time. Because it is in everyday decisions that the ontologically problematic bifurcations and misconceptions of derivative time emerge and persist by means of a fixation with substantiality and actuality, inauthenticity must be challenged and reoriented in terms of a courageous acceptance and creative affirmation of radical contingency. As existence is authentically reclaimed, ontology can be appropriately reinterpreted and refashioned. Thus the effectiveness in overcoming derivative time and substance ontology for each thinker is largely determined and reflected by the extent of the unity established in the analysis of the three tenses, self and other, time and beings as well as the convergence of the existential and ontological dimensions themselves. The aim of the disclosure of primordial time is not, however, to reduce existence to a monolithic or monistic uniformity, but to uncover the flexible and multi-dimensional yet integral framework which makes possible and is fulfilled by the diversified factors of existence.

Heidegger's philosophy seems to be haunted by a variety of ontological gaps or separations that fall short of a fully unified and non-substantive disclosure of primordial time. These subtle bifurcations appear in several aspects and dimensions of his analysis throughout the two main phases of his thinking, such that he himself acknowledges that he is uncertain whether the rifts can be eliminated within the context of hermeneutic circularity. The existentialist approach of *Sein und Zeit* is grounded in the analysis of Dasein without penetrating the temporal nature of beings, and it thereby leaves unresolved the leading question of Being itself. The naturalistic orientation in some of Heidegger's later writings, however, highlights the temporality of Being as such with a reduction in the significance of the existential dimension of time. In order for Heidegger to compensate for a drawback in one approach, another hermeneutic difficulty emerges or is created.

Heidegger's most significant philosophical achievement seems to be his disclosure of the unity of ecstatic temporality, or the underlying interrelatedness between Being and time in terms of an analysis of the totality of Dasein as Being-in-the-world thrown-projection, prior to the traditional bifurcations of subject/object, theory/non-theory, understanding (or "reason")/state-of-mind (or "emotion"). Heidegger's hermeneutic circle interprets ontology itself as an enterprise inseparable from the *existenziell* concern or ontical priority of Dasein, which is in every case uniquely "mine." Yet the hermeneutic framework of fundamental ontology also presupposes distinctions between *existenzial* analysis, interpretation or disclosure and Dasein's *existenziell* concrete choices, which are themselves divided into inauthentic and authentic possibilities, the latter further distinguished in terms of the aspects of projective anticipation and factical resolve. On the basis of these separations, Heidegger concludes that the unity of ecstatic temporality is subtly divided by the priority of future and past over the present.

Heidegger II seeks to disclose the mutually appropriative event of belonging-together which primordially links the temporal dimensions in the selfsameness of nearness. But the approach undertaken in the later writings also accentuates the futural orientation of temporality by counselling man to await through poetic thanksgiving to receive the redemptive call to an anticipated and long-sought homecoming with the neighborhood of Being. In his fundamental ontology, Heidegger attempts an analysis of Dasein's way to be that is executed for the sake of ontological disclosure, and he intends to ultimately leave existential concerns behind as a stepping-stone — no longer philosophically significant — on the pathway of thought. As Heidegger II further reduces the importance of the existential dimension for the unveiling of Being, Heidegger expresses a sense of increasing perplexity or inconclusiveness concerning the overriding ontological matter: "It looks as if thinking were continually being led, or driven like a fool, as though in a magic circle around the Sameness without ever being able to approach this Sameness. But perhaps the circle is a hidden spiral."[48]

The central thrust of Dōgen's approach is to remove any separation between past, present and future and between ontology and existence as problematical deficiencies which distort a genuine understanding and experience of the totalistic and insubstantial passage of being-time. From Dōgen's standpoint, it appears that Heidegger's conception of ecstatic temporality aggravates rather than overcomes the existential and ontological dilemmas inherent in the conventional view of time. In contrast to the futurally-based philosophy of Heidegger, Dōgen stresses the harmonious simultaneity of the three tenses. As opposed to Heidegger's notion of *Ereignis* as a mirror-play generated by virtue of the "nearness" of the configuration of participating elements, Dōgen's notion of *gyōji-dōkan* accentuates and stimulates the existential imperative for each individual to act without restraint right here-and-now. The Way which encompasses all temporal possibilities, according to Dōgen, is a harmonious network of interpenetrating relationships and non-substantive situations and perspectives, and it is perpetuated only by means of utmost or exhaustive exertion at this very moment and throughout the simultaneous realization of past, present and future. The foremost existential injunctive for Dōgen is activity itself — not in order to accomplish a specific end or for any particular motive — but dynamic movement fully integrated with the totality of existence in, of and through its own exertive power, non-obstructively enhancing, reflecting and reverberating through all other beings at all times each and every moment.

Heidegger seems to suggest that the proper time for the presencing of Being is for the most part withheld from man due to the inherently limiting condition of finitude which pervades existence. The notion of the withholding of the "right time" is depicted existentially in *Sein und Zeit* in terms of Dasein's anticipation of the imminent possibility of its end, and ontologically in Heidegger II through the notion of the epochal self-concealment of Being. Heidegger does point in *Sein und Zeit* to the authentic moment of vision realized by a resolution which takes action in a concrete Situation. "Resoluteness does not first take cognizance of a Situation and put that Situation before itself," he writes. "It has put itself into that Situation already. As resolute, Dasein is already *taking action* . . . 'activity' will also embrace the passivity of resistance."[49] But such an emphasis on the actualization of the possibility for authenticity in the situational context of the present moment is not further explored by Heidegger.

Dōgen stresses that there is absolutely no time which is not manifestly the "right time" for sustained exertion here-and-now. Since time has in every case already completely arrived without pause, lack or interruption, each and every moment must be affirmed and enacted through strenuous yet purposeless effort. No time is concealed, or to be anticipated, lost or only partially disclosed, obscured or forgotten. "Sometimes," Dōgen writes in "Gyōji," "these merits of [sustained exertion] do not appear and are neither seen nor heard nor perceived. Even without appearing, they are not concealed and must be realized, because they are not diffused or defiled whether they appear or disappear, are manifest or withheld."[50] The proper time is not withheld so long as one does not refrain from dedicated and sustained exertion. Furthermore, no being is excluded from active immersion in the totality of selfless exertion that makes possible full diversity, multiplicity and individuality in all the ten directions (*jippō*) of the universe: "The manifestation of each and every thing is nothing other than the ten directions realized as the individual self. Because it is the individual self, the ten directions is all selves. The ten directions of all selves is thoroughly interpenetrating the ten directions of individual selves."[51]

Thus the central existential difference between Heidegger and Dōgen is that Dōgen insists that the True Man must not await, expect or anticipate the arrival of the presencing of time because he penetrates insubstantiality here-and-now. For example, Dōgen reorients the Zen notion of *juki*, generally understood as a "prediction of the attainment of Buddhahood," in order to fully eliminate any notion of futural arrival. *Juki*, he maintains, is "invariably in our present life." "Although 'past', 'future', and 'present' are used to describe the instability, potentiality, and fluidity of things, you must realize the past, future, and present which have not yet arrived,"[52] and are manifest as the totalistic dwelling place of being-time. Anticipation, for Dōgen, is neither more nor less authentic than expectation. Both anticipation and expectation represent an unenlightened hesitation or self-centered deliberation concerning the right-now of being-time, thus reflecting a longing for the fabricated and unattainable "ruby palace" that must be spontaneously and completely cast off. Dōgen also stresses that the time of history is not a determining factor for existential awakening. Whether or not the historical epoch is suitable, the proper occasion is in every case here-and-now so long as there is utmost and sustained exertive power. The time for realization is not a futural advency; nor must any moment of time be allowed to pass by fruitlessly. There should be no holding back from a spontaneous manifestation of the Buddha-nature in all activities at this very moment.

The difference in ontology between the two thinkers is apparent in Dōgen's emphasis that time itself does not occur without thorough existential involvement and active immersion each moment. Time must not be conceived of or represented in any subtle sense as a landscape or setting divorced from action, or as a process severed from experiential affairs in each situational context. No element of spectatorship is permissible. Dōgen maintains that man must not wait for time because *uji* itself does not wait. The moment is neither automatic nor acquirable but immediately realized anew with each occasion of the totalistic harmony of doing and being, living and understanding. "Furthermore," he writes in "Bendōwa," "to think worldly affairs hinder the Buddha *Dharma* is to believe that there is no Buddha *Dharma* in daily life, without realizing that there are no 'worldly affairs' in the Buddha *Dharma*."[53] All activities — even the seemingly mundane — are extraordinarily unique occasions to realize the Way of being-time. Thus, Dōgen's doctrines of being-time and total dynamism (*zenki*) can be said to at once encompass and surpass the Heideggerian notions of ecstatic temporality and the event of belonging-together, of resoluteness and releasement. Dōgen fully integrates the existential and ontological dimensions of being-time radically oriented in terms of the preeminence of present activity. Heidegger's shifting from one hermeneutic approach to the other without a satisfactory conclusion highlights his need for a new foundation to guide the aims and scope of his thinking.

On the basis of Dōgen's view of the non-differentiation of ontology and existence, or of the truth of Buddha-nature and the appearance of all beings, he seems to be more successful than Heidegger in overcoming substance fixations in terms of the here-

and-now manifestation (*genjō*) encompassing the simultaneity of past, present and future. It may appear that Heidegger emphasizes the future (anticipation of advency) and past (historicality), and that Dōgen in contrast emphasizes the present. Yet, the dual notions of *nikon* and *kyōryaku* indicate that Dōgen by no means overlooks past and future but fully integrates them in the dynamic and insubstantial unity of the moment, so that there is no priority of one dimension over and above the others. The primordial standpoint, for Dōgen, is the flexibility and multidirectionality of their ultimate identity, which discovers and captures the meaning of each. Dōgen writes that "there is passage (*kyōryaku*) from tomorrow to tomorrow." Thus, the future *may* have priority at any given occasion, but this is not absolute and should be seen as a shifting perspective within the holistic, self-generating and self-renewing moment of being-time. Heideggcr's view of futural temporality seems to be somewhat attached to the conventional view. This highlights the point that Heidegger may be caught between depicting phenomenologically and overcoming ontologically the ordinary conception of time, between uncovering an awareness of the Western tradition's presuppositions or limitations and surpassing them. Heidegger's modification of the linear, sequential view he seeks to refute is not fully successful in overcoming substance ontology.

The differences concerning the issues of non-reductionism and non-anthropocentrism in Heidegger and Dōgen are illustrated by the following passage from "Uji":

> The mountain is time; the sea is time as well. If they were not time, there would be no mountain or sea. You must not think that there is no time right-now of the mountain and sea. If time should deteriorate, the mountain and sea will deteriorate as well; and if time does not deteriorate, neither will the mountain or sea. For this reason, the bright star appears, the Tathāgata appears, the [*Dharma*-]eye appears, the uplifted flower appears.[54]

First, whereas Heidegger tends to either reduce space and beings to the temporality of Dasein in *Sein und Zeit* or to reduce Dasein to the naturalistic presencing of *Ereignis* in later writings, Dōgen emphasizes the full and unimpeded inseparability of being-time and all spatial manifestations, without accentuating one realm over and above any other. The mountain and sea as well as anyone who stands on or walks in them are nothing other than being-time. They depend on time and are not manifested separable from time; time depends on the mountain and sea and is not manifested separable from them. Second, Dōgen stresses that the sameness-in-difference of all manifestations of space and being-time constitutes the impersonal and insubstantial moment of existential awakening, symbolized by the bright star and uplifted flower. Thus, Dōgen is neither reductionist nor anthropocentric, but existentialist within the holistic or non-substantive context of being-time.

Conclusions

The following hierarchical schema reviews the basic distinctions between Heidegger's and Dōgen's approaches to primordial time, as well as the differences between their views and the derivative conceptions they have refuted. The first three positions are deficient, according to Heidegger and Dōgen, because they presuppose substantiality and overlook contingency:

1. *Inauthentic time* — the views of the average man who feels subjugated by "time flies" and clings without reflection to the very source of his problem; his fearfulness of time and death is the hidden basis for substance ontology.

2. *Clock-time* — a neutral or value-free category in itself, because although derivative, it is not necessarily deficient; useful and even essential for everyday activity, clock-time becomes obstructive if (as is usually the case) it is mistaken for absolute and it obscures primordial time.

3. *Eternalism* — the varieties of theological, mystical and metaphysical claims of an infinity either removed from contingency through the suspension of time or imminent in the world of endless now-time, ranging from the most naive monotheistic

conceptions of a transcendent deity to the most sophisticated (but equally derivative) conceptions of eternity manifested "in" time (such as Nietzsche's eternal recurrence and the Senika heresy).

The next two views represent attempted disclosures of primordial time because they undermine substance-fixations in terms of radical contingency:

4. *Heidegger's ecstatic temporality* — based on finitude, it reverses the traditional preoccupation with actuality, but is limited because it separates present from past and future, Dasein from beings, theory from practice, and the question of Being as such from temporality itself.

5. *Dōgen's being-time* — based on impermanence, it seems to be more universal (encompassing all beings at all times without partiality, limitation or exception), naturalistic (embracing the human and phenomenal realms), holistic (as a total manifestation at each and every moment), and existential (emphasizing an imperative for selfless exertion without the Heideggerian separation of *existenziell* and *existenzial* levels).

Thus, the differences which emerge from this comparative examination of Heidegger and Dōgen concerning the unity and insubstantiality of the three tenses and their relation to activity reflect fundamental and critical points of philosophical contention. Heidegger can be criticized, for example, for a reluctance to accentuate total existential involvement in the ontological disclosure of the presencing of time, at least on the grounds that it limits the success of his inquiry. To a large extent, the differences which appear in their respective notions of primordial time can be traced to the method of Heidegger's analysis of derivative time and disclosure of finitude. Because, as previously shown, Heidegger associates making present-at-hand with falling, and because he connects finitude with the inherent non-power of existence or the prior incapacity of man to attain truth, he is led to two points of ambivalence. First, he is unwilling to propose existential awakening as a "*genjō*-oriented" (here-and-now manifestation of all tenses at the present moment) realization rather than as a futural possibility. Secondly, he is unable to formulate an ontology which genuinely encompasses the temporal unity and activity of human existence and other beings. On the one hand, Heidegger seems to indirectly suggest a negative evaluation of human existence as falling for the most part into inauthenticity because of its necessary concern with beings. Yet, by resisting a definite injunction for overcoming everydayness, he does not approach the totalistic and harmonious unity of being-time that is disclosed by Dōgen.

Heidegger's hermeneutic difficulties, however, appear to be more basic than a drawback in the procedure of investigation because the goals, range and accomplishments of his philosophical enterprise remain questionable and puzzling at the end of his career, even for Heidegger himself. The central problem in Heidegger's approach seems to pertain to the dimension of time which he has tried from the outset to exclude from his thinking — that is, the soteriological dimension, which necessarily involves personal experience, reflection, commitment and insight in the development and formulation of ontological understanding. If the very starting point of thinking is itself problematic, the conclusions will invariably be limited as well.

To clarify the reasons why differences between Heidegger and Dōgen concerning the soteriological dimension are of utmost importance for their understanding of the existential and ontological dimensions of temporality, it is necessary to briefly reframe how and why each thinker sets for himself the nature and significance of the question of time. Both Heidegger and Dōgen force the issue of time into the open, considering it afresh after a philosophical "slumber" that has taken time for granted as given and self-evident, and not subject to inquiry. They are eager to render time worthy of asking about in a positive, constructive way. It is important to realize, however, that although the question of time is necessary and essential as an integral part of the primary and overriding concerns which guide their philosophical tasks, this key issue is not in itself to be equated with their primary concerns. Heidegger and Dōgen are each propelled by one basic matter that is pursued with single-minded persistence and intensity. But a theory of time is not necessarily a solution to the central issue, even as the issue itself cannot be separated from the question of time.

Heidegger's primary concern is the *Seinsfrage*, and why ontology is increasingly confused and problematic despite — or, rather, because of — the metaphysical tradition's smug indifference to the paramount question of all thinking. After attempting various non-substantive approaches to Being through a disclosure of temporality, however, Heidegger remains uncertain about the relationships between Being and time, time and man, man and beings; the long-sought primordial unity underlying these elements is still elusive. The notion in his later writings that they "belong-together" is not necessarily more fruitful as a disclosure of the dynamic integralness of time than the *existenzial* analysis of ecstatic temporality. In each of Heidegger's approaches, there are dimensions and perspectives which are left unsettled and are continually troubling to him.

Dōgen's concern is why the gap between original and acquired Buddhahood had been fabricated and perpetuated in Buddhist theories and approaches to practice. An ontological understanding of Buddha-nature was considered self-evident in Japanese Buddhism, although it did not satisfactorily account for Dōgen's personal experience of impermanence. He concludes that the temporal nature of *busshō* is not an issue which can be isolated or abstracted from personal insight into the realization of the truth of being-time. The attainment of Buddhahood is obstructed by an inauthentic and inadequate understanding of time, which can in turn only be clarified and corrected through spontaneous and renewable dedication and discipline in pursuit of the Way of non-self.

The significance of the question of time for Heidegger's thought is the role time plays as the "first name" of Being. Any personal involvement or interest in this matter is bracketed until the disclosure of *Sein* is accomplished. Heidegger seems to claim that only by solving the *Seinsfrage* first of all will an appropriate basis have been established for a personal realization of authenticity. Despite Heidegger's attempted avoidance of the issue of personal involvement in the question of Being and time, however, soteriological implications do not disappear but continually emerge as unacknowledged tendencies or unclarified tangential elements which obstruct and perhaps prohibit a resolution to the *Seinsfrage*. The question thus remains whether any separation between ontology and personal experience is, indeed, possible or even reasonable in terms of Heidegger's hermeneutic method and philosophical aims. Such a separation seems to violate the unity of *Seinsverständnis* and mineness, of man's way to be and the potentiality for illumination, which is the very ground and framework of his thought.

From Heidegger's own interpretive standpoint, soteriology cannot and should not be added on after or in addition to ontology, nor subtracted from it beforehand. Otherwise, personal experience would stand in an ontical or *vorhanden* relation to Being, which thereby becomes objectified — and that is precisely the position of substantiality Heidegger struggles to overcome. For example, Heidegger does note in *Humanismusbrief* that there must be a unity of ontology and human experience which neither negates nor transcends either dimension, but also does not merely attach one to the other. "The thinking that inquires into the truth of Being and so defines man's essential abode from Being and toward Being is neither ethics nor ontology. Thus the question about the relation of each to the other no longer has any basis in this sphere."[55] Yet, he does not use that insight as an occasion to articulate the primordially temporal basis of an existentialist ethics in its inseparability from ontology, but rather to further avoid or delay that very matter until Being has been disclosed.

Heidegger bases ontology on the *existenziell* way to be of Dasein, which is always already intimately involved as its own-most concern in the question which is ultimately at stake. But, by presupposing that man cannot help but be inauthentic by virtue of *existenzial* finitude and falling, Heidegger inherently limits the possibility for a fully non-substantive disclosure of temporality. Furthermore, the sense of urgency that he seeks to instill in his inquiry is dissipated without a personal commitment and a sense of wholehearted conviction in and pursuit of resolving the matter. Instead, the quasi-mystical approach of Heidegger II's "purposeless play" tends to reinforce rather than radically reorient traditional theology; and the ambivalent existentialism of *Sein und Zeit* is perhaps less challenging to traditional Western metaphysics than Kierkegaard's uncompromising imperative for the subjective realization of truth through the inwardness and passion of self-reflection and self-discovery which demands a transformation of the entire person. Heidegger does not adequately disclose either the existential or ontological dimension precisely because the soteriological concern has been excluded from his thinking. Just as Heidegger has criticized Kant, Nietzsche and other thinkers, it seems that by his holding back from a full disclosure of the primordial temporal unities he seeks to uncover, Heidegger reveals the poverty and entanglements as well as his own bondage to the very tradition of substance ontology he attempts to overcome. He is not free from the basic separations of theory and practice, philosophy and existential experience, which betray the presuppositions of onto-theo-logy, even though he does see that he must penetrate beyond them to achieve a breakthrough from the notion of substantiality.

Dōgen presupposes that man is always already involved in exertion at all times and at this very moment. He writes in "Uji," "I already am, so time cannot be said to slip away." The attempt to avoid exertion is a sham both philosophically and personally — it is an "impossible and unrighteous evasion," which is ontologically misleading and existentially self-deceptive in that it reveals a clinging to self, and therefore it is soteriologically obstructive and unedifying. Personal involvement in and realization of the true nature of being-time can never be bracketed or withheld in any subtle way. It is impossible to stand by as a spectator of time because the innate and unceasing dynamism, impermanence and insubstantiality of temporal reality does not permit, but rather continuously betrays such an evasion. Dōgen stresses that man cannot hold still in personal or existential development until the ontological issue is solved, in that the ontological nature of reality itself is nothing other than one's existential activity temporally interpenetrating all beings each and every and any occasion of *uji*. To attempt to stand back from full personal involvement in the matter of casting off body and mind by realizing the true nature of time is itself a self-destructive or debilitating inauthentic response to the passage of being-time.

For example, because each and every dwelling-place of being-time — at once possessed of and yet cut off from before and after — encompasses and is liberated from all possibilities of moral causation (karma), Dōgen does not withdraw from or hesitate in affirming a thoroughgoing ethical commitment on the part of the True Man. Rather, in contrast to Heidegger, he insists that the moment-to-moment presencing of being-time offers innumerable and inexhaustible occasions by which the enlightened person must continually and diligently attempt to "refrain from all evil" (shoaku-makusa) as the natural and spontaneous outflow of his utmost selfless exertion. "Where evil is already not produced," he writes, "the exertive power of practice is at once spontaneously realized. This spontaneous realization is measured through its manifestations in the whole earth, the entire world, every moment, and all dharmas. This measure is nothing other than the measure of refraining [from all evil]."[56] The fulfillment of the moral imperative is inseparably related to the realization and expression of being-time as the manifestation of non-self. The totalistic moment of spontaneous compassion and renewed ethical discipline is itself the overcoming of a fixation with self by means of the dynamic dwelling-place of uji.

The religious question for Dōgen is not undertaken for the sake of ontological disclosure; nor does ontological clarification necessarily lead to personal realization. Dōgen neither reduces the dimensions of time into a sheer (derivative) identity nor elevates the priority of one dimension over and above the others. Nor does Dōgen expect, in a way which would violate the true nature of being-time, for one dimension to appear first or last, before or after any other one. "As soon as one begins to seek the Dharma [apart from himself], he drifts far away from its true location. When the Dharma has been received through right transmission, the True Man is immediately realized."[57] Theory must spring from and be in perfect accord with authentic practice, just as realization is enhanced and renewed by personal effort. Theory is not a mere consequence of practice, but neither can it be isolated from practice. Theory and practice are only fulfilled by means of complete realization of their inseparability. Dōgen points directly to the three-fold and ultimately unified interpenetration of the existential authenticity of renewed selfless practice, the soteriological deliverance of *nirvāṇic* awakening, and the ontological penetration of the truth of *uji* by the True Man of *shinjin-datsuraku*. The creative activities and expressions of the True Man's self-forgetfulness are at once grounded in, realized through and sustaining of the harmonious simultaneity and insubstantiality of the totalistic passage (*kyōryaku*) of being-time.

Appendix

A Translation of Dōgen's "Uji" (Being-Time)

Introductory Comments

"Uji" is one of the central fascicles of Dōgen's monumental philosophical work, the *Shōbōgenzō*, and it is crucial to an understanding of the philosophy of time which is the centerpiece of his thought, practice and unique interpretation and appropriation of the Buddhist *Dharma*. In "Uji," Dōgen introduces several key notions, such as *uji* (being-time), *jiji* (time's occurrence at each, every and any moment), and *kyōryaku* (passage, encompassing the simultaneity of past, present, future), which do not appear in other fascicles of the work. He also discusses terms such as *nikon* or *shikin* (right-now) and *jū-hōi* (*dharma*'s dwelling-place) which are treated rather more extensively elsewhere. This does not, however, suggest a discontinuity between "Uji" and the rest of the *Shōbōgenzō*. To the contrary, the notions dealt with here are fully compatible with other doctrines concerning time, particularly *mujō* (impermanence), *mujō-busshō* (impermanence-Buddha-nature), *zenki* (total dynamic activity), *kikan* (dynamic engagement), *genjōkōan* (immediate and complete realization of Zen *kōan*), *gyōji* (sustained exertion), and *gyōbutsu* (active Buddha). All these ideas must be understood in their interrelatedness in order to comprehend Dōgen's philosophy of Zen as a whole. Therefore, although *uji* is not mentioned in other fascicles, it can well be considered one of the foremost of the doctrines he formulates to creatively "express the Way" (*dōtoku*). And although this chapter does not refer specifically to *mujō*, Dōgen's understanding and experience of impermanence is inseparable from his explication of the meaning (*dōri*) of *uji*.

The aim of this fascicle is to expose and overcome fundamental existential deceptions and ontological misconceptions concerning time that arise in the views of the average man (*bonbu*), and lead to deficient interpretations of the process of enlightenment and the attainment of Buddhahood. Because the average man mistakes the unity and total dynamism of being-time presencing each and every occasion for a mere sequential time-unit "flying by," enlightenment is seen as a matter of linear development toward some futural goal. For Dōgen, each and every totalistic moment of being-time encompassing past, present and future, life and death, all Buddhas and all beings, is the essential experience of self, triple world and Buddha-nature which must be penetrated and realized here-and-now as the basic aim of Buddhist theory and practice. Any view which proposes enlightenment as a supratemporal realm, beyond the incessant vicissitudes of momentary existence, is to be considered a basically non-Buddhistic position (*gedō*).

Japanese editions consulted:

Dōgen (*Nihon shisō taikei*, vols. 12 and 13). Edited by Terada Tōru and Mizuno Yaoko, Tokyo, Iwanami shoten, 1970 and 1972, vol. I, pp. 256–263. This is the main edition I have used.

Dōgen zenji zenshū, 2 volumes. Edited by Ōkubo Dōshū, Tokyo, Chikuma shobō, 1970, vol. I, pp. 385–395.

Zenyaku Shōbōgenzō, 4 volumes. Trans. Nakamura Sōichi, Tokyo, Seishin shobō, 1970, vol. I, pp. 385–395.

Gendaigoyaku Shōbōgenzō, 8 volumes. Trans. Masutani Fumio, Tokyo, Kadakawa shoten, 1971, vol. I, pp. 193–213.

Dōgen shū. Trans. Tamaki Kōshirō, Tokyo, Chikuma shobō, 1969, pp. 175–182.

Translation of "Uji" (Being-Time)

An ancient Buddha's words[1]:

> Sometimes (*uji*)[2] standing so high up on the mountain top;
> Sometimes walking deep down on the bottom of the sea;
> Sometimes a three-headed eight-armed [demon or *Acala*];
> Sometimes a sixteen- or eight-foot [Buddha];
> Sometimes a Zen master's staff or *hossu*;[3]
> Sometimes a round pillar or stone lantern;
> Sometimes this man or that fellow;
> Sometimes the great earth or the empty sky.

The so-called "sometimes" (*uji*) means: time (*ji*) itself already is none other than being(s) (*u*); being(s) (*u*) are all none other than time (*ji*). The sixteen-foot golden body itself is time, and just because it is time there is the luminous glow of the radiance (*kōmyō*)[4] of time, and you must study the matter right within this twenty-four hours.[5] The three-headed eight-armed [demon] itself is time, and just because it is time it must be the same as the time right within this twenty-four hours. Although the time span for each day is generally not actually measured out, it is said to be twenty-four hours. Because of the clear tracks left by the coming and going [of time], people do not doubt the duration of daily time, but even though they do not doubt it, this does not mean that they know what it really is. Whenever people for the most part doubt any thing or any event unknown to them, their doubting is so inconsistent that the doubts at the previous moment do not necessarily correspond to the doubts at the present moment. Nevertheless, doubting itself, for the time being, is indeed time.[6]

The configuration of my-self makes up the entire [*Dharma-*]realm, and you must examine each being and each thing in the entire [*Dharma-*]realm as time's occurrence at each, every and any moment (*jiji*). The mutual non-obstruction of things and things is the same as the mutual non-obstruction amongst all times.[7] Therefore, the arousing of aspiration [in different] minds at the selfsame time is the arousing [at different] times of the selfsame mind.[8] It is just the same with practice and attainment of the [Buddhist] Way. [Projecting] the configuration of my-self is to behold this. The truth of my-self's being time is just like this.

You must realize that it is by this very reason[9] that there are all the phenomena and all the many grasses in the whole world as well as each particular blade of grass and each particular phenomenon in its own place in the whole world. To survey the matter in this way is the initiation of practice. When you reach such a standpoint, each particular blade of grass and each particular phenomenon is seen as it is. There may or may not be an understanding of phenomena or of grass. [But] it is by virtue of this very time that being-time [appears at] all times and being-a-grass and being-a-phenomenon alike are time. All beings of the entire [Dharma-]realm are time's occurrence at each, every and any moment. You should seriously consider whether or not any being in the entire [Dharma-]realm lies outside this moment of time.[10]

When, however, the average man (bonbu)[11] unlearned in the Buddhist teaching hears the word "uji," it becomes an occasion for all sorts of conjectures that "sometimes" (arutoki) [it is] a three-headed eight-armed [demon] and "sometimes"[it is] a sixteen- or eight-foot [Buddha].[12] This can be likened by metaphor to crossing a river and climbing a mountain. Although the mountain and river are indeed here right-now, I seem to think that I have left them far behind and I act as if I occupy a palace made of rubies, thereby believing that there is a separation between my-self and the mountain and river [as great] as that between heaven and earth.[13]

But the truth is not only this. When I climbed the mountain and crossed the river I existed, so in myself there must be time. I already am, and time cannot be said to slip away.[14] If time is not the form (sō, Skt. laksana) of going and coming, then the time of ascending the mountain is the right-now (nikon) of being-time. Suppose that time does maintain the form of going and coming, then in myself there is the right-now of being-time; this itself is being-time. Does or does not the very moment of ascending the mountain and crossing the river chew up and spit out the time of the palace made of rubies?[15]

The three-headed eight-armed [demon] is yesterday's time; the sixteen- or eight-foot [Buddha] is today's time. Nevertheless, the truth of yesterday-and-today lies precisely in the moment of setting forth up the mountain to overlook so many different peaks. The three-headed eight-armed [demon] passes around in my being-time (*waga uji*), not as it may appear over there, but right here-and-now. The sixteen- or eight-foot [Buddha] passes around in my being-time, not as it may appear down yonder, but right here-and-now.[16]

Likewise, the pine tree is time and so also the bamboo. You must not understand and account for time in terms of its flying ever away; you must not learn "time flies" as the one and only function of time. If time had only this one function of flying by, there would have to be a gap [between t1 and t2].[17] If someone does not heed the way of being-time, it's because he sees it as something merely slipping away. In short, all beings in the entire [*Dharma-*]realm are linked together as time's occurrence at each, every and any moment. Because of being-time I am [being-]time.

In being-time there is the distinctive function of [totalistic] passage (*kyōryaku*);[18] there is passage from today to tomorrow, passage from today to yesterday, passage from yesterday to today, passage from today to today, and passage from tomorrow to tomorrow. This transpires because passage itself is the distinctive function of time.

Since the times of past and present neither pile up on top of one another nor line up side by side, Ch'ing-yüan is time, Huang-po is time, Ma-tsu and Shih-t'ou are time.[19] Because self and other already are time, practice and realization take place at all times. In the same way, entering into the mud and water is time.[20] The views now held by the average man as well as the conditioned origination (*innen*, Skt. *pratītya-samutpāda*) of the views by which he tries to account for his existence are by no means the *Dharma* of the average man; the *Dharma* for now sets the stage for the origination of his [*karmic*] conditions.[21] It is because this very time and this very being are learned as something other than the *Dharma* that the sixteen-foot golden body is not recognized as myself. But even the evasion of [the truth] that I am the sixteen-foot golden body is a fragment of being-time.[22] The person who has not realized this had better take a look at the matter again and again.[23]

The arrangement of the "horse" [noon] and the "sheep" [two

o'clock] in the world is due to the ascending and descending fluc-
tuations of things such as they are dwelling in their appropriate
dharma-positions.[24] The "mouse" [midnight] is time, the "tiger"
[four o'clock] is time; sentient beings and Buddhas are time as
well. At this very moment, the entire [*Dharma*-]realm is realized in terms of a three-headed eight-armed [demon] or in terms
of a sixteen-foot golden body. To fully enlighten the entire
[*Dharma*-]realm is ultimate and complete realization (*kyūjin*). To
fully enlighten the sixteen-foot golden body by means of the sixteen-foot golden body is to spontaneously manifest (*genjō*) resolve
(*hosshin*), practice (*shugyō*), *bodhi* (*bodai*), and *nirvāṇa* (*nehan*);
this itself is being, this itself is time. Ultimate and complete
realization of all times as all beings is to have no left-over *dharma*
because the left-over *dharma* is itself a *dharma* left-over. A [full]
being-time half known is a half being-time fully known.[25] Any
false step taken is still being[-time]. Moreover, even before and
after the misjudgement is shown, still there is found the dwelling-
place of being-time. The incessant vigorous activity of a *dharma*'s
dwelling-place itself is being-time. Don't jump to the conclusion
that it is non-being, but don't be constrained to assume that it
is being. Discerning only the aspect of time that passes away,
there is no understanding of the time which has not-yet come.[26]
To realize this is time; but time itself is not conditioned by
[whether it is realized or not]. Discerning going and coming, it
is impossible for a "stubborn fool"[27] to clearly perceive the
dwelling-place of being-time, let alone reach the moment of
breaking through the barrier [to realization]. Even discerning
the dwelling-place [of being-time], who can express how to maintain such [a dwelling place]? Even if there is a person who has
been able to express this for a long time, still he is groping in
the darkness for his original face. Left up to the being-time of
the average man, *bodhi* and *nirvāṇa* are only being-time in the
form of going and coming.[28]

　　Freedom from all entanglements is the spontaneous here-and-
now manifestation of being-time (*uji genjō*).[29] The heavenly kings
and their heavenly court appearing in the right realm and the
left realm are at this moment the being-time of my utmost exertion (*jinriki*).[30] The being-time of the multitudes outside [that

universe] on land and in the water is the spontaneous manifestation of my utmost exertion. The being-time of every single thing in "this" world and in "that" world are all in all the spontaneous manifestation and the passage of my utmost exertion. You should realize that without the passage of my utmost exertion at this very moment, there would be neither the manifestation of one single *dharma* or one single phenomenon, nor the passage of one single *dharma* or one single phenomenon.

Don't conceive of this passage as something like the wind and rain moving from east to west. There is nothing in the whole world that is not moving around, nothing that is not advancing or retreating, [nothing that is not in] passage. Pasage is like spring in that all the various manifestations of spring themselves are passage. You must realize that there is passage nowhere else than in spring. For example, the passage of spring is necessarily that which passages in-and-through spring. Passage is not [just] spring; however, since it is the passage of spring, passage now completes the Way at the very time spring appears.[31] You must carefully examine the matter backwards and forwards. When those who do not concentrate single-mindedly on the Buddhist Way speak of passage, they tend to think it is something outside of which the objective world stands; and the *Dharma* that makes passage is misunderstood as moving eastward a hundred thousand worlds and a hundred thousand epochs away.[32]

One time Master Shih-t'ou instructed his disciple Master Yüeh-shan Hung-tao to visit Master Chiang-hsi Ta-chi. Yüeh-shan asked Ta-chi,, "I have searched through all the essential doctrines of the three vehicles and the twelve schools, but what is the meaning of the Bodhidharma's coming from the West? [Hearing] this, Ta-chi replied:

Sometimes teaching him to raise his eyebrows and blink his eyes;
Sometimes not teaching him to raise his eyebrows and blink his eyes;
Sometimes teaching him to raise his eyebrows and blink his eyes is right;
Sometimes teaching him to raise his eyebrows and blink his eyes is not right.

Upon hearing these words, Yüeh-shan experienced a great enlightenment (*daigo*) and said to Ta-chi: "When I was Shit-t'ou's disciple, I was as hard-headed as a mosquito trying to bite an iron cow."

What Ta-chi expresses here is essentially different from all others' expressions. The eyebrows and eyes must be the mountain and sea because the mountain and sea are the eyebrows and eyes. This "teaching him to raise" must be to see the mountain, this "teaching him to blink" is to overlook the sea. "It is right" is to become "his" common practice; "he" is persuaded by the "teaching." "It is not right" is not "not teaching him"; "not teaching him" is not "it is not right." These are one and all being-time.[33]

The mountain is time; the sea is time as well. If they were not time, there would be no mountain or sea. You must not think that there is no time right-now of the mountain and sea.[34] If time should deteriorate, the mountain and sea will deteriorate as well; and if time does not deteriorate, neither will the mountain or sea. For this reason, the bright star appears, the Tathāgata appears, the [*Dharma-*]eye appears, the uplifted flower appears. These are all time.[35] If there were no time, they would not be such as they are.

Zen Master Kuei-hsing of the Yeh district was a *Dharma-*successor of Lin-chi and transmitter of Master Shou-shan's teaching. One time, holding forth before a congregation, he said:

Sometimes the intended meaning (*i*) gets there (*tō*), but the expression (*ku*) does not get there;
Sometimes the expression gets there, but the intended meaning does not get there;
Sometimes both the intended meaning and the expression get there concurrently;
Sometimes neither the intended meaning nor the expression get there.[36]

"Intended meaning" and "expression" are both being-time; "getting there" and "not getting there" are both time as well. While the time of getting there is unfinished, the time of not getting there is already here.[37] Intended meaning is a donkey, expression is a horse, or the horse is taken as expression and the donkey as intended meaning.[38] "Getting there" itself is not forthcoming, "not getting there" is not not-yet [forthcoming]; such is being-time. Getting there is obstructed by getting there, and not by not getting there. Not getting there is obstructed by not getting there, and not by getting there. Intended meaning penetrates through intended meaning and realizes intended meaning. Expression penetrates through expression and realizes expression. Obstruction penetrates through obstruction and realizes obstruction. All this is time. [The average man tends to think that] obstruction can be used by other *dharmas*, but there has never been any obstruction that obstructs other *dharmas*.[39] I meet people, people meet people, I meet myself, meeting meets meeting.[40] If these [matters] were not time, no such [meeting] would ever happen. Furthermore, intended meaning is the very moment of the immediate and complete realization of the *kōan* (*genjōkōan*).[41] Expression is the very moment of advancing upward and breaking through the barrier. Getting there is the very moment of casting off body[-and-mind]. Not getting there is the very moment of staying-here and leaving-here.[42] You should discern in this way, you should fully realize being-time [*as* being-time] (*uji subeshi*).[43]

Previous Zen masters have expressed it in all these ways; is there anything further to be expressed? Yes, I should add:

Intended meaning and expression that get half way there are being-time;
Intended meaning and expression that do not get half way there are also being-time.

You must investigate in this way.

Teaching him to raise his eyebrows and blink his eyes is a half way being-time;
Teaching him to raise his eyebrows and blink his eyes is a mistaken being-time;
Not teaching him to raise his eyebrows and blink his eyes is an even more misleading being-time.

In such a way, careful examination backwards and forwards, getting all the way there and not getting there are both this very moment of being-time.[45]

Composed on November 1, 1240 at Kōshōhōrinji temple [in Fukakusa], and copied by Ejō in the summer of 1243 in Echizen Province.

Notes

Chapter 1

1. See SZ 330 (BT 379) and 425 (BT 478); SBGZ "Uji," vol. I, p. 258.

2. SBGZ "Uji," vol. I, p. 257.

3. Heidegger's term "primordial time" (*ursprüngliche Zeit*) is used here to refer to both philosophers' conceptions of genuinely realized time prior to, underlying, and the disguised basis of the conventional view, keeping in mind that despite the common elements in their philosophies, there are also major and significant differences which will subsequently be explored. "Primordial time," to be discussed in detail in Chapter 4, is the eminently active, dynamic, non-substantial and unified foundation of the multiple dimensions of existence, including authenticity and inauthenticity, language, space, history, etc. Heidegger's term "derivative time" (*abkünftige Zeit*) is also used to refer to the conventional view, which is not a logical error or mistake, but is inauthentically derived from primordial time.

4. In *The Confessions of Saint Augustine* (Book XI), trans. Edward Pusey (New York: Collier, 1975), p. 194: "For what is time? Who can readily and briefly explain this? Who can even in thought comprehend it, so as to utter a word about it? . . . If no one asks me, I know: If I wish to explain it to one that asketh, I know not. . . ."

5. The term "existential" is used to refer to the dimension of concrete human encounters with and decisions concerning time which, in turn, reflects and determines the dimension of ontological understanding of the meaning and structure of existence. "Existential" in this sense is closely related to, but must be distinguished from Heidegger's term *existenzial* (the ontological structure of Dasein) and *existenziell* (Dasein's ontical affairs and factual decisions), which will always be cited in the German, even in translations of passages (since Macquarrie and Robinson translate "*existenzial*" as "existential," misleading from our point of view). The suggestion to be made in this comparative examination is that the "existential" dimension of time, perhaps as an

implication in Heidegger's thought although he tends to deny it, must represent an inseparability of experience and understanding, decision and disclosure, practice and insight; in other words, "existential" is a unity of Heidegger's *existenzial* and *existenziell* from the higher point of view. The question of the relationship between the two levels of Heidegger's inquiry, the *existenzial*-ontological and the factical-*existenziell*, and of whether it is appropriate or fair to refer to Heidegger's thinking as "existential" will receive attention in later chapters in light of Dōgen's philosophy of *genjōkōan* (spontaneous here-and-now realization) which does not presuppose, but rather seems to consistently overcome any distinction between "theory" (*existenzial*) and "practice" (*existenziell*) from the standpoint of the ultimate identity of existential awakening and ontological seeing.

6. Cited in SZ 421 (BT 473) from Aristotle, *Physica*, Book Delta II, 219b, 1 ff.

7. Heidegger's critique is mainly directed at those modern thinkers whom he feels have both fulfilled the greatness and revealed the poverty of the traditional metaphysical conception of time — Kant, Hegel, and Nietzsche. He does not generally deal with other modern philosophers who challenge the conventional view of linear and sequential calculative time, such as Bergson and Whitehead, who attempt to formulate a comprehensive and creatively dynamic temporal unity of reality. Heidegger does briefly mention in SZ 432 ftn. xxx (BT 500–501) that Bergson's philosophical project is derivative of the Aristotelian conception, and limited in that it has not first disclosed the primordial *existenzial* origins of temporality. His interpretation of Whitehead would probably run along similar lines. Yet, Whiteheadean process philosophy of the harmonious and dynamic universe of prehensive events and developing organisms perhaps poses a significant challenge to Heidegger's Dasein-oriented approach to the question of time.

8. The phrase "skin, flesh, bones, marrow," repeatedly used by Dōgen, refers to the traditional Zen story of Bodhidharma (the first Zen patriarch to transmit the *Dharma* from India to China) who tells four disciples in response to their various expressions of Zen realization that they "possess," respectively and metaphorically, his skin, flesh, bones and marrow (the last is reserved for the one who communicates by silence). In SBGZ "Kattō," Dōgen refutes any gap between external/internal, speech/silence, superficiality/profundity which may be implied in traditional interpretations of the legend; he maintains that all expressions are spontaneous manifestations (*genjō*) of being-time.

9. The Mahāyāna literature, particularly in the *Tathāgata-garbha* (matrix or potentiality for "Thus-come" attainment) tradition, includes the *Mahāparinirvāṇa Sūtra*; the *Mahāyānaśraddotpāda Śāstra* (*The Awakening of Faith*, trans. Yoshito Hakeda, New York: Columbia University Press, 1967); *Śrī-mālā-sūtra* (*The Lion's Roar of Queen Śrīmālā*, trans. Alex and Hideko Wayman, Columbia University Press, 1974); and the *Ratnagotravibhāga-Mahāyānottaratantra-śāstra*. See the Waymans' "Introduction" for a review of the history and doctrines of this literature in light of related Mahāyāna philosophical developments.

10. SBGZ "Sokushinzebutsu," vol. I, p. 83. Dōgen also critiques the Senika heresy in SBGZ "Busshō" and "Bendōwa."

11. Dōgen's critique of Hui-neng is in SBGZ "Shizen-biku," in which he postulates that the doctrine of *kenshō* attributed to the sixth patriarch may not have actually been formulated by him since it seems to represent, from the standpoint of being-time, an heretical or non-Buddhistic tendency.

12. Martin Heidegger, *Einführung in die Metaphysik*, trans. *An Introduction to Metaphysics* by Ralph Mannheim (New Haven: Yale University Press, 1959), p. 5.

13. SZ 312 (BT 360).

14. Heidegger refers, for example, to the danger wherein grows the "saving power" for man, as the shepherd of Being, to attend the arrival of the truth of Being, in the essay, "The Turning" in *The Question Concerning Technology and Other Essays*, trans. William Lovitt (New York: Harper and Row, 1977), p. 42.

15. The "ambivalence" in Heidegger's approach, which leads him to vacillate between his emphasis on Dasein's concrete decisions and affairs and his refraining from any experiential concern or espousing a practical proposal, will be explored in subsequent chapters as to its roots in and consequences for his disclosure of the primordial *unity* of temporality. It seems that Heidegger's reluctance to speak of practice may still presuppose in a subtle way the traditional distinction between *theoria* and *praxis* which he seeks to overcome.

16. SBGZ "Hakujushi," vol. I, p. 451.

17. SBGZ "Genjōkōan," vol. I, p. 35. For a fuller analysis of this profound yet elusive passage in light of different translations in both English and modern Japanese, see my "Multiple Dimensions of Impermanence in Dōgen's 'Genjōkōan,'" *Journal of the International Association of Buddhist Studies*, vol. 4, no. 2, pp. 44–62.

18. SBGZ "Uji," vol. I, p. 258.

19. SBGZ "Genjōkōan," vol. I, p. 36.

20. SZ 18 (BT 39).

21. It is interesting that Heidegger assisted in editing Husserl's work on the phenomenological analysis of time, *Phenomenology of Internal Time-Consciousness*, near the time he was preparing *Sein und Zeit* for publication, and that his hermeneutic approach toward *existenzial* investigation differs so greatly from his mentor's method. In a telling comment, noted by Herbert Spiegelberg in *The Phenomenological Movement* (The Hague: Nijhoff, 1960, p. 302), which Heidegger makes on the draft of the *Encyclopedia Brittanica* article in which Husserl says, "If I carry out the [transcendental] reduction for myself, I am not a human ego," Heidegger underlines the final phrase and adds, "or perhaps I am precisely that in its most specific, most amazing (*wundersamst*) existential possibility."

22. SZ 18 (BT 40).

23. SZ 14 (BT 34).

24. See Heidegger's "Preface" to William Richardson, *Heidegger: Through Phenomenology to Thought* (The Hague: Nijhoff, 1974), p. x.

25. Martin Heidegger, *Phänomenologie und Theologie*, trans. The Piety of Thinking by James Hart and John Maraldo (Bloomington: Indiana University Press, 1976), p. 20.

26. Martin Heidegger, "Der Rückgang in den Grund der Metaphysik," trans. "The Way Back into the Ground of Metaphysics," by Walter Kaufmann in *Existentialism from Dostoyevsky to Sartre* (New York: Meridian, 1967).

27. Heidegger, *An Introduction to Metaphysics*, p. 171.

28. *Ibid.*, pp. 171–172.

29. Martin Heidegger, *Was Heisst Denken?*, trans. *What is Called Thinking?* by Fred D. Wieck and J. Glenn Gray (New York: Harper and Row, 1968), p. 103.

30. Heidegger repeatedly and consistently stresses the neutrality or value-free status of his notions of authenticity (*eigentlich*) and inauthenticity (un-*eigentlich*) as varying *existenziell* modifications and possibilities of Dasein. Authenticity is not prior to or higher than the latter, which is not a moral imperfection or loss of purity. Both are variations of the unified totality of Being-in-the-world: authenticity is not

Selfhood removed or isolated from the world; nor is inauthenticity merely a lostness into the world and elimination of self; the two are overlapping, simultaneous and by no means mutually exclusive possibilities.

31. SZ 15 (BT 35).

32. SZ 43 (BT 69), SZ 133 (BT 171), SZ 145 (BT 185).

33. Otto Pöggeler, "Being as Appropriation" trans. Rudiger H. Grimm in *Heidegger and Modern Philosophy* (New Haven: Yale University Press, 1978), p. 87.

34. SZ 23 (BT 45).

35. SZ 48 (BT 73).

36. *The Confessions of Saint Augustine* (Book XI), p. 204.

37. SZ 153 (BT 37).

38. SZ 16 (BT 37).

39. *Ibid.*

40. SZ 13 (BT 33).

41. James Demske, *Being, Man, and Death* (Lexington, Kentucky: University of Kentucky Press, 1970), p. 59.

42. Biographical material on Dōgen largely taken from the following sources: Kōdō Kawamura, *Eihei kaizen Dōgen zenji gyōjō — Kenzeiki* (Tokyo: Daishūkan shoten, 1975); Dōshū Ōkubo, *Dōgen zenji-den no kenkyū* (Tokyo: Chikuma shobō, 1966; Michio Takeuchi, *Dōgen* (Tokyo: Yoshikawa kobunkan, 1962); Hee-jin Kim, *Dōgen Kigen — Mystical Realist* (Tucson: University of Arizona Press, 1975); and Takashi James Kodera, *Dogen's Formative Years in China* (Boulder: Prajña Press, 1980).

43. Dōgen, *Shōbōgenzō Zuimonki*, trans. Reihō Masunaga in *A Primer of Sōtō Zen* (Honolulu: University of Hawaii Press, 1975), p. 66.

44. Dōgen,"Shūshō-gi" trans. Yūhō Yokoi in *Zen Master Dōgen* (New York and Tokyo: Weatherhill, 1976), p. 58.

45. SBGZ "Immo," vol. I, p. 223.

46 Dōgen, "Fukanzazengi," *Dōgen zenji zenshū*, ed. Dōshū Ōkubo (Tokyo: Chikuma shobō, 1969–1970), vol. 2, p. 3.

47. The term "great doubt" mentioned in Dōgen's biography, *Kenzeiki* (Kawamura, p. 10), seems to refer to Dōgen's soteriological impasse caused by the apparent gap between the theory of an eternal

Buddha-nature and his own painful experience of transiency as well as his inability, at that point, to liberate himself from attachments to a fixated concept of self.

It should be noted that the doctrine of the "great doubt" is usually associated with Zen thinkers who have made it an integral part of their approach, including Hakuin and the modern Kyoto-school philosopher, Nishitani Keiji. It implies a direct encounter with emptiness, stripping one of ego fixations and attachments, leading to a realization of non-self or the formless Self.

48. SBGZ "Genjōkōan," vol. I, pp. 38–39.

49. Dōgen, *Shōbōgenzō Zuimonki*, p. 67: "I regarded the great teachers of my country as so much dirt and broken tile," Dōgen writes of the time after he read the biographies of the authentically dedicated Buddhist priests of China.

50. This encounter is related by Dōgen in "Tenzokyōkun" in *Dōgen zenji zenshū*, vol. 2.

51. SBGZ "Bendōwa," vol. I, p. 11.

52. SBGZ "Busshō," vol. I, p. 53.

53. It has been suggested by Jikidō Takasaki in *Kobutsu no manebi* (with Takeshi Umehara) (Tokyo: Kadokawa shoten, 1969), as a matter of personal conjecture, that Dōgen deliberately altered or "creatively misunderstood" the meaning of Ju-ching's phrase from "cast the dust off the mind," which perhaps has a subtle substantialist implication, as if there were an enduring mind which could be defiled and purified. Because the expressions are pronounced slightly differently in Chinese (though identical in Japanese), Takasaki's point seems to be unfounded.

54. In contrast to Rinzai's doctrine of the "True Man of no rank," Dōgen proposes the "True Man with rank" (*ui-shinjin*) to emphasize the concrete personal embodiment of Buddha-nature in all affairs here-and-now, in SBGZ "Sesshin sesshō," vol. II, p. 22.

55. SBGZ "Busshō," vol. I, p. 46.

56. SBGZ "Uji," vol. I, p. 256.

57. Hajime Nakamura in *Ways of Thinking of Eastern Peoples* (Honolulu: East-West Center Press, 1964), p. 353, shows several ways in which Dōgen deliberately and creatively revises or even distorts key textual phrases to expose what he considers their fundamental and essential meanings and implications. Dōgen's creative philosophical reading and interpretation will be examined in Chapter 2 in light of

his notion of the totalistic passage (*kyōryaku*) of the *Dharma* simultaneously extending throughout past, present and future. Also, see my: "Temporality of Hermeneutics in Dōgen's *Shōbōgenzō*," *Philosophy East and West*, vol. 33, no. 2 (April, 1983), pp. 139–147.

58. SBGZ "Zenki," vol. I, pp. 275–276.

59. SZ 176 (BT 220).

60. SBGZ "Bendōwa," vol. I, pp. 17–18.

61. Martin Heidegger, "Aus Einem Gespräch Von Der Sprache" trans. "A Dialogue on Language" by Peter D. Hertz and Joan Stambaugh in *On the Way to Language* (New York: Harper and Row, 1971).

Chapter 2

1. Martin Heidegger, *Humanismusbrief (Brief uber Humanismus)* trans. "Letter on Humanism" by David F. Krell in *Basic Writings* (New York: Harper and Row, 1977), p. 219.

2. SZ 206 (BT 250).

3. Heidegger's later works on the overcoming of Western onto-theo-logy include, among others, *Nietzsche* (Pfullingen: Neske, 1961) (on modern philosophy of subiectität from Descartes through Nietzsche grounded in "European nihilism"); *Holzwege* (Frankfurt: Klostermann, 1950) (essays on Anaximander, Descartes, Hegel and Nietzsche); *Identität Und Differenz* (Pfullingen: Neske, 1956) (discussion of the "step back" from modern technological *Gestell* or "framing"). For the use and meaning of "Heidegger II," a distinction acknowledged by and apparently acceptable to Heidegger himself, see William Richardson, *Heidegger: Through Phenomenology to Thought* (The Hague: Nijhoff, 1971).

Heidegger coins the term "onto-theo-logy" to imply that the seemingly separate disciplines of ontology, theology, and logic have come together to form the Western metaphysical tradition.

4. Dōgen, "Fukanzazengi," p. 3.

5. *Ibid.*

6. See SBGZ "Gyōbutsu-igi" for a discussion of *butsu-baku.*

7. SBGZ "Uji," vol. I, pp. 258–259.

8. Bodhidharma's dictum:

"A special transmission outside the scriptures,
Without reliance on words and letters,
Direct pointing to the mind,
Seeing into one's own nature and attaining Buddhahood."

Dōgen believes that Rinzai Zen overemphasis on kōan exercise may create a false bifurcation between silence and expression. Although Dōgen does hold that ultimate and complete realization is incommunicable, this only accentuates rather than negates the need for creative divulgences which convey its innumerable dimensions and manifestations. See SBGZ "Kenbutsu" for a critique of Rinzai.

9. SZ 59 (BT 85).

10. SZ 64 (BT 92).

11. SZ 350 (BT 401).

12. SZ 56 (BT 82).

13. SZ 304 (BT 351).

14. Heidegger acknowledges in SZ and other works an apparent similarity in his analysis of falling, temporality, and Being with Hegel, and he is careful to distinguish his emphasis on finitude in contrast to Hegelian absolutism. See also *Identitat und Differenz* and "Hegel und die Griechen" in *Wegmarken*.

15. SZ 425 (BT 478).

16. SZ 425 (BT 477)

17. SZ 391 (BT 443)

18. SZ 348 (BT 400)

19. Heidegger, *An Introduction to Metaphysics*, p. 36.

20. SZ 235 (BT 278).

21. Heidegger, *What is Called Thinking?*, p. 185.

22. Martin Heidegger, "Der Spruch des Anaximander" in *Holzwege* trans. "The Anaximander Fragment" in *Early Greek Thinking* by David F. Krell and Frank A. Capuzzi (New York: Harper and Row, 1975), p. 50.

23. Martin Heidegger, *Zur Sache des Denkens* trans. *On Time and Being* by Joan Stambaugh (New York: Harper and Row, 1972), p. 7.

24. Martin Heidegger, *Die Frage nach dem Ding* trans. *What is a Thing?* by W.B. Barton and Vere Deutsch (Chicago: Regnery, 1967), pp. 150–151.

25. Heidegger, *Nietzsche*, vol. II, p. 287.

26. SBGZ "Busshō," vol. I, p. 56.

27. The threefold body of Buddha consists of the Body of Law (*Dharmākāya, hōsshin*) Body of Bliss (*Sambhogakāya, hōjin*) and Body of Transformation (*Nirmānakāya, ōjin*). According to Dōgen's radical interpretation, the three bodies are ultimately equalizable through sustained here-and-now practice of the active Buddha (*gyōbutsu*).

28. SBGZ "Busshō," vol. I, pp. 57 and 59.

29. SBGZ "Uji," vol. I, p. 256.

30. SBGZ "Kūge," vol. I, p. 153.

31. SBGZ "Uji," vol. I, p. 259.

32. SBGZ "Uji," vol. I, p. 257.

33. SBGZ "Uji," vol. I, p. 258.

34. SBGZ "Uji," vol. I, p. 261.

35. SBGZ "Uji," vol. I, p. 262.

36. SBGZ "Kankin," vol. I, p. 345.

37. SBGZ "Uji," vol. I, p. 259.

38. SBGZ "Uji," vol. I, p. 258.

39. SBGZ "Uji," vol. I, p. 260.

40. SBGZ "Uji," vol. I, p. 262.

41. Dōgen, *Shōbōgenzō Zuimonki*, p. 72.

42. SBGZ "Dōtuku," vol. I, p. 385. Also, in SBGZ "Shisho," there is a recorded conversation in which Dōgen asks master Ju-ching how the *Dharma* of aeons past could be transmitted by Buddhas of the present. Ju-ching responds that the question itself presupposes a fixation with linear sequential time and reduces the spontaneous transmission of *Dharma* to the mere coming and going of something 'in' time.

43. Dōgen, "Hōkyō-ki" in *Dōgen zenji zenshū*, vol. 2.

44. See SBGZ "Kattō" for Dōgen's reinterpretation of the traditional Zen legend.

45. SBGZ "Bendōwa," vol. I, p. 14.

46. SBGZ "Busshō," vol. I, p. 47.

47. SBGZ "Busshō," vol. I, p. 48.

48. SBGZ "Busshō," vol. I, p. 48.

49. SZ 346 (BT 397).

50. SZ 167 (BT 211).

51. SZ 420 (BT 472).

52. SBGZ "Genjōkōan," vol. I, p. 37.

53. SBGZ "Gyōji," vol. I, p. 165.

54. SBGZ "Uji," vol. I, p. 259.

55. SBGZ "Uji," vol. I, p. 257.

56. SZ 21, 386 (BT 42, 438–439).

57. SBGZ "Uji," vol. I, p. 259.

Chapter 3

1. Martin Heidegger, *Vom Wesen des Grundes*, trans. *The Essence of Reasons* by Terence Malick (Evanston: Northwestern University Press, 1969), pp. 129–131.

2. Dōgen, "Gakudō-yōjinshū" trans. Yūhō Yokoi in *Zen Master Dōgen* (New York and Tokyo: Weatherhill, 1976), p. 48.

3. Dōgen, *Shōbōgenzō Zuimonki*, p. 39.

4. Martin Heidegger, *Kant und das Problem der Metaphysik*, trans. *Kant and the Problem of Metaphysics* by James S. Churchill (Bloomington: Indiana University Press, 1962), p. 236.

5. Heidegger, *Kant and the Problem of Metaphysics*, p. 224.

6. SZ 285 (BT 331).

7. SZ 284 (BT 330).

8. SZ 245 (BT 289).

9. SZ 287 (BT 333).

10. SZ 331 (BT 379).

11. Heidegger, *On Time and Being*, p. 54.

12. Martin Heidegger, *Was ist Metaphysik?*, trans. "What is Metaphysics?" by David F. Krell in *Basic Writings* (New York: Harper and Row, 1977), pp. 110, 108.

13. Martin Heidegger, "Das Ding," trans. "The Thing" by Albert

Hofstadter in *Poetry, Language, Thought* (New York: Harper and Row, 1971), p. 179.

14. Martin Heidegger, *Vom Wesen der Wahrheit*, trans. "On the Essence of Truth" by John Sallis in *Basic Writings*, p. 132.

15. Heidegger, "On the Essence of Truth," p. 135.

16. SBGZ "Sesshin sesshō," vol. II, p. 22.

17. SBGZ "Busshō," vol. I, p. 55.

18. Dōgen, *Shōbōgenzō Zuimonki*, p. 86.

19. Dōgen, *Shōbōgenzō Zuimonki*, p. 87.

20. SBGZ "Busshō," vol. I, p. 54.

21. *Ibid.*

22. SBGZ "Busshō," vol. I, p. 55.

23. Dōgen's *waka* appears in Nanboku Ōba, *Dōgen zenji waka-shū shin shaku* (Tokyo: Nakayama shobo, 1972), p. 342. Although the authenticity of this verse has been challenged by Ōba and other scholars (it appears that it may have been added to Dōgen's collection by a later editor as it is not included in some of the early manuscripts), it does seem consistent with the form and content of Dōgen's expression in his other writings. Another *waka* of uncontested authenticity also illustrates his sensitivity to the importance of an aesthetic attunement to impermanence:

Asahi matsu	Dewdrops, like tears, on a blade of grass
Kusaba no tsuyu no	Having so little time
Hodonaki ni	Before the sun rises;
Isogina tachi so	Let not the autumn wind
No be no aki kaze	Blow so quickly in the field.

24. SBGZ "Genjōkōan," vol. I, p. 37.

25. Dōgen, *Shōbōgenzō Zuimonki*, p. 24.

26. SBGZ "Udonge," vol. I, p. 218.

27. SBGZ "Baige," vol. I, pp. 122–123, 127.

28. SBGZ "Genjōkōan," vol. I, p. 36.

29. SBGZ "Shōji" in *Dōgen zenji zenshū*, vol. I, p. 778. This is one of several fascicles not included in the 88-fascicle Terada-Mizuno edition.

30. SBGZ "Shinjingakudō," vol. I, pp. 78–79.

31. SBGZ "Zenki," vol. I, p. 276.

32. *Ibid.*

33. SZ 330 (BT 378–379).

34. "Shinjingakudō," vol. I, p. 80.

35. SBGZ "Genjōkōan," vol. I, p. 36.

36. SBGZ "Bendōwa," vol. I, p. 31.

37. Heidegger, *Kant and the Problem of Metaphysics*, p. 241.

Chapter 4

1. SBGZ "Gyōji," vol. I, p. 166.

2. Heidegger, *On Time and Being*, pp. 3–4.

3. SBGZ "Zenki," vol. I, p. 276.

4. SZ 316 (BT 364).

5. SZ 310 (BT 357).

6. SZ 262 (BT 307).

7. SZ 287 (BT 333).

8. SZ 273 (BT 318).

9. SZ 325, 329 (BT 372, 377).

10. SZ 326 (BT 374).

11. SZ 350 (BT 401).

12. SZ 396 (BT 448).

13. SZ 436, 437 (BT 487, 488).

14. Heidegger, *On Time and Being*, p. 70.

15. *Ibid.*, p. 73.

16. *Ibid.*, p. 16.

17. Of the term *Ereignis*, also translated "E-vent" (Richardson) and "self-spectacle" (Vail), Heidegger writes in *Identität und Differenz* (trans. *Identity and Difference* by Joan Stambaugh (New York: Harper and Row, 1969), p. 36: "The words event of appropriation, thought of in terms of the matter indicated, should now speak as a key term in the service of thinking. As such a key term, it can no more be translated than the Greek *Logos* or the Chinese *Tao*. The term event of appropriation here

no longer means what we would otherwise call a happening, an occurrence. It now is used as a *singulare tantum*. What it indicates happens only in the singular, no, not in any number, but uniquely."

18. Heidegger, *On Time and Being*, p. 24.

19. Martin Heidegger, *On the Way to Language*, p. 166.

20. Martin Heidegger, "Überwindung der Metaphysik" (from *Vorträge und Aufsatze*) trans. "Overcoming Metaphysics" in *The End of Philosophy* by Joan Stambaugh (New York: Harper and Row, 1973), p. 90.

21. In "The Anaximander Fragment" (p. 18), Heidegger stresses that the "eschatology of Being" is not to be understood in an onto-theological (or teleological) way in that it does not lead inexorably and inevitably to a supreme and attainable goal. Rather, the richness and greatness of the *eschaton* lies at the beginning, which is not left behind, but is coming-towards man: "If we think within the eschatology of Being, then we must someday anticipate the former dawn in the dawn to come; today we must learn to ponder this former dawn through what is imminent." The "former dawn" is the early Greek thinking on Being as dynamic temporal presencing in terms of the notions, according to Heidegger's interpretation, of *physis*, *logos* and *aletheia*.

22. Heidegger, "The Thing," p. 180. In *Der Satz vom Grund* ((Pfullingen: Neske, 1957), p. 69), Heidegger explores the meaning of Being ontologically "without ground" (*ab-grund*) and existentially "without why" ("*ohne Warum*") by citing the mystical poem of Angelius Silesius: "The rose is without why; it blooms because it blooms/It does not care about itself, does not ask if it's being seen." Heidegger also writes (p. 188): "The 'because' is submerged in the play. . . The question remains whether we and how we, heeding the passage of this play, play along with and acquiesce to the play."

23. Martin Heidegger, *Gelassenheit*, trans. *Discourse on Thinking* by John Anderson and E. Hans Freund (New York: Harper and Row, 1966), p. 62.

24. Martin Heidegger, "Nur Noch ein Gott Kann uns Retten," trans. "Only a God Can Save Us Now" from *Der Spiegel* interview by David Schendler in *Graduate Faculty Philosophy Journal*, vol. 6, no. 1 (Winter, 1977), p. 19. This material was first published in *Der Spiegel* immediately after Heidegger's death, in keeping with his request at the time the interview was conducted.

25. SBGZ "Gyōji," vol. I, p. 165.

26. SBGZ "Uji," vol. I, p. 267.

27. SBGZ "Uji," vol. I, p. 267.

28. SBGZ "Uji," vol. I, p. 267.

29. SBGZ "Shinjingakudō," vol. I, p. 77.

30. SBGZ "Uji," vol. I, p. 262.

31. SBGZ "Tsuki," vol. I, p. 278.

32. SBGZ "Uji," vol. I, p. 260.

33. SBGZ "Busshō," vol. I, p. 47.

34. In addition to the various temporal dimensions of Buddha-nature, Dōgen also examines in "Busshō" two other significant dimensions — no-Buddha-nature (*mu-busshō*) and emptiness-Buddha-nature (*kū-busshō*) — to overcome any subtle clinging to substantiality. According to Dōgen, *mu-busshō* does not indicate the absence, negation or denial of Buddha-nature (as in the traditional interpretations), but full liberation from an objectified concept of *busshō*. Furthermore, *mu-busshō* directly points to and is ultimately (groundlessly) grounded in *kū-busshō*, which is not an abstract emptiness, nor merely a synthesis with form, but each and every non-substantial concrete particularity or manifestation. "One does not say 'no' (*mu*), because it is nothing. One says 'no' because it is Buddha-nature-emptiness. Thus, each aspect of 'no' is a means of expressing emptiness; emptiness is the power in expressing 'no'. Here emptiness is not the emptiness of 'form is emptiness'. . . . The emptiness of 'emptiness is emptiness' is that each and every element is a concrete manifestation of emptiness." (In SBGZ "Busshō," vol. I, p. 52).

35. SBGZ "Kobusshin," vol. I, p. 115.

36. SBGZ "Shisho," for Dōgen's refutation of Rinzai practices.

37. SBGZ "Bendōwa," vol. I, p. 15.

38. SBGZ "Gyōji," vol. I, p. 166.

39. SBGZ "Hotsu-mujōshin," vol. II, pp. 210–211.

40. *Ibid.*, p. 211.

41. SBGZ "Bendōwa," vol. I, p. 20.

42. SBGZ "Genjōkōan," vol. I, p. 36.

43. SBGZ "Uji," vol. I, pp. 259–260.

44. SBGZ "Gyōji," vol. I, p. 165.

45. *Gyōji* is a Zen term for *zazen* practice which Dōgen explores

for its deeper philosophical significance — *gyō* means activity, movement, exertive effort; *ji* means to hold, maintain or sustain unrelentingly. Thus, *gyōji* signifies the dynamism and universality of temporal reality, grounded in the existential imperative for selfless activity; or, the totalistic moment ceaselessly renewed.

46. SBGZ "Gyōji," vol. I, p. 166.

47. SBGZ "Gyōji," vol. I, p. 165.

48. Martin Heidegger, *Zur Seinsfrage*, trans. *The Question of Being* by William Kluback and Jean T. Wilde (New Haven: College and University Press, 1958), p. 81.

49. SZ 300 (BT 347).

50. SBGZ "Gyōji," vol. I, p. 165.

51. SBGZ "Jippō," vol. II, p. 146.

52. SBGZ "Juki," vol. I, p. 273.

53. SBGZ "Bendōwa," vol. I, p. 25.

54. SBGZ "Uji," vol. I, p. 261.

55. Heidegger, "Letter on Humanism," p. 236.

56. SBGZ "Shoaku makusa," vol. I, p. 357.

57. SBGZ "Genjōkōan," vol. I, p. 36.

Appendix

1. "An ancient Buddha . . . " refers to Zen Master Yüeh-shan Wêi-yen (751–834).

2. *Uji*, the central notion discussed in this chapter, has two meanings, according to Dōgen. In everyday or conventional discourse, it means "sometimes" or "at a certain time" in the sense that something takes place in a particular time-point. This implies that time is a realm separable from existence "in which" events transpire that are conceived as mutually exclusive oppositions — "sometimes" it is either a demon *or* a Buddha, enlightened or unenlightened, fitting and appropriate or unmanageable and out of season. In the opening sentence of the paragraph below, Dōgen points to the second or primordial meaning of *uji* disclosed through a profound philosophical pun or creative linguistic "twist," by showing that all beings (*u*) are originally time (*ji*) and time

is already beings. Beings are invariably and without exception temporal occurrences. Being and time are absolutely inseparable, constituting two-fold aspects of the selfsame reality, which is not conceived as a monistic identity, but represents the fundamental experience that generates the full manifold of differentiation. Spring, for example, does not merely take place at a certain time, but all the various expressions of spring — the colors, fragrances, ambience and vistas — are the immediate manifestations of the being-time of spring.

3. The staff or *hossu* is used by Zen masters to train, discipline, and stimulate their disciples during meditation.

4. *Kōmyō*, generally used in Buddhism to describe the distinctive features of an illuminative Buddha, and sometimes used synonymously with the Pure Land of Amitābha, is for Dōgen fully integrated and harmonious with the ever-varying manifestations of being-time. In SBGZ "Kōmyō" he writes that *kōmyō* is not beyond or the ground of existence, but it radiates through each and every element and dimension of *shohō-jissō* (true form of all *dharmas*).

5. *Uji* in its primordial meaning is inseparable from daily time and is found nowhere else than right within this very twenty-four hours. In SBGZ "Busshō" Dōgen writes: "Because non-dependence on any thing is within the twenty-four hours, it is the clear seeing of the Buddha-nature. There is no occasion when the twenty-four hours (of daily time) do not arrive." Yet, to merely measure the day into twenty-four identically recurring sequences and to equate this with *uji* — the standpoint of the average man — is to perpetuate a self-deception which misses the true nature of time.

6. Linear, sequential time needs to be so self-evident, beyond doubt, and free from the need for inquiry that it is generally not questioned. The lack of doubt indicates not a genuine understanding, but that the conventional view of time is increasingly problematic and removed from insight into the primordial significance of *uji*. Underlying the false sense of certainty, however, lurks the suspicion that the true nature of time is unknown or misrepresented. The very act of doubting, though frequently subliminal, is a manifestation of *uji*. The inconsistencies of doubting reveal that doubt itself, and even an apparent lack of doubt (or false certainty), is invariably shaped by and inseparable from time.

7. This passage shows both the profound influence of Kegon (Ch. Hua-yen) philosophy on Dōgen's thinking and his unique existentially-oriented appropriation of it. As a Sōtō (Ts'ao-Tung) master, Dōgen relies

heavily on Kegonian ontology of totality and non-obstruction, but he uses it to express his own experience and understanding of Buddhist *Dharma*. According to the Kegon school, suchness is the mutually reciprocal and harmoniously interpenetrating non-obstruction of all phenomena (*jiji-muge*) manifested in the simultaneity of ten periods of time. Dōgen stresses below, however, that the totality of phenomena unfolds without hindrance, not on its own as a mere abstract process, but by virtue of the exertive projection of the configuration of my-self which mirrors and contains the entire *Dharma*-realm.

8. A fascinating sentence which illustrates Dōgen's profoundly rich literary style: *kono yoheni dōji ho(tsu)shin ari, dōshin hotsuji ari*. By reversing the order of the two characters, *ji* (time) and *shin* (mind) in the two clauses, Dōgen offers a concrete expressional illustration of the meaning of interpenetration. Times and minds are both the self-same in that the awakening of spiritual intentions or authentic resolve in one mind at one time awakens all minds at times, and different in that each and every mind is a unique occurrence of *uji* at any moment.

9. " . . . this very reason . . . " (*immo no dōri*). *Inmo* can imply suchness (Skt., *tathātā*), but it is generally used in this chapter more modestly in the sense of "just as," "such as," or "this very" — in the same way that *tathā* can be so used in Sanskrit. Yet, the deeper implication may be kept in mind; it is explored more fully in SBGZ "Immo," in which Dōgen says that to know *immo* one must become a "man of *immo* (*immo no hito*)."

10. Dōgen stresses that the primordial significance of *uji* is in accord with concrete experience, in which no being or occasion can be isolated, separated or abstracted from this very occasion of being-time.

11. The term *bonbu* refers to the unreflective, existentially self-deceptive and ontologically misconceived standpoint of average worldlings, corresponding to Heidegger's critique of the they-self (*das Man*), who obstinately and continuously perpetuate and reinforce their misunderstandings by clinging to partial and one-sided perspectives.

12. In this case, Dōgen uses the *kana* form *"arutoki"* for "sometimes," perhaps to stress that the term here represents the conventional view of a fixed time-point, rather than the primordial significance of *uji* which seems to be unknown to the *bonbu*.

13. The example of climbing the mountain is a central passage which illustrates the conventional preoccupation with linear, sequential time. Even while man is fixated on the supposed constancy of now-

points, he feels that the points are connected in an irreversible series leading towards a goal only obtainable in the future. Obsessed with the fabricated and romanticized future symbolized by the palace made of rubies, which may or may not exist or ever be reached, the past is considered to be left far behind, and the current activity of traversing the path in the present here-and-now is overlooked or discounted. The palace represents man's deficient attempts to escape from the responsibilities for authentic exertion in terms of an idealized and anticipated futural attainment. Dōgen is implicitly critical here (and explicitly in SBGZ "Busshō") of Buddhist doctrines and practices which misrepresent Buddha-nature or enlightenment as an objectified endpoint which arrives in the future. The average man's views create existential-ontological gaps or gulfs, which violate the primordial selfsameness of being-time, between self and time, self and world, present and future, and t1 and t2, that seem of enormous and insurmountable proportions.

14. The misconceptions concerning time are not considered false in the sense that they constitute a logical error or inconsistency that can either be proven or disproven. Rather, they are partial, misguided views arising from one's existential deficiencies and reflecting a lack of ontological understanding. Dōgen's point is that since there is no way of talking about or experiencing oneself apart from time, even the unenlightened one's existence is inherently temporal.

15. Dōgen here considers two basic forms of time — not going and coming, and going and coming. In both cases *uji* manifests itself right-now, which is altogether experientially more significant and ontologically more primordial than the supposed time of the ruby palace. *Nikon*, the "eternal now," is able to both encompass ("chew up") and to surpass ("spit out") the conventional misconception of time.

16. Yesterday and today are not separable time–units, the one gone away and the other having arrived. Rather, both dimensions interpenetrate each other right here-and-now, just as the many different mountain peaks are at once unique manifestations linked together in the mountain range.

17. The conventional, ontologically misleading and existentially inauthentic view that "time flies" is reprehensible if taken as the exclusive understanding of time. It implies a gap between t1 and t2, which are thought to be connected in a series forever passing man by and able to sweep him away should he relinquish his grasp on the supposed constancy of the derivative now-point. Yet, "time flies" is, in a

profound sense unknown to the *bonbu*, close to the truth in that the incessant movement of *uji* is never detained.

18. *Kyōryaku* (literally "undergo" or "passing through") is one of the central notions in Dōgen's philosophy of time. Here, Dōgen deals with the continuity of time in a way fundamentally distinct from the conventional view, which holds that fixed time-units are passing, flying or slipping away and flowing in irreversible succession toward some destination. *Kyōryaku*, on the other hand, refers to the process of a journey actively engaging the passenger and passage-way as well as the full context of their experiential reality. It is multi-dimensional, flexible and dynamic, moving in and through multiple directions simultaneously — a projection of man's ontological understanding and enlightened experience of time into past, present and future, which are ultimately equalizable yet experientially differentiable dimensions of being-time. All tenses of time interpenetrate, reverberate through and influence one another.

19. Because time is not linear, successive time-points do not accumulate. Thus, the lives of previous Zen masters are not counted or added up backwards in terms of chronological sequence, but are to be understood as interpenetrating occasions of the here-and-now transmission of the true passage (*kyōryaku*) of *Dharma* encompassing the simultaneity of past, present and future.

20. " . . . entering into the mud and water . . . " is symbolic of the *bodhisattva*'s fulfillment of his compassionate vow to aid the soteriological aspirations of all beings within the here-and-now context of being-time.

21. This is a complex sentence which seems to suggest that the *Dharma* is not in the least bound or reduced by the *bonbu*'s misconceptions about it; rather, the vastness and inexhaustibility of the *Dharma* presencing as being-time prevails, and it makes possible the provisional and/or partial standpoints of men who are unable to fully comprehend the *Dharma*. In the second part of the sentence, dependent origination is used as a verb: *innen shite*.

22. Even the evasion of the truth of being-time, like doubting or not knowing enough to doubt the conventional view (ftn. 6), is shaped by and inseparable from *uji*.

23. " . . . had better take a look at the matter again and again." Literally, *kan-kan*, "look, look," with the force of a Zen master's injunction to awaken his disciple.

24. *Dharma*-position (*jū-hōi*), another key notion explored more fully in SBGZ "Genjōkōan," suggests the total situational complex of each and every occasion of being-time, encompassing the continuity of *kyōryaku* and the immediacy of *nikon* as well as the simultaneity of past, present and future and of life and death. *Jū-hōi* is characterized by incessantly vigorous activity, always moving around — thus, it is neither stable and fixed nor chaotic and abrasive.

25. This passage suggests that the particular contains the totality and the totality is manifest in-and-through each and every particular. Each fully penetrating experience at every moment of being-time embraces the simultaneity of the four stages of awakening — resolve, practice, *bodhi*, and *nirvāṇa* — which must not be conceived as sequential segments. Furthermore, nothing is excluded from the totality (which is not a mere collection or random grouping of items) because if a particular is left out of one group, it is still a unique occurrence of *uji* which embodies and reflects the totality. Thus, half of anything if fully realized is of equal significance as the whole partially realized, because half and whole are terms relative to the totality which is always disclosed in each phenomenon.

26. " . . . the time which has not-yet come" is not flying by or passing away, nor is it simply stationary; it is the right here-and-now of *jū-hōi* acting vigorously through itself.

27. "Stubborn fool" is literally "leather sack" or "wine-skin," and it is used in Zen as a deprecatory term for someone who is too obstinate to ever seek or realize the Way. The term is stronger than *bonbu*, which is a neutral designation of the average person, because it expresses a highly negative value judgement.

28. Dōgen traces here a step-by-step progression to show the limitations of human language and expressions in attempting to convey the full meaning of *uji*. The "stubborn fool" certainly cannot express the truth of being-time. Yet, those who have a clear perception, and even those whose insight is maintained for a long time, are still groping in their human ways to divulge the trans-ultimate standpoint. The danger always lurks that an inadequate understanding and expression will reduce *bodhi* and *nirvāṇa* to the mere aspect of going and coming, which is the only form of time the average man sees.

29. This sentence is literally, "The net and the cage are useless in trying to snare the spontaneous here-and-now manifestations of being-time."

30. All possible realms, both the heavenly and the worldly, both in this universe and in any other one, both in "this" life and the "next" life, are dependent upon the *genjō* (spontaneous here-and-now manifestations) and *kyōryaku* (totalistic passage) of one's own utmost exertion, exhaustive power, or sustained effort (*jinriki*), which implies not only *zazen* and other Buddhist practices, but every aspect of human activity which is itself an occurrence of being-time. Here, Dōgen stresses again the existential dimension in interpreting the Kegonian doctrine of totality. Being-time, indeed incessantly dynamic, is not an abstract realm, but only completed through each being's dedicated yet ultimately purposeless endeavors. Dependence upon *jinriki*, however, does not suggest a subjectivistic causal principle. One's own efforts are equally dependent upon the exertions of all other beings. In SBGZ "Gyō-ji," Dōgen writes that the unrelenting activity of sustained exertion (*gyō-ji*) right-now is the basis of all selves and all Buddhas, all moments and all phenomena, and it is more fundamental than dependent origination.

31. The passage of spring is by no means separable from spring itself; it does not happen "in" spring, or vice-versa, but is realized through the ever-varying display and diversified expressions, contexts, situations, and occurrences of spring. The flowers, hues, fragrances, sunlight, warmth, ambience, etc. are all passage. Yet, spring and passage are not merely identical since passage perpetually occurs at any and at every moment of being-time. As each phenomenon of spring appears, passage and spring continually complete and fulfill each other.

32. The *bonbu*'s conception of *kyōryaku* is linear, unidirectional, remote and removed from human existence, beyond man's reach, yet sweeping him away as it rushes by with the incessance and indifference of a rainstorm. Furthermore, the average man confuses the transmission of the *Dharma* — symbolized by the Bodhidharma's coming from the West (from India to China) — with the mere physical passing of doctrine from one country to another one.

33. Teaching and not-teaching, right and wrong are all temporal; none has absolute status or significance over and above the others. Here Dōgen recalls the *Diamond Sutra* dictum, "*Nirvāṇa* is not *nirvāṇa*, therefore *nirvāṇa*." The appropriateness of teaching or not-teaching in Zen instruction is determined by the concrete temporal context; each is realized in terms of its negation, just as *uji* is neither exclusively the mountaintop nor the depths of the sea (in the first poem of the chapter), but both occurrences interpenetrating one another simultaneously. The particular vantage point to be realized is continually shifting.

34. Dōgen shows the undifferentiable unity or identity of space and being-time. The mountain and sea as well as anyone who stands on or walks in them are nothing other than *uji*. They depend on time and are not manifested separable from time; time depends on them and is not manifested separable from them.

35. The bright star is symbolic of the dawn of Śākyamuni's awakening and triumph over the temptations and taunting of Mara at the age of thirty-five under the Bo tree; Tathāgata or "thus come" (*nyorai*) is the name for one who has clearly realized the thusness or suchness of conditioned phenomena, or the truth of reality such as it is without one-sided views or conceptual fabrications imposed upon and distorting it; the *Dharma*-eye is symbolic of a Buddha's unique power of insight and comprehension; the uplifted flower is symbolic of the origins of Zen when Śākyamuni silently presented a flower to Mahākāśyappa, the only monk who understood the meaning of his silence, thus initiating the spontaneous transmission from selfsame mind-to-selfsame mind which Bodhidharma, Dōgen's master Ju-ching, Dōgen, and all other Zen masters continually perpetuate as the *kyōryaku* of *Dharma*. The four appearances occur simultaneously as manifestations of *uji*; otherwise, there would be no appropriation, evaluation and duplication of Śākyamuni's experience throughout all ages.

36. This poem is attributed to a Lin-chi (J. *Rinzai*) disciple and recalls the content and structure of Lin-chi's own famous saying: "Sometimes I snatch away the man but not the environment; sometimes I snatch away the environment but not the man; sometimes I snatch away both man and environment; sometimes I snatch away neither man nor environment" (from *The Zen Teaching of Rinzai*, trans. Irmgard Schloegl, Berkeley, Shambala, 1976, p. 19). Dōgen makes the point below that since getting there and not getting there are both eminently temporal, there is no superiority of the former over the latter.

I means both intention and meaning as well as attention, care, and thought, implying that which is prior to what is said and what any saying actually conveys; it also signifies disposition, will(ing), etc. *I* has been used in Chinese Buddhist texts as a translation of *manas* (thought). In the Terada-Mizuno edition, *kokoro* is written in *kana*-form next to *i*, which is the *kun-yomi* for *shin* (mind, heart-mind, will), frequently used as a Chinese translation for *citta* (mind). *Ku* could mean generally language or expression, or specifically sentence, words and phrase, implying that which articulates and gives concrete expression to what is intended as the meaning to be conveyed. *I* and *ku* may be identical, or there may be great variance between them. *Tō* means reach or arrive in the sense of getting the point across or hitting the mark; it also implies arrival at the "other shore" of *nirvāṇa*.

37. Dōgen shifts the priority from the linear accomplishment of completion to the acting or the process itself. Not getting there is not a lesser or merely preliminary stage leading up to the arrival, but it is nothing other than *uji* already realized here-and-now.

38. Neither intended meaning nor expression, neither the horse nor the donkey should be considered first or second as if in a sequence.

39. Each of the four factors of experience cited in the poem "obstructs," that is, existentially penetrates and realizes itself. Obstruction here, recalling the Kegonian view, is paradoxically to be understood not as hindrance or impediment, but as the non-obstruction of a totalistic self-generating, self-fulfilling and self-renewing moment. Obstruction itself, as explained in the last two sentences, is a temporal event involving the mutual dependence, containment and reflection of harmoniously interpenetrating *dharmas*; it makes use of other *dharmas*, as do all interdependent phenomena, but it never hinders them in the conventional sense.

40. A uniquely concrete illustration of the above notion. Myself and people, the particular and the totality, the individual and the universal, the phenomenon and the principle all "meet" (*hō*) or are mutually engaged in existential encounter of intersubjective lived-experience. That is, all factors and perspectives penetrate, realize and "obstruct" each other. " . . . meeting meets meeting" (literally, "going out, *shutsu*, meets going out") conveys the ontologically non-obstructive interpenetration of all simultaneous manifestations of being-time.

41. *Genjōkōan* is one of the central notions in Dōgen's philosophy of Zen, and is the subject of the first chapter of SBGZ. Dōgen uses it in contrast to the Rinzai view of *kōan* as a puzzle intuitively and suddenly solved, as if that in itself were *satori*. For Dōgen, the *kōan* is more than a riddle, but the *Dharma* fully and spontaneously disclosed, presented, revealed, or manifested right-now and perpetually renewed in each and every concrete activity and expression of the True Man (*shinjin*). In other words, *satori* is not necessarily "getting there" to a futurally anticipated goal, but is the "not getting there" or the time which has "not-yet come."

42. The first two sentences in this sequence imply an ascention from *genjōkōan* realized in everyday life to the upward slashing of barriers in the supramundane world. But the point of the third sentence

is that attainment is not as significant as the temporal process, whether manifest as getting there or not getting there.

43. This sentence is almost impossible to translate because it uses *uji* as a verb, thus accentuating and intensifying its dynamic and existential nature.

44. Instruction is limited in that whatever teaching is conveyed and understood invariably falls short of the whole truth of *uji*; but to refrain from teaching and not attempt to get any point across is an existential evasion of being-time.

45. Even if one does not achieve genuine realization of being-time, the ontological truth of *uji* still prevails; otherwise, enlightened realization would be conceived of as an attainment in linear time.

Glossary of Japanese Terms

Amida (Buddha of Pure Land)

阿弥陀

Baige (Plum blossoms)

梅華

bendō (practice of the Way)

辨道

Bendōwa (Discourse on the practice of the Way)

辨道話

bodai (bodhi, wisdom)

菩提

bonbu (prthagjana, unenlightened mortal being, average person's standpoint)

凡夫

Busshō (Buddha-ksetra, Buddha-nature)

仏性

butsu-baku (bounded by seeking Buddhahood external to oneself while not
　　　　　realizing that it already exists within oneself)

仏縛

Butsukōjōji (Continuous development beyond Buddhahood)

仏向上事

daigo (great awakening)

大悟

daimoku (sacred title)

題目

Dōgen (Japanese Zen master, 1200-1253)

道元

dōri (truth, reason, meaning)

道理

Dōtoku (Fully expressing the Way)

道得

engi (pratītya-samutpāda, dependent origination)

縁起

fukan (constant application)

普勧

Fukanzazengi (Universal admonition for zazen)

普勧坐禪儀

ga (ātman, self)

我

Gabei (Painted rice-cake)

画餅

Gakudō-yōjinshū (Advice on learning the Way)

学道用心集

gedō (anya-tirthiya, heresy or non-Buddhistic standpoint)

外道

gendaigoyaku (modern Japanese translation)

現代語訳

genjō (manifestation, realization)

現成

Genjōkōan (Immediate and complete realization of Zen enlightenment)

現成公按

goshiki (karmic consciousness)

業識

gyōbutsu (active Buddha)

行仏

Gyōbutsu-igi (Majestic activities of the active Buddha)

行仏威儀

Gyōji (Sustained exertion)

行持

gyōji-dōkan (perpetuation of the Way through sustained exertion)

行持道環

hakanashi (fleeting, uncertain)

はかなし

Hakujushi (Cypress tree)

栢樹子

Heian (Japanese era, 794-1192)

平安

hō (dharma, experiential factor; Dharma, Law)

法

hō (meet, encounter)

逢

Hōkyō-ki (Record of Hōkyō period)

寶慶記

hōjin (sambhoga-kāya, body of bliss)

報身

Hōnen (founder of Jōdo sect, 1133-1212)

法然

hosshin (bodhicitta-samutpāda, arising of the enlightenment-mind;
        resolve for enlightenment)

発心

hosshin (Dharma-kāya, body of Law)

法身

Hosshō (True nature of dharmas; Dharma-nature)

法性

hossu (Zen staff)

払子

Hotsu-bodaishin (Arising of the enlightenment-mind; same as hosshin)

発菩提心

hotsu-mujōshin (arising of the supreme mind)

発無上心

i (intended meaning)

意

Ikkya-myoju (One bright pearl)

一顆明珠

Immo (Suchness; being-such)

恁麼

innen (dependent origination; same as engi)

因縁

ji (instant)

次

ji (time)

時

jiji (time's occurrence at any moment)

時々

jiji-muge (non-obstruction of events and events)

事事無礙

jinen-gedō (heresy that all things arise in natural ways)

自然外道

jinen-hōni (naturalism)

自然法爾

jinriki (utmost exertive power)

尽力

Jippō (Ten directions)

十方

jiriki (self-power)

自力

jisetsu (time, occasion)

時節

jisetsu kishi (the time has already arrived, or a passed moment)

時節既至

jisetsu nyakushi (if the time arrives, or at a future moment)

時節若至

jissō (true form)

実相

jōbutsu (attainment of Buddhahood)

成仏

jū-hōi (dharma's dwelling place)

住法位

Juki (Prediction of future Buddhahood)

授記

Kamakura (Japanese era, 1192-1338)

鎌倉

Kankin (Silent reading of sūtras)

看経

kan-kan (look!)

看々

kannō-dōkō (reciprocal spiritual communion)

感応道交

Kattō (Spiritual vines or entanglement)

葛藤

Kegon (Japanese Mahāyāna sect; Hua-yen in Chinese)

華厳

kenshō (seeing into one's own original nature)

見性

kikan (dynamic engagement)

機関

kōan (catechistic technique for Zen realization)

公案

Kobusshin (Original Buddha-mind)

古仏心

Kōmyō (Radiant light)

光明

ku (expression)

句

ku (duhkha; suffering)

苦

kū (śūnyatā; emptiness, voidness)

空

kū-busshō (emptiness-Buddha-nature)

空仏性

Kūge (Flowers in the sky; false perception of seeing "flowers in emptiness," i.e., assigning self-nature to things)

空華

kūshu-genkyō (returning empty-handed to the native land)

空与還郷

kyōryaku (totalistic passage)

経歴

kyūjin (ultimate and complete realization)

究尽

mappō (age of degenerate Law)

末法

mi-ten (prior-to-turning)

未 転

mi-tō (not-yet come)

未 到

mondō (Zen dialogue)

問 答

mono no aware (poignant sadness at the passing of things)

ものの あわれ

mu-busshō (no-Buddha-nature)

無 仏 性

muchū (dream, or dream-like nonsense)

夢 中

muga (anātman, non-self, insubstantiality of phenomena)

無 我

mui-shinjin (true man of no rank)

無 位 真 人

mujō (anitya, impermanence)

無 常

mujō-busshō (impermanence-Buddha-nature)

無 常 仏 性

Mumonkan (Gateless gate)

無 門 関

mu-u-hennyaku (non-existence of change)

無 有 変 易

nehan (nirvāna)

涅 槃

nembutsu (recitation of the Buddha's name)

念 仏

Nichiren (founder of Nichiren sect, 1222-1282)

日 蓮

nikon (right here-and-now)

而 今

Nyojō (Dōgen's Chinese Zen master, Ju-ching, 1163-1228)

如 浄

nyorai (Tathāgata, thus-come)

如来

nyūnan-shin (soft and flexible mind)

柔軟心

ōjin (nirmāna-kāya, body of transformation)

応身

Rinzai (founder of Rinzai Zen sect, d. 867; Lin-chi in Chinese)

臨済

saidan (cut off from, beyond)

際断

Sansuikyō (Mountain and river sutras)

山水経

satori (Zen enlightenment)

悟り

sennigedō (Senika heresy that an eternal realm underlies temporal reality)

先尼外道

Sesshin sesshō (Explaining mind, explaining nature)

説心 説性

shikan-taza (zazen-only)

只管打坐

shin (heart-mind)

心

shingen (manifesting body)

身現

shingi (authenticity)

真偽

shinjin (true man)

真人

Shinjin-gakudō (Learning the Way through body and mind)

身心学道

shinjin-datsuraku (cast off body and mind)

身心 脱落

Shinran (founder of Jōdo-shin sect, 1173-1262)

親鸞

Shisho (Transmission records)

嗣書

shitsu-u-bussho (all beings are, or have, Buddha-nature)

悉有仏性

sho (realization)

証

Shoaku makusa (Refrain from evil)

諸悪莫作

shobo (true Law)

正法

Shoho jisso (True form of all dharmas)

諸法実相

Shobogenzo (Treasury of the true Dharma-eye)

正法眼蔵

Shobogenzo Zuimonki (Gleanings from Dogen's talks)

正法眼蔵随聞記

Shoji (Life-and-death)

生死

shugyo (practice)

修行

Shusho-gi (Meaning of practice and realization)

修証義

shutsu (going out)

出

so (laksana, form)

相

Sokushinzebutsu (This mind itself is Buddha)

即心是仏

Soto (Zen sect founded in Japan by Dogen; Ts'ao-tung in Chinese)

曹洞

Tendai (Japanese Mahāyāna sect; T'ien-t'ai in Chinese)

天台

Tenzokyokun (Instructions to the chief cook)

典座教訓

tō (get there, or to arrive, to attain)

到

tōdatsu (penetration)

透脱

Tsuki (Moon)

月, 都機

u (being)

有

u-busshō (being-Buddha-nature)

有仏性

Udonge (Udambara flower)

優曇華

Uji (Being-time)

有時

ui-shinjin (true man of rank)

有位真人

waka (31-syllable Japanese poem)

和歌

Yuibutsu-yobutsu (Only between a Buddha and a Buddha)

唯仏與仏

zazen (seated meditation)

坐禅

Zen (dhyāna, meditation; Mahāyāna sect, Ch'an in Chinese)

禅

Zenki (Total dynamism)

全機

Index

Abhidharma, 6–7, 76
Age of Degenerate Law (*mappō*), 22, 40, 56, 66, 69, 103
Age of Right Law (*shōbō*), 38, 40
anatman. See non-self
Anaximander, 15, 47, 123, 169*n*
anxiety, 14, 17, 20, 71, 74, 80
Aristotle, 5, 15, 16, 17, 20, 48, 74, 78, 117, 164*n*
atman. See self
Augenblick. See moment-of-vision *under* ecstatic temporality
Augustine, 3, 17, 19, 74, 163*n*, 167*n*
average man (*bonbu*), 28, 39, 50–51, 52–53, 60, 154, 156, 179–181*n*, 182*n*, 183*n*
awakening, 111, 145–146; Dōgen's interpretation of, 134–137, 141–142; unity of practice and realization, 135–136

Being (*Sein*), 4, 5, 6, 10, 13, 107; and beings, 5, 36–37, 85, 121; and Dasein, 17, 20–21, 37–38, 40–46, 79–82, 85, 112–114, 117; and history, 47, 63–64, 75, 85–86, 98, 121–123, 175*n*; and non-substantiality, 108; and nothingness, 20, 83–84, 113; and time, 15–16, 29, 108–109, 121–122, 147; -as-*Ereignis* (event), 125; as presence, 5, 36, 46; as present-at-hand (*vorhanden*), 5, 36–37, 40–41, 44, 45, 62, 78, 108, 113, 115, 118, 121, 145, 148; as such, 64; forgetfulness of (*Seinsvergessenheit*), 47, 84–86, 103–104; horizon of, 31; -in-the-world, 41, 139, 166*n*; in contrast to time, 5–6, 48; meaning of, 14–15, 16–17, 36, 40; power of, 20, 79;

question of (*Seinsfrage*), 10, 13, 16, 20, 22, 40, 65, 67, 109, 147; temporal determinateness of, 5; traditional view of, 14–16, 40, 121; -toward-the-end (*or* -unto-death), 20, 73, 75, 82–83, 102, 114; understanding of (*Seinsverständnis*), 12, 14–17, 30, 41, 68, 74, 103, 148
being-time (*uji*), 3, 11, 13, 23, 28, 32, 33, 39, 49, 99, 111, 134, 144, 155–161, 164*n*, 165*n*; derivative view of, 2, 39, 50–53, 58–60, 126–127, 154, 156–157, 177*n*, 179–181*n*; Dōgen's interpretation of, 51–60, 61–62, 65–66, 125–128, 135, 142, 145, 146, 149–151, 153–154, 155–157, 177–178*n*, 179*n*, 181–183*n*, 185–186*n*; passage (*kyōryaku*), 36, 39, 52, 54–58, 68–69, 108, 111, 127, 129–134, 143, 151, 153, 157, 159, 169*n*, 181–184*n*; right now, *or* here-and-now (*nikon*), 31, 39, 53–54, 61–62, 66, 108, 110–111, 127, 128–131, 133, 137,143, 153, 156–157, 180*n*, 182*n*, 185*n*
Bergson, Henri, 164*n*
Bodhidharma, 55, 57, 164*n*, 169–170*n*, 183*n*
bonbu. See average man
Brentano, Franz, 14
Buddha (Śākyamuni), 23, 28–29, 56, 68, 77, 88, 177*n*, 178*n*, 184*n*
Buddha, active (*gyōbutsu*), 28, 39, 153, 171*n*
Buddha, Amida, 56
Buddha, bonds of, 39
Buddha-body (*Trikāya*), 50, 171*n*
Buddha-nature (*busshō*), 4, 7–8, 11, 21, 31, 38, 39, 52, 106, 107, 176*n*; being-, 131–132, 176*n*; derivative view of, 7–8, 24–26, 39, 50–51, 58, 67, 127–128,

129; Dōgen's interpretation of, 26–28, 31, 58–60, 110–111, 131–133, 142, 147, 176n, 178n, 180n; emptiness-, 176n; eternalized, 7, 25, 39, 58, 91, 110, 167–168n; impermanence-, 8, 28, 29, 58, 76–77, 90–91, 102, 147, 153; original, 111; traditional view of, 7, 25, 50, 59, 129, 131
bussho. *See* Buddha-nature

cast off body and mind (*shinjin datsuraku*), 27, 58, 76, 77, 90, 91, 92, 99–100, 110, 125, 134–136, 149, 151, 161, 168n

das Man. See they-self
death, 8–9, 17, 71–73; and life (or life/death), 6, 11, 23, 27, 28, 76, 88, 90, 92–96, 98–100; as nothingness, 82–84, 98; derivative view of, 8, 112; Dōgen's interpretation of, 23, 93–96, 98–99; Heidegger's interpretation of, 44–45, 74, 81–84, 98, 112–114; primordial view of, 8–9, 96–99, 112. *See also* Being-toward-the-end; finitude; impermanence; radical contingency
Demske, James, 21–22, 167n
Descartes, Rene, 5, 18, 64, 120, 169n
dharma-position. *See dharma*-stage
dharma-stage (*jū-hōi*), 39, 58, 65, 77, 93–96, 100–101, 127, 129–130, 150, 153, 158, 182n
Diamond Sutra, 183n
Dilthey, Wilhelm, 17
Dōgen: aesthetic-naturalistic dimension in, 77, 89, 91–93, 173n; background and development of, 22–29; biography of, 22–27, 56, 86–87, 167n; existential and ontological dimensions in, 7, 10–12, 13, 25, 27–28, 49, 53, 55, 59–60, 65–66, 75, 77, 86, 88–89, 100, 125–127, 131, 137, 140–143, 164n,

183n, 185–186n; great doubt, 25; relation to Buddhist tradition, 6–8, 22–29, 34, 39–40, 49–50, 54–60, 86, 88–89, 103, 129, 131–132, 147, 165n, 178n, 181n, 183n; relation to Japanese cultural tradition, 22, 77, 87, 103; relation to Rinzai Zen, 39–40, 54, 57, 133, 169n, 176n, 184n, 185n; soteriological dimension in, 7, 10–12, 13, 26, 30, 100, 108, 147, 149–151; view of language and interpretation in, 28–29, 39–40, 57–58, 66, 68–69, 131–132, 168–169n, 171n, 177n, 179n, 182n, 182n, 184–185n
Dōgen, works of: "Fukanzazengi," 38, 167n; "Gakudō-yōjinshū," 23, 172n; "Hōkyō-ki," 171n; "Mujō," 91; *Shōbōgenzō*, 1, 23, 34, 39, 92, 99, 133, 153, 154; *Shōbōgenzō Zuimonki*, 23, 34, 89, 92, 167n, 168n, 171n, 172n, 173n; "Shūshō-gi," 167n; "Tenzokyōkun," 168n. *See also* *Shōbōgenzō*, chapters of
dwelling-place. *See dharma*-stage

ecstatic temporality, 41, 43, 45–46, 61, 63, 109, 114–117, 138–140, 145, 147; and nearness, 122–123; and transcendence, 116–117; future, 41, 102, 114–116, 120, 124–125, 140, 143; moment-of-vision (*Augenblick*), 19, 107–108, 115–116; past, 45–46, 115, 118–119
Endlichkeit. See finitude
Ereignis. See event
event (*Ereignis*), 34, 108–110, 122–125, 143, 174–175n; historical dimension of, 123; naturalistic dimension of, 123–124
exertion (*gyōji*), 26, 38, 57, 60, 108, 125, 136–137, 140, 149–150, 153, 158–159, 176–177n, 183n
existentialism, 17, 22, 84, 121, 148, 163–164n

falling, 42–44, 62–63, 146, 148
finitude, 8, 9, 17, 71–75, 109; finite
  transcendence, 10, 66; in contrast to
  infinitude, 20, 37, 48, 77, 83, 101; in
  Heidegger, 20, 45, 73–75, 77–82,
  83–86, 101–104, 112–114; in Kant, 18,
  48; in-itself, 83; the non-power of, 75,
  79
flowers in the sky (*kūge*), 57–58
fundamental ontology. *See*
  phenomenology
future Buddhahood, prediction of (*juki*),
  141–142

ga. See self
genjokoan. See spontaneous realization
gyōji. See exertion

Hakuin, 168*n*
Hegel, Georg W. F., 6, 43, 48–49, 64,
  117, 164*n*, 169*n*
Heian, 87
Heidegger, Martin: approach to
  Daseinanalytik in, 10, 12, 37–38,
  41–44, 64, 74–75, 109, 120–121, 143,
  164*n*, 166–167*n*; approach to
  hermeneutics in, 13, 20–21, 29, 30,
  36–37, 46–48, 63–64, 67–68, 109,
  111–112, 121, 138–139, 146, 166*n*;
  background and development of,
  13–22; existential and ontological
  dimensions in, 13, 36, 42, 64, 100,
  138–140, 145, 163–164*n*; *existenziell*
  and *existenzial* dimensions in, 10, 12,
  13, 20–21, 29, 30, 37, 42, 45, 64, 65,
  68–69, 74, 80, 81–82, 99–100, 100–101,
  109, 111–114, 120, 139, 145, 147–148,
  163–164*n*; Heindegger II, 34, 37, 47,
  64, 68, 85, 98–99, 109, 123, 139–140,
  148, 169*n*; question of soteriological
  dimension in, 10, 13, 29, 108, 114,
  146–149; relation to metaphysical
  tradition, 5–6, 10, 13–22, 32–33,

36–37, 46–49, 73–75, 78–80, 98,
  102–104, 106, 108–109, 117, 121–123,
  143, 147–149, 164*n*, 169*n*, 175*n*;
  relation to theological tradition, 15,
  73, 102, 104, 149; view of nothingness
  in, 79–81
Heidegger, works of: "Das Ding" ("The
  Thing"), 84, 172*n*, 175*n*; "Der
  Rückgang in den Grund der
  Metaphysik" ("On the Way Back into
  the Ground of Metaphysics"), 16,
  166*n*; "Dialogue with a Japanese," 32,
  169*n*; *Die Frage nach den Ding (What
  is a Thing?)*, 170*n*; *Der Satz vom
  Grund*, 175*n*; *Early Greek Thinking*,
  170*n*; *Einführung in die Metaphysik
  (An Introduction to Metaphysics)*, 15,
  46, 165*n*, 166*n*, 170*n*; *Gelassenheit
  (Discourse on Thinking)*, 22, 175*n*;
  Holzwege, 123, 169*n*; *Humanismusbrief*
  ("Letter on Humanism"), 22, 36, 64,
  149, 169*n*, 177*n*; *Identität und
  Differenz* (Identity and Difference),
  169*n*, 170*n*; *Kant und das Problem der
  Metaphysik (Kant and the Problem of
  Metaphysics)*, 78, 172*n*, 174*n*;
  Nietzsche, 123, 169*n*, 171*n*; "Nur Noch
  ein Gott Kann uns Retten" ("Only a
  God Can Save Us Now"), 175*n*;
  *Phanomenologie und Theologie
  (Phenomenology and Theology)*, 166*n*;
  Poetry, Language, Thought, 173*n*; *The
  Question Concerning Technology*, 165*n*;
  Sein und Zeit (Being and Time), 1, 5,
  16, 21, 22, 29, 30, 33, 34, 37, 40, 47,
  48, 64, 79, 83, 98, 99, 102, 109, 120,
  121, 122, 124, 138, 140, 143, 149, 163*n*,
  166*n*, 167*n*, 169*n*, 170*n*, 172*n*, 174*n*;
  "Uberwindung der Metaphysik"
  ("Overcoming Metaphysics"), 175*n*;
  *Unterwegs zur Sprache (On the Way to
  Language)*, 169*n*, 175*n*; *Vom Wesen des
  Grundes ("The Essence of Reason")*, 75,
  172*n*; *Vom Wesen der Wahrheit (On
  the Essence of Truth")*, 84, 173*n*; *Was
  Heisst Denken? (What is Called*

Thinking?), 33, 102, 166*n*, 170*n*; *"Was ist Metaphysik?"* ("What is Metaphysics?"), 84, 172*n*; *Wegmarken*, 170*n*; *Zur Sache des Denkens* (On Time and Being), 33, 83, 109, 170*n*, 172*n*, 174*n*, 175*n*; *Zur Seinsfrage* (On the Question of Being), 177*n*
history, 33, 63; as historicality (primordial view), 46, 68, 108, 118–120, 143; as historiology (derivative view), 45, 119–120; Dōgen's interpretation of, 55–56, 68–69, 102–103; Heidegger's interpretation of, 45–46, 47–48. *See also* Being; being-time; ecstatic temporality
Hōnen, 40
Husserl, Edmund, 13, 17, 18
Huai-hai, 59, 69
Hua-yen. *See* Kegon
Hui-neng: view of seeing into [one's own-] nature (*kenshō*) in, 8, 76, 88, 129, 165*n*

impermanence (*mujō*), 6–8, 9, 11, 13, 27, 32, 33, 75, 153–154; -as-impermanence, 23, 88; as fleetingness, 22, 87, as transiency, 23–24, 77; derivative view of, 6–8, 75–76, 86; Dōgen's interpretation of, 10–11, 22–24, 76–77, 89–96, 99, 102–104, 149; existential and ontological dimensions of, 10–11, 88. *See also* Buddha-nature, impermance-

jinen-gedō. *See* naturalistic heresy
jippō. *See* ten directions
Ju-ching (J. Nyojō), 26–27, 37, 90, 171*n*, 184*n*
jū-hōi. *See dharma*-stage
juki. *See* future Buddhahood, prediction of

Kamakura, 56, 77, 87
Kant, Immanuel, 5, 17, 18, 48, 64, 74, 78–79, 100, 120, 149
Kegon, 7, 128, 178–179*n*, 183*n*, 185*n*
kenshō. *See* seeing into [one's own-] nature *under* Hui-neng
Kenzeiki, 23, 27, 167*n*. *See also* Dōgen, biography of
Kierkegaard, Soren, 17, 19, 74, 149
kūge. *See* flowers in the sky
kyōryaku. *See* passage *under* being-time

Lotus Sutra, 56

Madhyamika, 7
mappō. *See* Age of Degenerate Law
metaphysics, 1, 4, 6, 73, 121; ousiology, 20; trans-metaphysical, 121. *See also* Heidegger, relation to metaphysical tradition
Myōyu, 89
Myōzen, 89–90, 92
muga. *See* non-self
mujō. *See* impermanence
mujo-busshō. *See* Buddha-nature, impermanence-

Nāgārjuna, 50
Nakamura, Hajime, 168*n*
naturalistic heresty (jinen-*gedō*), 8, 38, 88, 127
nembutsu, 56
neo-Platonism, 19
Nichiren 40, 56
Nietzsche, Friedrich, 6, 15, 17, 19, 31, 47, 49, 64, 117, 119–120, 123, 145, 149, 164*n*, 169*n*
nihilism, 9
nikon. *See* right-now *under* being-time
Nirvāna Sutra, 59, 131
Nishitani, Keiji, 168*n*

non-self (J. *muga*, Skt. *anatma*), 65, 75, 76–77, 86, 90, 95, 100–101, 125, 128, 134, 137, 168*n*
non-substantialty, 29, 32, 71, 76, 96, 106–107, 127–128, 138, 140, 144, 163*n*
nothingness, 17, 71, 73, 79, 113
Nyojō. *See* Ju-ching

onto-theo-logy, 117, 124, 149, 169*n*, 175*n*

passage (*kyōryaku*). *See under* being-time
phenomenology, 21, 30, 38, 46, 63, 79–80, 120, 143; and fundamental ontology, 10, 12, 13, 18, 20, 46, 63, 73–74, 98, 102, 139; and phenomenological ontology, 21; in Husserl, 17, 18–19. *See also* Heidegger, approach to Daseinanalytik
Plato, 6, 17, 48, 117
Pöggeler, Otto, 17
pre-Socratics, 123
Pure Land, 56, 178*n*

radical contingency, 34, 69, 71–73, 96–98, 106, 144–145. *See also* death; finitude; *and* impermanence
right-now (*nikon*). *See under* being-time
resoluteness, 8, 100, 112–114, 121, 140, 142; and releasement, 122, 142; and resolution, 116
Rinzai. *See* Dōgen, relation to Rinzai Zen
ruby palace, image of, 2, 53, 58–59, 62, 88, 141, 156, 180*n*

Śākyamuni. *See* Buddha
Scheler, Max, 17, 18, 74
seeing into [one's own-] nature. *See* under Hui-neng

Sein. *See* Being
Sein und Zeit. *See* Heidegger, works of
Seinsfrage. *See* Being, question of
Seinsvergessenheit. *See* Being, forgetfulness of
Seinsverständnis. *See* Being, understanding of
self (J. *ga*; Skt. *atman*), 8, 53, 141
selfhood, 19, 40, 101, 167*n*
Senika heresy (*sennigedō*), 8, 31, 38, 76, 86, 88, 127, 145, 154
sennigedō. *See* Senika heresy
Shinran, 40
shinjin datsuraku. *See* cast off body and mind
shōbō. *See* Age of Right Law
Shōbōgenzō, chapters of: Baige, 173*n*; Bendōwa, 30, 103, 135, 142, 165*n*, 168*n*, 169*n*, 171*n*, 174*n*, 176*n*, 177*n*; Busshō, 1, 39, 49, 58, 76, 90, 131, 133, 165*n*, 168*n*, 171*n*, 172*n*, 173*n*, 176*n*, 178*n*, 180*n*; Dōtoku, 171*n*; Genjōkōan, 11, 25, 66, 90, 92, 93, 165*n*, 166*n*, 168*n*, 172*n*, 173*n*, 174*n*, 176*n*, 177*n*, 182*n*; Gyōbutsu-igi, 169*n*, Gyōji, 125, 136, 141, 172*n*, 174*n*, 175*n*, 176*n*, 177*n*, 183*n*, Hakujushi, 165*n*; Hotsu-Mujōshin, 176*n*; Immo, 167*n*, 179*n*; Jippō, 177*n*; Juki, 177*n*; Kankin, 171*n*; Kattō, 164*n*, 171*n*; Kenbutsu, 169*n*; Kobusshin, 176*n*; Kōmyō, 178*n*; Kūge, 171*n*; Sansuikyō, 67; Sesshin sesshō, 168*n*, 173*n*; Shinjingakudō, 173*n*, 174*n*, 176*n*; Shisho, 171*n*; 176*n*; Shizen-biku, 165*n*; Shoaku-makusa, 177*n*; Shōji, 94, 173*n*; Sokushin-zebutsu, 165*n*; Tsuki, 129, 176*n*; Udonge, 173*n*; Uji, 1, 12, 39, 50, 110, 125–126, 136, 143–144, 149, 153–162, 163*n*, 166*n*, 168*n*, 169*n*, 171*n*, 172*n*, 175*n*, 176*n*, 177*n*; Zenki, 110, 169*n*, 173*n*, 174*n*
spontaneous realization (*genjōkōan*), 11, 28, 131, 133–134, 137, 153, 161, 164*n*, 185*n*

ten directions (*jippō*), 136, 141
Tendai, 7, 24–25
they-self (*das Man*), 17, 42, 112–114, 179*n*
time: and non-substantiality, 6, 32, 106–107; derivative view of, 1–4, 6, 8, 14, 16, 31, 35–36, 42–45, 50–51, 60–61, 96, 105–106, 137–138, 144–145, 163*n*, 178*n*, 179–180*n*; existential and ontological dimensions of, 1–2, 4, 5–9, 13, 31, 33, 35–36, 44, 59, 63, 72, 96–97, 106–107, 137–138; "now-time," 2, 5, 6, 9, 17, 18, 31, 35–36, 37, 43–44, 48–49, 61, 63, 66, 71, 96–98, 103, 105–106, 111, 115, 179–180*n*; primordial view of, 3–4, 9, 16, 29, 30–33, 35–36, 61, 66, 69, 96, 105–108, 116–117, 125, 144–145, 163*n*, question of, 10, 146; "time flies," 1, 2, 8, 9, 12, 39, 54, 72, 97, 106, 144, 157, 180–181*n*. *See also* being-time; death; ecstatic temporality; history; radical contingency; *and* ruby palace

total dynamism (*zenki*), 28, 94–96, 108, 110, 142, 153
Trikāya. See Buddha-body
True Man(hood), 7, 11, 27, 30, 38, 40, 55, 57, 58, 60, 65–66, 92, 108, 137, 141, 150–151, 168*n*, 185*n*

uji. See being-time
Upanishads, 8

vorhanden. See Being, as present-at-hand

Whitehead, Alfred North, 164*n*

zenki. See total dynamism